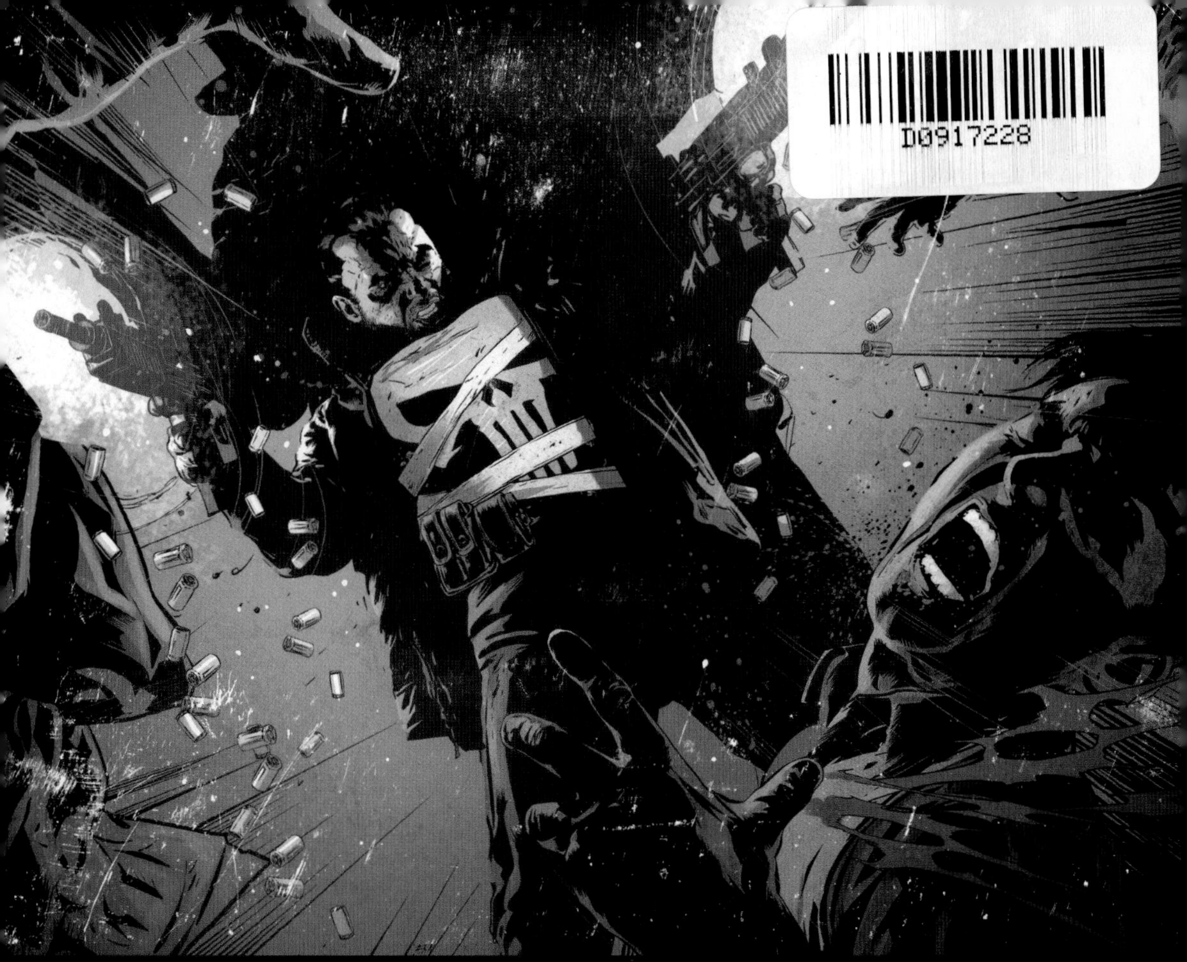

THE PUNISHER

LD WAR FRANK

COLLECTION EDITOR:
MARK D. BEAZLEY

ASSISTANT EDITOR:
CAITLIN O'CONNELL

ASSOCIATE MANAGING EDITOR:
KATERI WOODY

SENIOR EDITOR, SPECIAL PROJECTS:
JENNIFER GRÜNWALD

VP PRODUCTION & SPECIAL PROJECTS:
JEFF YOUNGQUIST

SVP PRINT, SALES & MARKETING:
DAVID GABRIEL

BOOK DESIGNER:
RODOLFO MURAGUCHI

EDITOR IN CHIEF:
C.B. CEBULSKI

CHIEF CREATIVE OFFICER:
JOE QUESADA

PRESIDENT:
DAN BUCKLEY

EXECUTIVE PRODUCER:
ALAN FINE

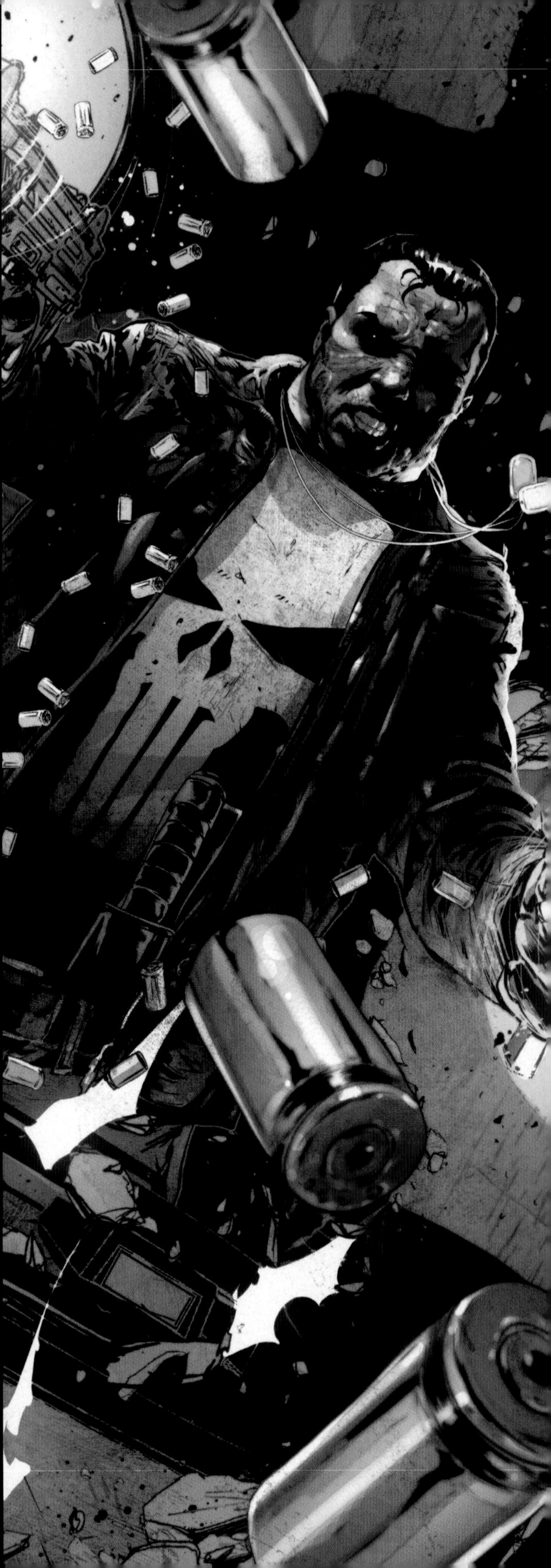

THE PUNISHER VOL. 1: WORLD WAR FRANK. Contains material originally published in magazine form as THE PUNISHER #1-5. First printing 2018. ISBN 978-1-302-91347-2. Published by MARVEL WORLDWIDE, INC., a subsidiary of MARVEL ENTERTAINMENT, LLC. OFFICE OF PUBLICATION: 135 West 50th Street, New York, NY 10020. **Printed in the U.S.A.** DAN BUCKLEY, President, Marvel Entertainment; JOHN NEE, Publisher; JOE QUESADA, Chief Creative Officer; TOM BREVOORT, SVP of Publishing; DAVID BOGART, SVP of Business Affairs & Operations, Publishing & Partnership; DAVID GABRIEL, SVP of Sales & Marketing, Publishing; JEFF YOUNGQUIST, VP of Production & Special Projects; DAN CARR, Executive Director of Publishing Technology; ALEX MORALES, Director of Publishing Operations; DAN EDINGTON, Managing Editor; SUSAN CRESPI, Production Manager; STAN LEE, Chairman Emeritus. For information regarding advertising in Marvel Comics or on Marvel.com, please contact Vit DeBellis, Custom Solutions & Integrated Advertising Manager at vdebellis@marvel.com. For Marvel subscription inquiries, please call 888-511-5480. **Manufactured between 12/14/2018 and 1/29/2019 by LSC COMMUNICATIONS INC., KENDALLVILLE, IN, USA.**

0 9 8 7 6 5 4 3 2 1

Frank Castle was a decorated Marine, an upstanding citizen and a family man. Then his family was taken from him when they were accidentally killed in a brutal mob hit. From that day, he became a force of cold, calculated retribution and vigilantism. Frank Castle died with his family. Now, there is only…

THE PUNISHER

During the Secret Empire, the deceptive Evil Steve Rogers conscripted the Punisher to unknowingly do his dirty work. After, Frank got his hands on a War Machine suit and tried to pay for his actions by taking out Evil Steve. He no longer has the armor, but the mission to atone for his role in Hydra Nation—as well as the taste the War Machine armor gave him for bigger game—remains.

WORLD WAR FRANK

WRITER:
MATTHEW ROSENBERG

ARTIST:
SZYMON KUDRANSKI

COLORIST:
ANTONIO FABELA

LETTERER:
VC's CORY PETIT

COVER ARTIST:
GREG SMALLWOOD

ASSOCIATE EDITOR:
MARK BASSO

EDITOR:
JAKE THOMAS

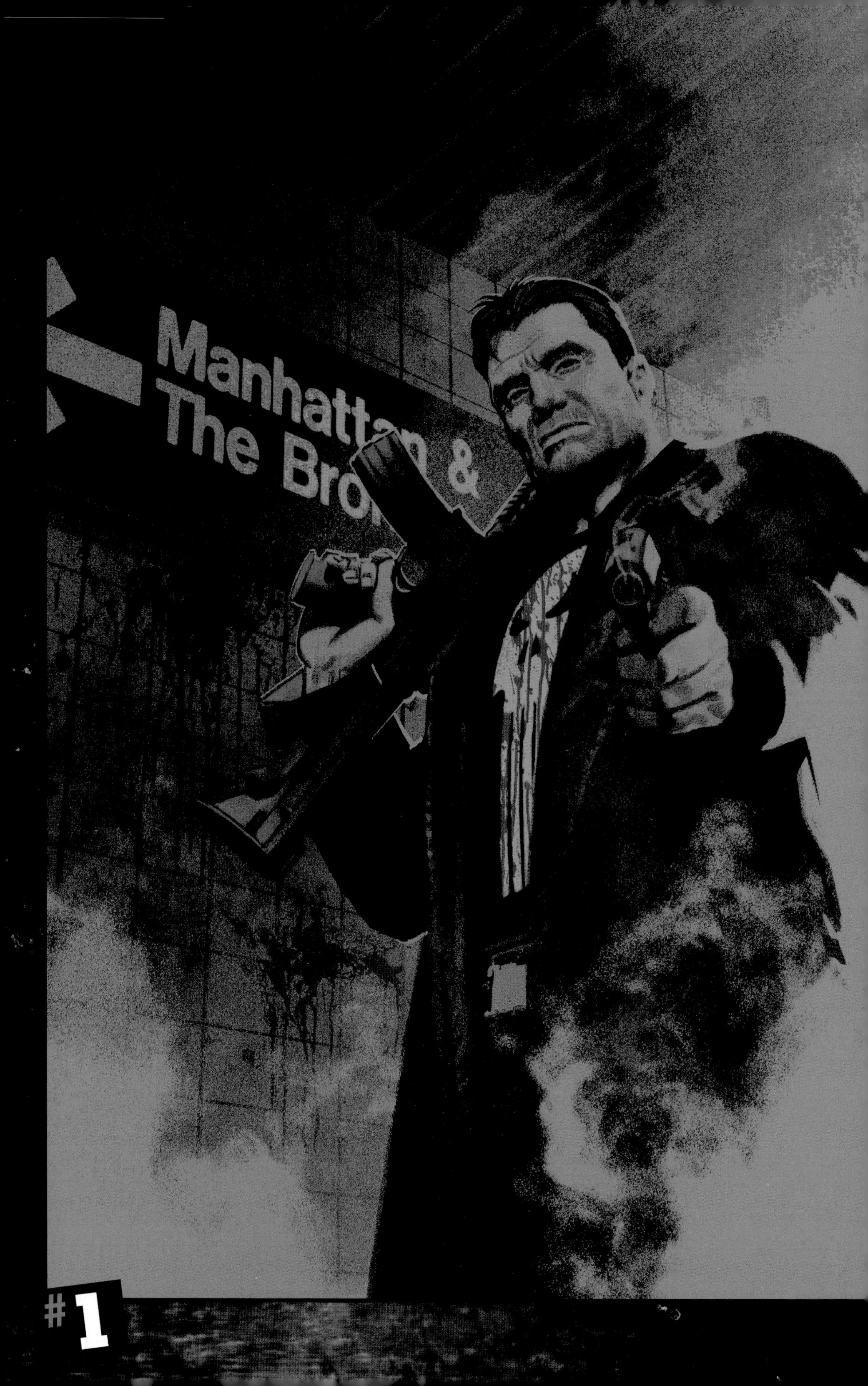
Manhattan &
The Bro
#1

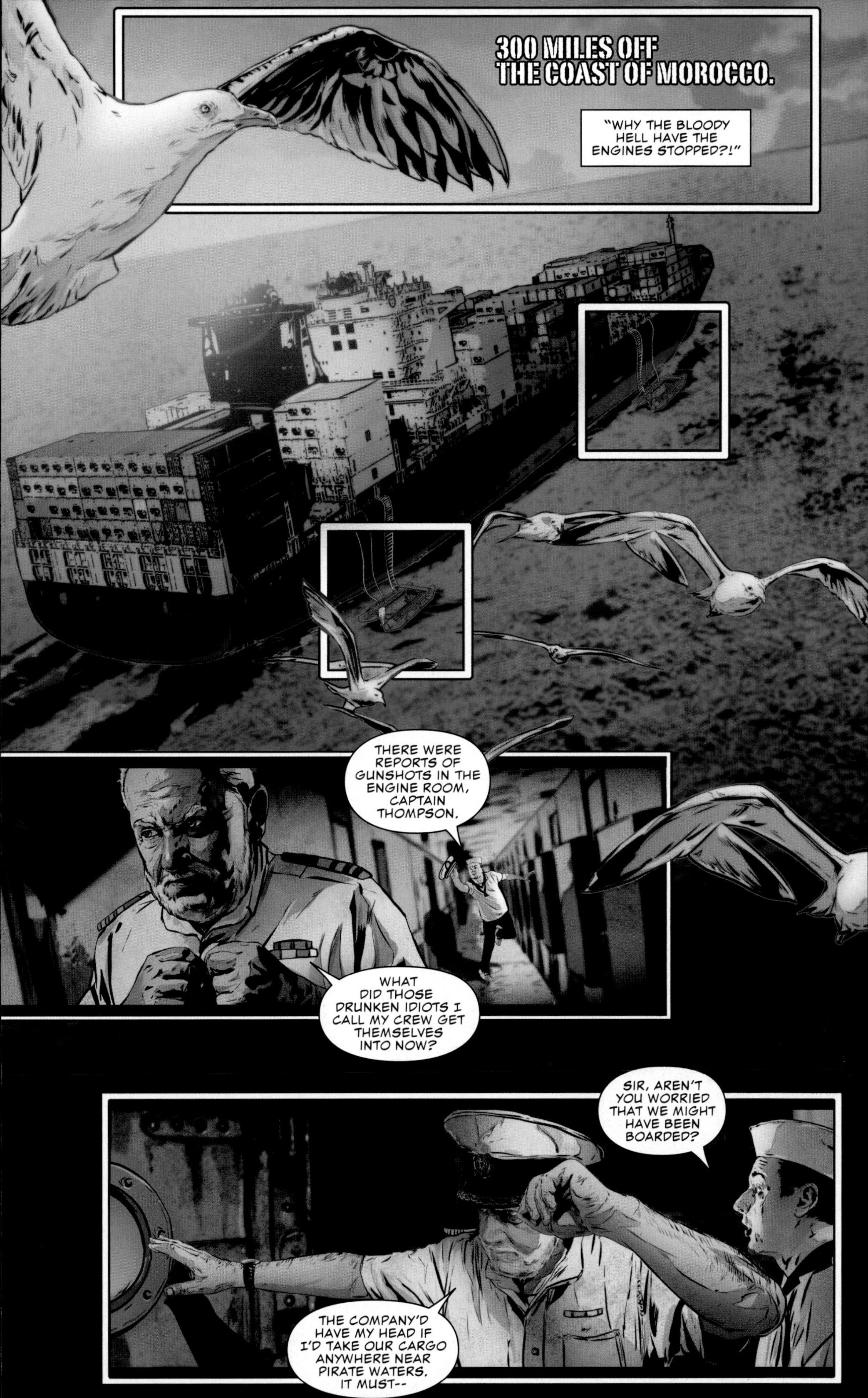
300 MILES OFF THE COAST OF MOROCCO.
"WHY THE BLOODY HELL HAVE THE ENGINES STOPPED?!"
THERE WERE REPORTS OF GUNSHOTS IN THE ENGINE ROOM, CAPTAIN THOMPSON.
WHAT DID THOSE DRUNKEN IDIOTS I CALL MY CREW GET THEMSELVES INTO NOW?
SIR, AREN'T YOU WORRIED THAT WE MIGHT HAVE BEEN BOARDED?
THE COMPANY'D HAVE MY HEAD IF I'D TAKE OUR CARGO ANYWHERE NEAR PIRATE WATERS. IT MUST--

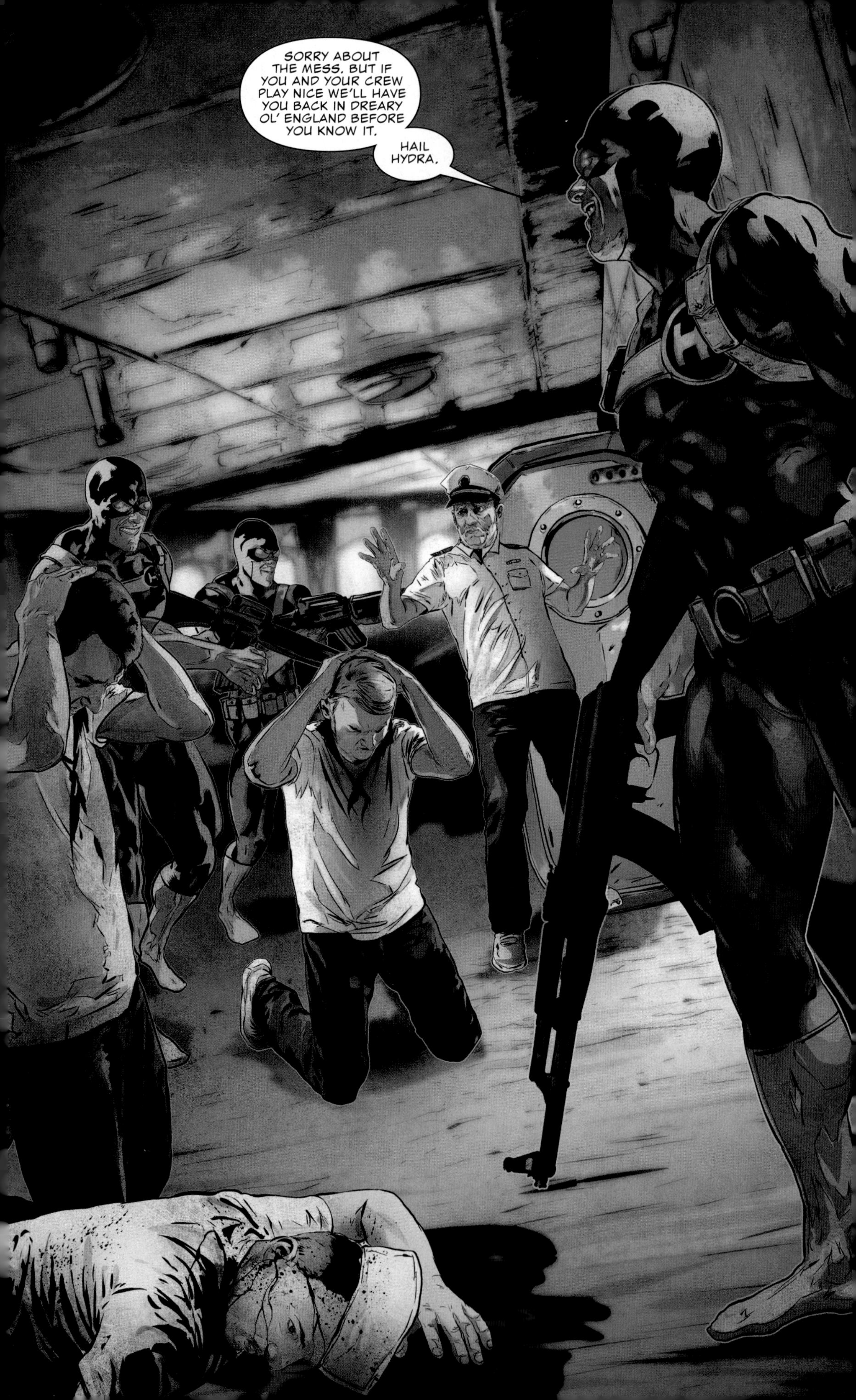
SORRY ABOUT THE MESS, BUT IF YOU AND YOUR CREW PLAY NICE WE'LL HAVE YOU BACK IN DREARY OL' ENGLAND BEFORE YOU KNOW IT.
HAIL HYDRA.

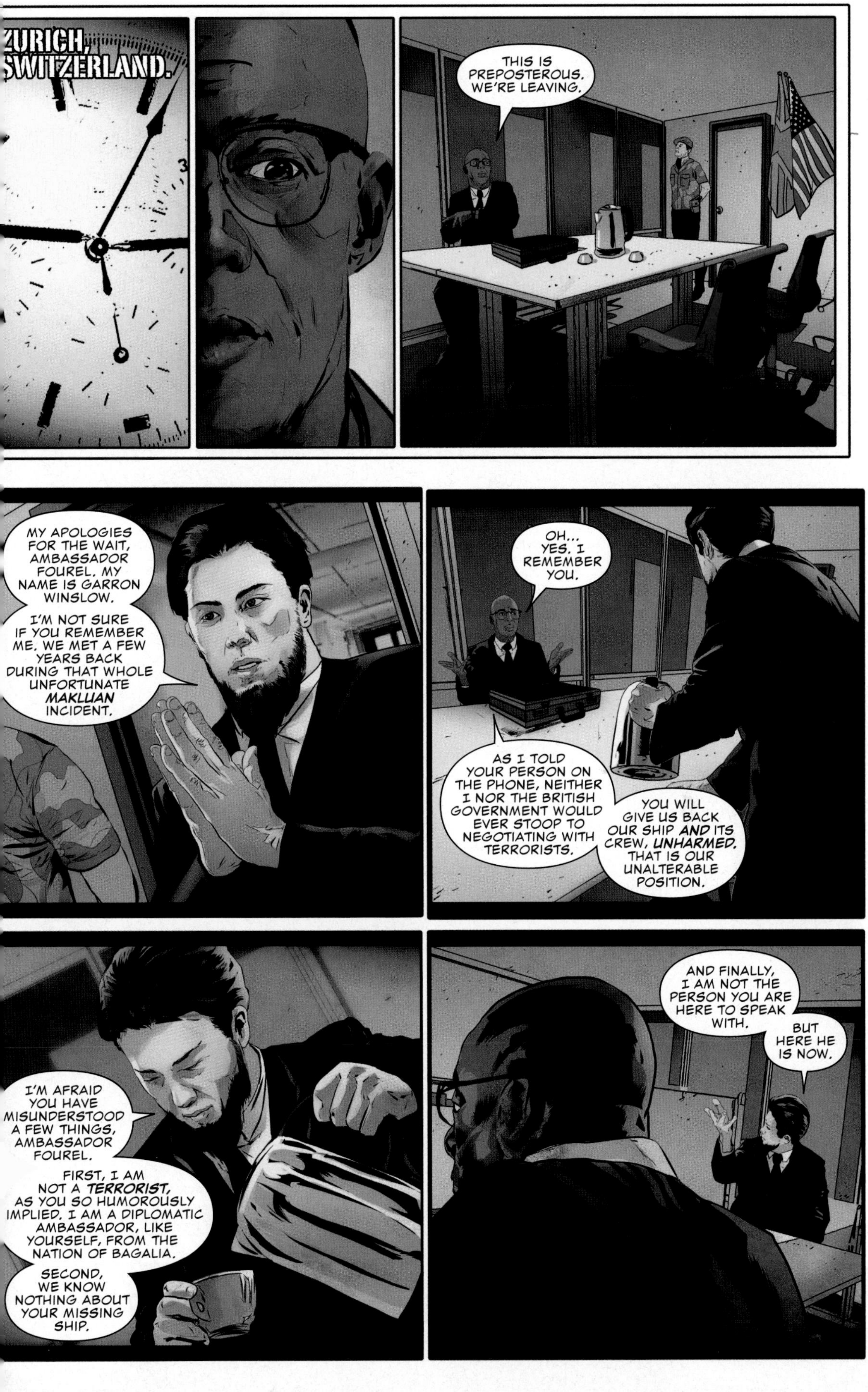

ZURICH, SWITZERLAND.
THIS IS PREPOSTEROUS. WE'RE LEAVING.
MY APOLOGIES FOR THE WAIT, AMBASSADOR FOUREL. MY NAME IS GARRON WINSLOW.
I'M NOT SURE IF YOU REMEMBER ME. WE MET A FEW YEARS BACK DURING THAT WHOLE UNFORTUNATE *MAKLUAN* INCIDENT.
OH... YES. I REMEMBER YOU.
AS I TOLD YOUR PERSON ON THE PHONE, NEITHER I NOR THE BRITISH GOVERNMENT WOULD EVER STOOP TO NEGOTIATING WITH TERRORISTS.
YOU WILL GIVE US BACK OUR SHIP ***AND*** ITS CREW, ***UNHARMED.*** THAT IS OUR UNALTERABLE POSITION.
I'M AFRAID YOU HAVE MISUNDERSTOOD A FEW THINGS, AMBASSADOR FOUREL.
FIRST, I AM NOT A ***TERRORIST,*** AS YOU SO HUMOROUSLY IMPLIED. I AM A DIPLOMATIC AMBASSADOR, LIKE YOURSELF, FROM THE NATION OF BAGALIA.
SECOND, WE KNOW NOTHING ABOUT YOUR MISSING SHIP.
AND FINALLY, I AM NOT THE PERSON YOU ARE HERE TO SPEAK WITH.
BUT HERE HE IS NOW.

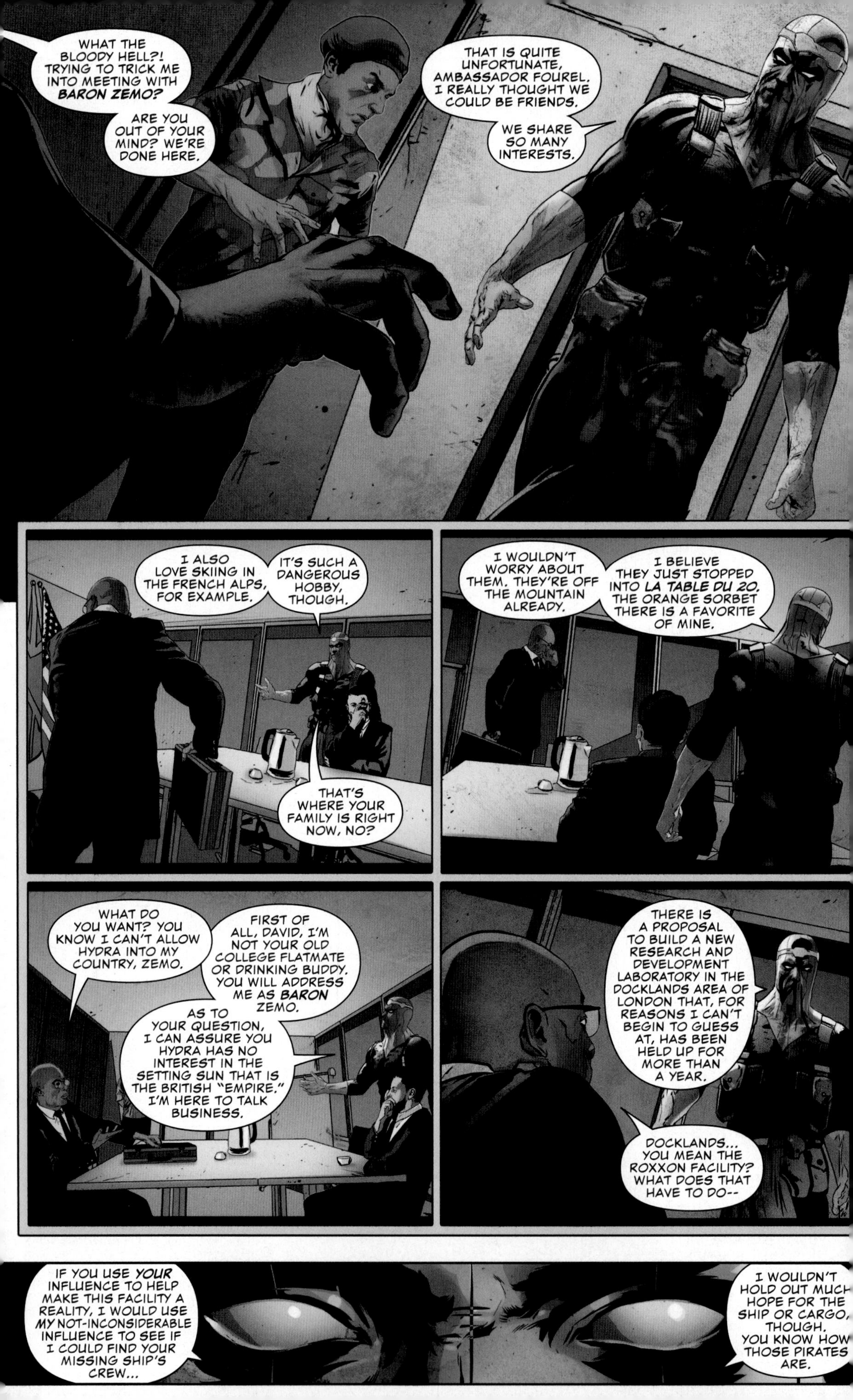
WHAT THE BLOODY HELL?! TRYING TO TRICK ME INTO MEETING WITH BARON ZEMO?
ARE YOU OUT OF YOUR MIND? WE'RE DONE HERE.
THAT IS QUITE UNFORTUNATE, AMBASSADOR FOUREL. I REALLY THOUGHT WE COULD BE FRIENDS.
WE SHARE SO MANY INTERESTS.
I ALSO LOVE SKIING IN THE FRENCH ALPS, FOR EXAMPLE.
IT'S SUCH A DANGEROUS HOBBY, THOUGH.
THAT'S WHERE YOUR FAMILY IS RIGHT NOW, NO?
I WOULDN'T WORRY ABOUT THEM. THEY'RE OFF THE MOUNTAIN ALREADY.
I BELIEVE THEY JUST STOPPED INTO LA TABLE DU 20. THE ORANGE SORBET THERE IS A FAVORITE OF MINE.
WHAT DO YOU WANT? YOU KNOW I CAN'T ALLOW HYDRA INTO MY COUNTRY, ZEMO.
FIRST OF ALL, DAVID, I'M NOT YOUR OLD COLLEGE FLATMATE OR DRINKING BUDDY. YOU WILL ADDRESS ME AS BARON ZEMO.
AS TO YOUR QUESTION, I CAN ASSURE YOU HYDRA HAS NO INTEREST IN THE SETTING SUN THAT IS THE BRITISH "EMPIRE." I'M HERE TO TALK BUSINESS.
THERE IS A PROPOSAL TO BUILD A NEW RESEARCH AND DEVELOPMENT LABORATORY IN THE DOCKLANDS AREA OF LONDON THAT, FOR REASONS I CAN'T BEGIN TO GUESS AT, HAS BEEN HELD UP FOR MORE THAN A YEAR.
DOCKLANDS... YOU MEAN THE ROXXON FACILITY? WHAT DOES THAT HAVE TO DO--
IF YOU USE YOUR INFLUENCE TO HELP MAKE THIS FACILITY A REALITY, I WOULD USE MY NOT-INCONSIDERABLE INFLUENCE TO SEE IF I COULD FIND YOUR MISSING SHIP'S CREW...
I WOULDN'T HOLD OUT MUCH HOPE FOR THE SHIP OR CARGO, THOUGH. YOU KNOW HOW THOSE PIRATES ARE.

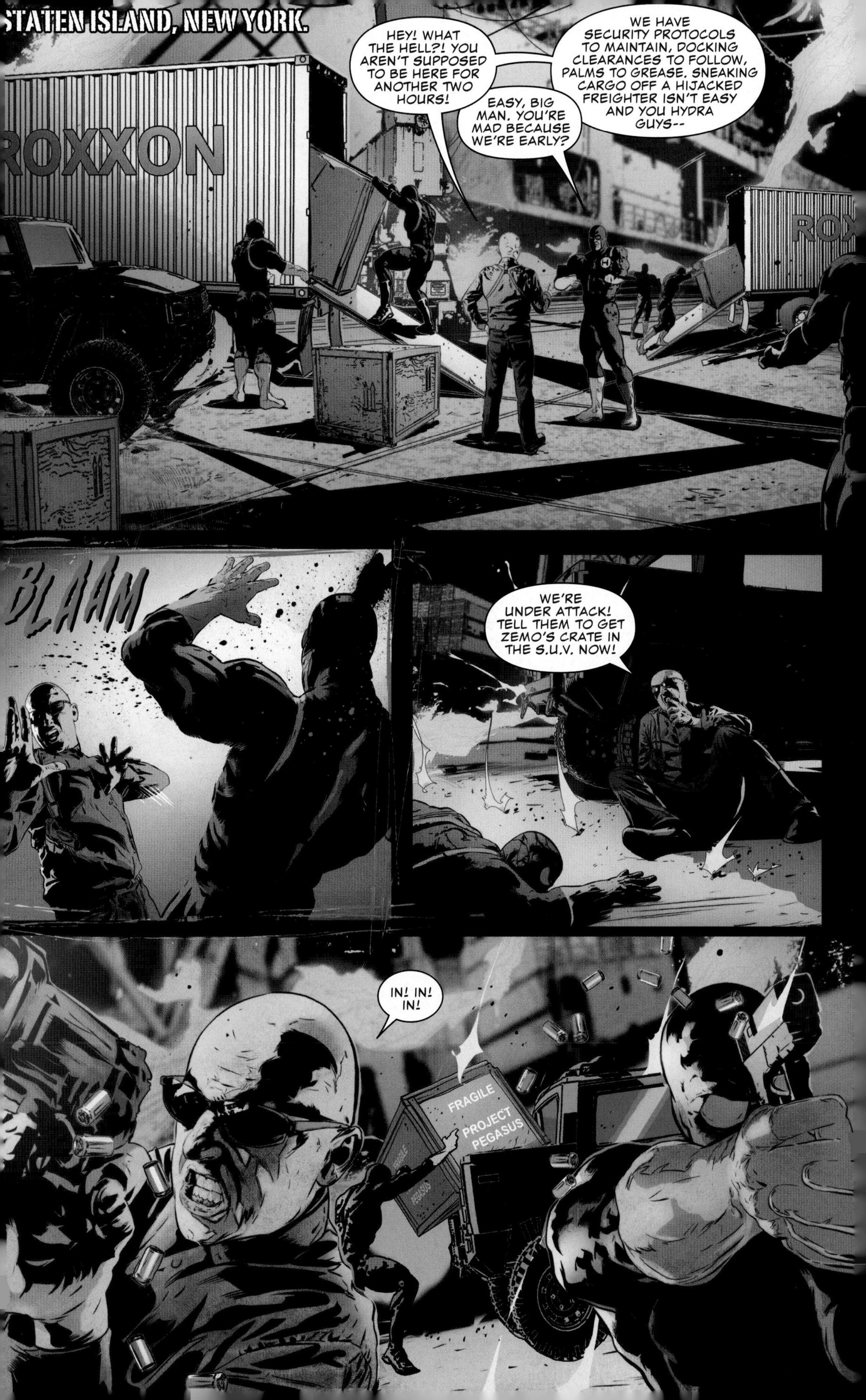
STATEN ISLAND, NEW YORK.
HEY! WHAT THE HELL?! YOU AREN'T SUPPOSED TO BE HERE FOR ANOTHER TWO HOURS!
EASY, BIG MAN. YOU'RE MAD BECAUSE WE'RE EARLY?
WE HAVE SECURITY PROTOCOLS TO MAINTAIN, DOCKING CLEARANCES TO FOLLOW, PALMS TO GREASE. SNEAKING CARGO OFF A HIJACKED FREIGHTER ISN'T EASY AND YOU HYDRA GUYS--
ROXXON
BLAAM
WE'RE UNDER ATTACK! TELL THEM TO GET ZEMO'S CRATE IN THE S.U.V. NOW!
IN! IN! IN!
FRAGILE
PROJECT PEGASUS

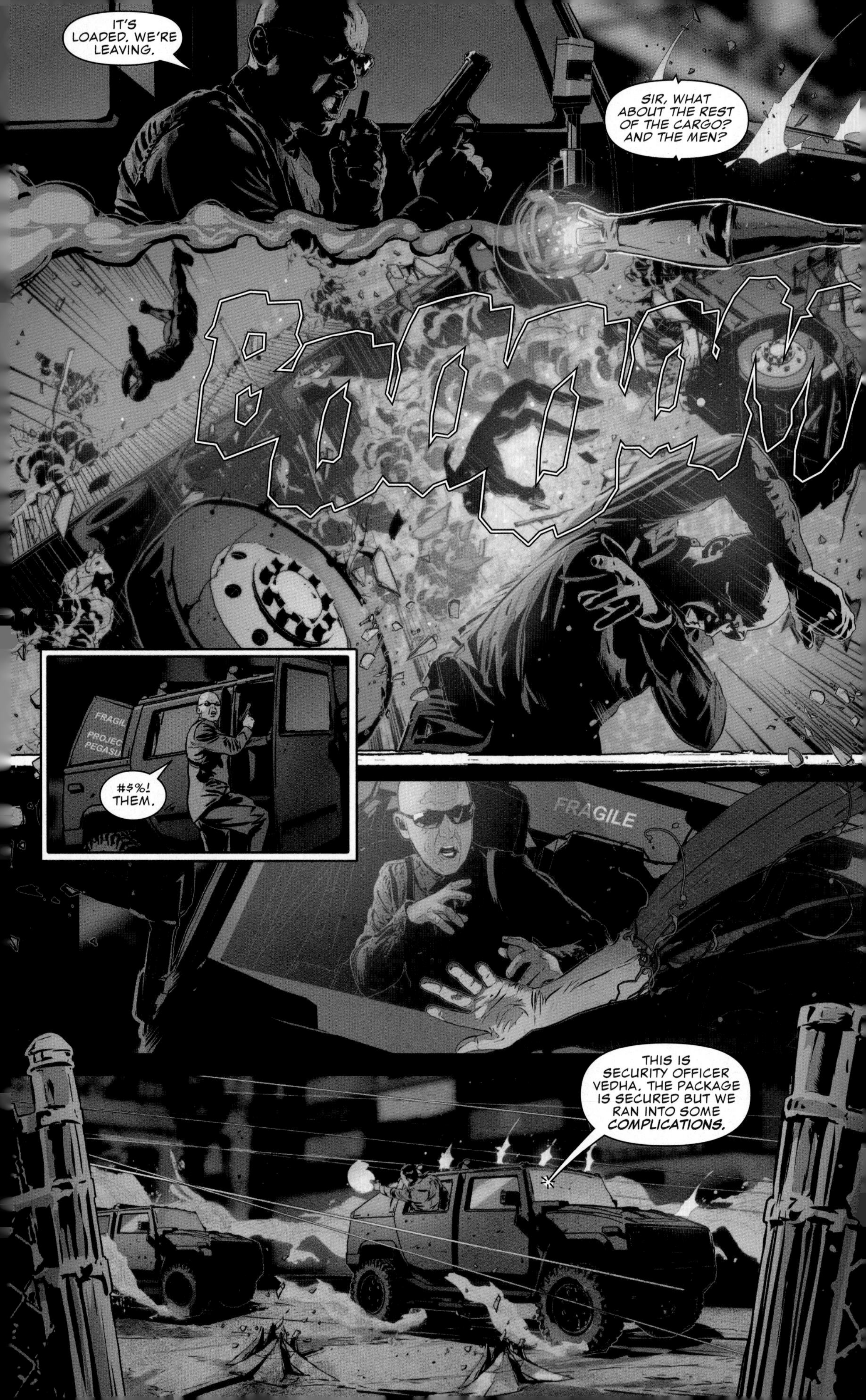

IT'S LOADED. WE'RE LEAVING.
SIR, WHAT ABOUT THE REST OF THE CARGO? AND THE MEN?
BOOOOOM
FRAGILE
PROJEC
PEGASU
#$%! THEM.
FRAGILE
THIS IS SECURITY OFFICER VEDHA. THE PACKAGE IS SECURED BUT WE RAN INTO SOME COMPLICATIONS.

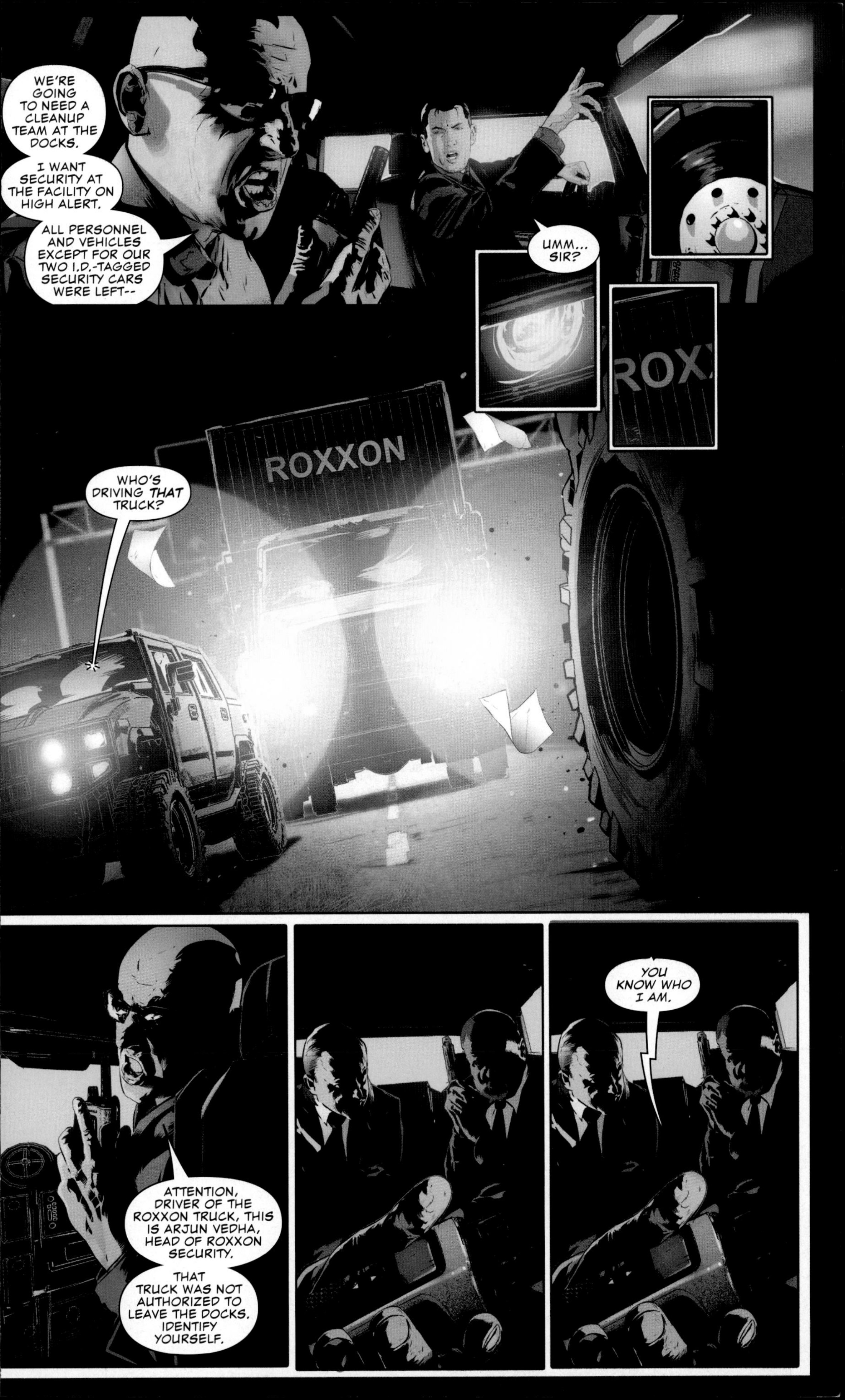
WE'RE GOING TO NEED A CLEANUP TEAM AT THE DOCKS.
I WANT SECURITY AT THE FACILITY ON HIGH ALERT.
ALL PERSONNEL AND VEHICLES EXCEPT FOR OUR TWO I.D.-TAGGED SECURITY CARS WERE LEFT--
UMM... SIR?
ROXX
ROXXON
WHO'S DRIVING *THAT* TRUCK?
ATTENTION, DRIVER OF THE ROXXON TRUCK, THIS IS ARJUN VEDHA, HEAD OF ROXXON SECURITY.
THAT TRUCK WAS NOT AUTHORIZED TO LEAVE THE DOCKS. IDENTIFY YOURSELF.
YOU KNOW WHO I AM.

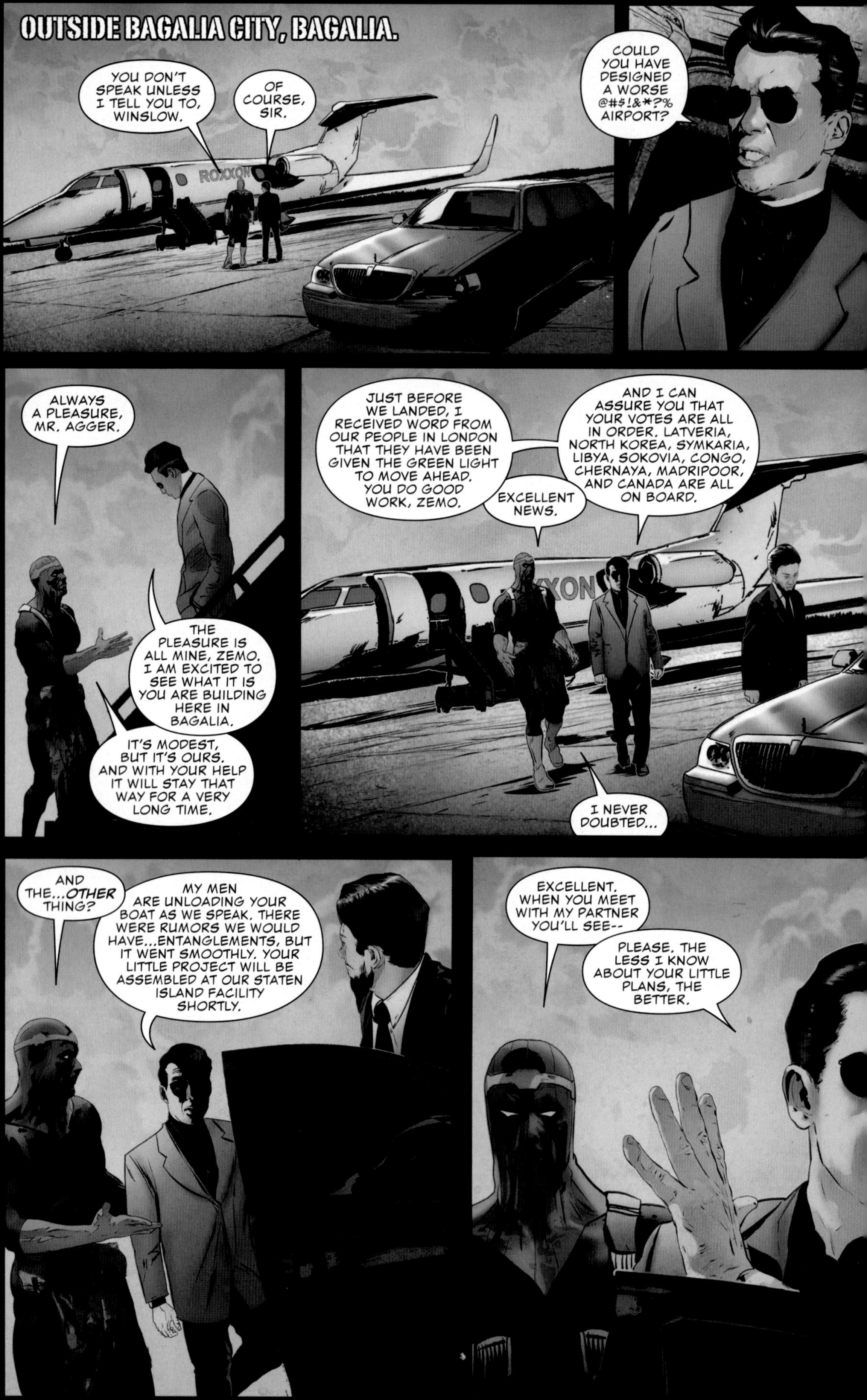
OUTSIDE BAGALIA CITY, BAGALIA.
YOU DON'T SPEAK UNLESS I TELL YOU TO, WINSLOW.
OF COURSE, SIR.
ROXXON
COULD YOU HAVE DESIGNED A WORSE @#$!&*?% AIRPORT?
ALWAYS A PLEASURE, MR. AGGER.
THE PLEASURE IS ALL MINE, ZEMO. I AM EXCITED TO SEE WHAT IT IS YOU ARE BUILDING HERE IN BAGALIA.
IT'S MODEST, BUT IT'S OURS. AND WITH YOUR HELP IT WILL STAY THAT WAY FOR A VERY LONG TIME.
JUST BEFORE WE LANDED, I RECEIVED WORD FROM OUR PEOPLE IN LONDON THAT THEY HAVE BEEN GIVEN THE GREEN LIGHT TO MOVE AHEAD. YOU DO GOOD WORK, ZEMO.
EXCELLENT NEWS.
AND I CAN ASSURE YOU THAT YOUR VOTES ARE ALL IN ORDER. LATVERIA, NORTH KOREA, SYMKARIA, LIBYA, SOKOVIA, CONGO, CHERNAYA, MADRIPOOR, AND CANADA ARE ALL ON BOARD.
I NEVER DOUBTED...
AND THE...*OTHER* THING?
MY MEN ARE UNLOADING YOUR BOAT AS WE SPEAK. THERE WERE RUMORS WE WOULD HAVE...ENTANGLEMENTS, BUT IT WENT *SMOOTHLY*. YOUR LITTLE PROJECT WILL BE ASSEMBLED AT OUR STATEN ISLAND FACILITY SHORTLY.
EXCELLENT. WHEN YOU MEET WITH MY PARTNER YOU'LL SEE--
PLEASE. THE LESS I KNOW ABOUT YOUR LITTLE PLANS, THE BETTER.

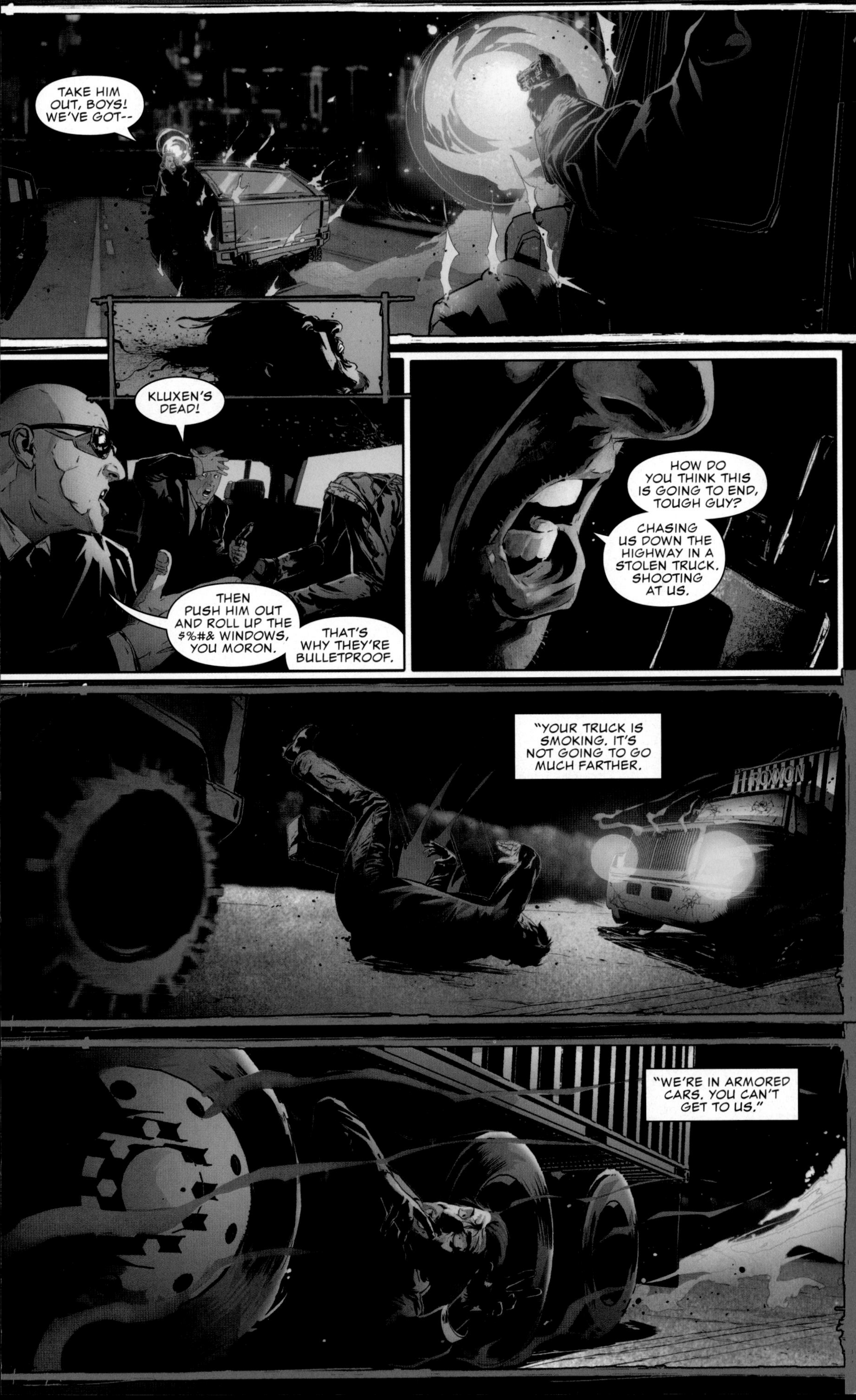
TAKE HIM OUT, BOYS! WE'VE GOT--
KLUXEN'S DEAD!
THEN PUSH HIM OUT AND ROLL UP THE $%#& WINDOWS, YOU MORON.
THAT'S WHY THEY'RE BULLETPROOF.
HOW DO YOU THINK THIS IS GOING TO END, TOUGH GUY?
CHASING US DOWN THE HIGHWAY IN A STOLEN TRUCK, SHOOTING AT US.
"YOUR TRUCK IS SMOKING. IT'S NOT GOING TO GO MUCH FARTHER.
ROXXON
"WE'RE IN ARMORED CARS. YOU CAN'T GET TO US."

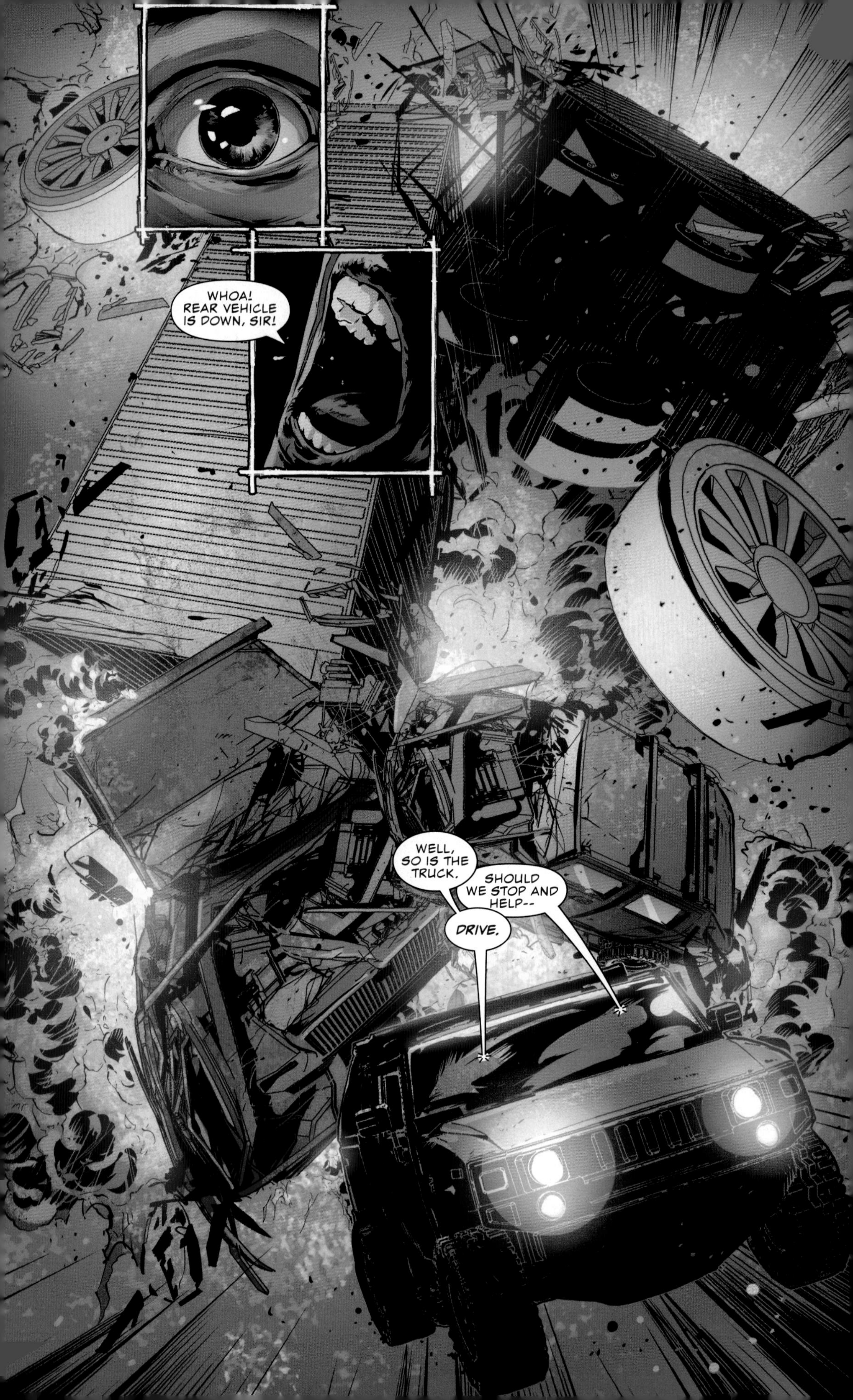
WHOA! REAR VEHICLE IS DOWN, SIR!
WELL, SO IS THE TRUCK.
SHOULD WE STOP AND HELP--
DRIVE.

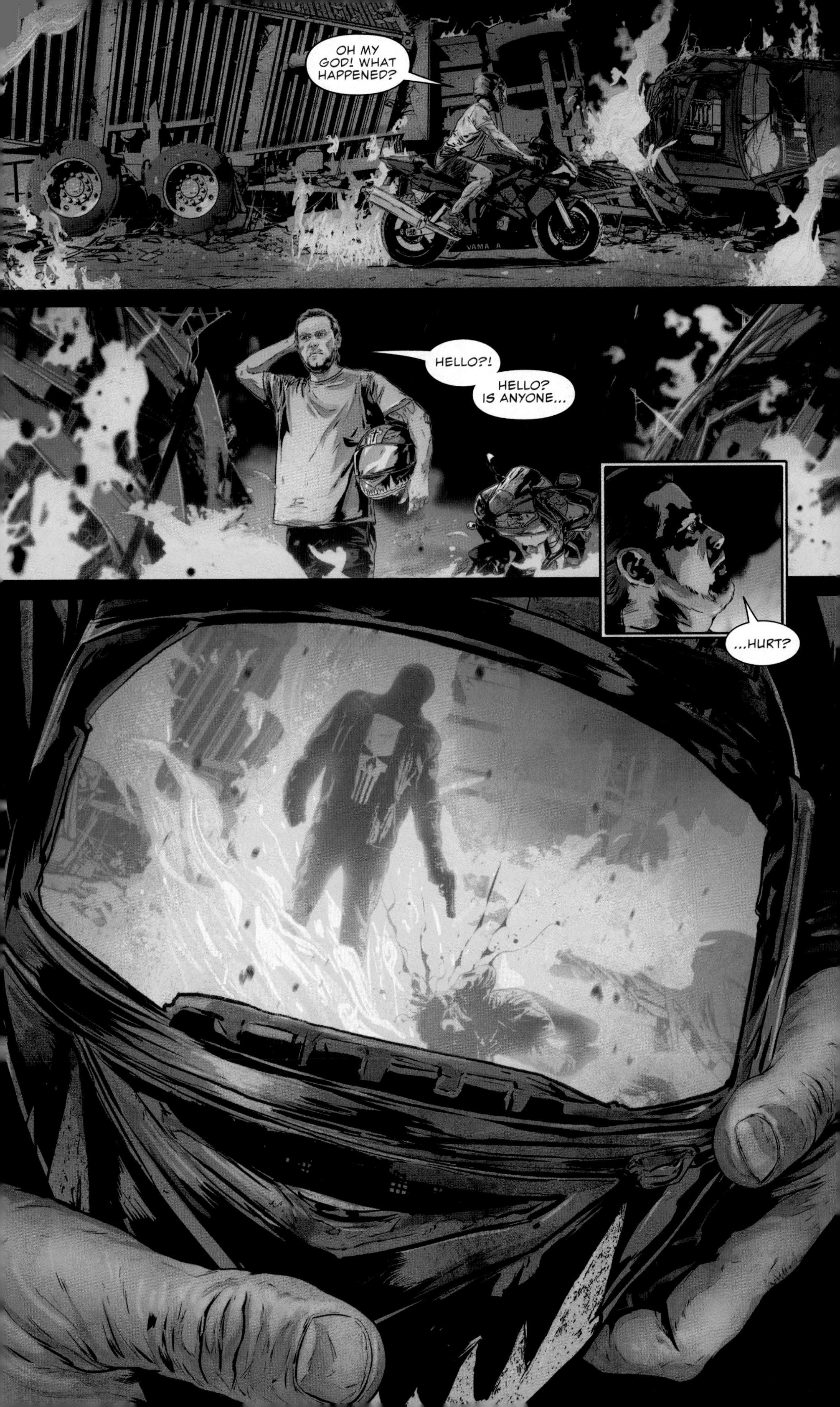
OH MY GOD! WHAT HAPPENED?
HELLO?!
HELLO? IS ANYONE...
...HURT?

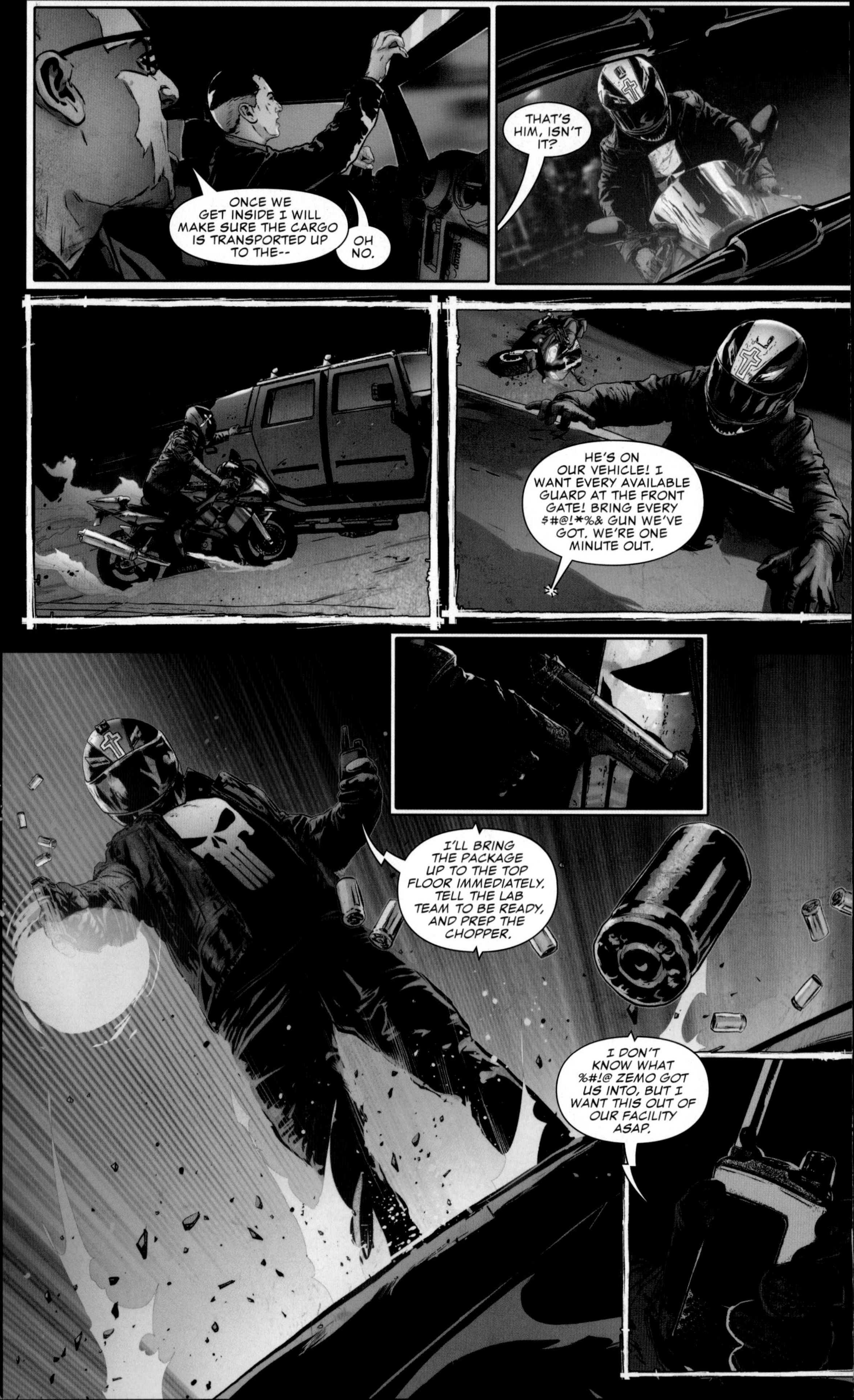
ONCE WE GET INSIDE I WILL MAKE SURE THE CARGO IS TRANSPORTED UP TO THE--
OH NO.
THAT'S HIM, ISN'T IT?
HE'S ON OUR VEHICLE! I WANT EVERY AVAILABLE GUARD AT THE FRONT GATE! BRING EVERY $#@!*%& GUN WE'VE GOT. WE'RE ONE MINUTE OUT.
I'LL BRING THE PACKAGE UP TO THE TOP FLOOR IMMEDIATELY. TELL THE LAB TEAM TO BE READY, AND PREP THE CHOPPER.
I DON'T KNOW WHAT %#!@ ZEMO GOT US INTO, BUT I WANT THIS OUT OF OUR FACILITY ASAP.

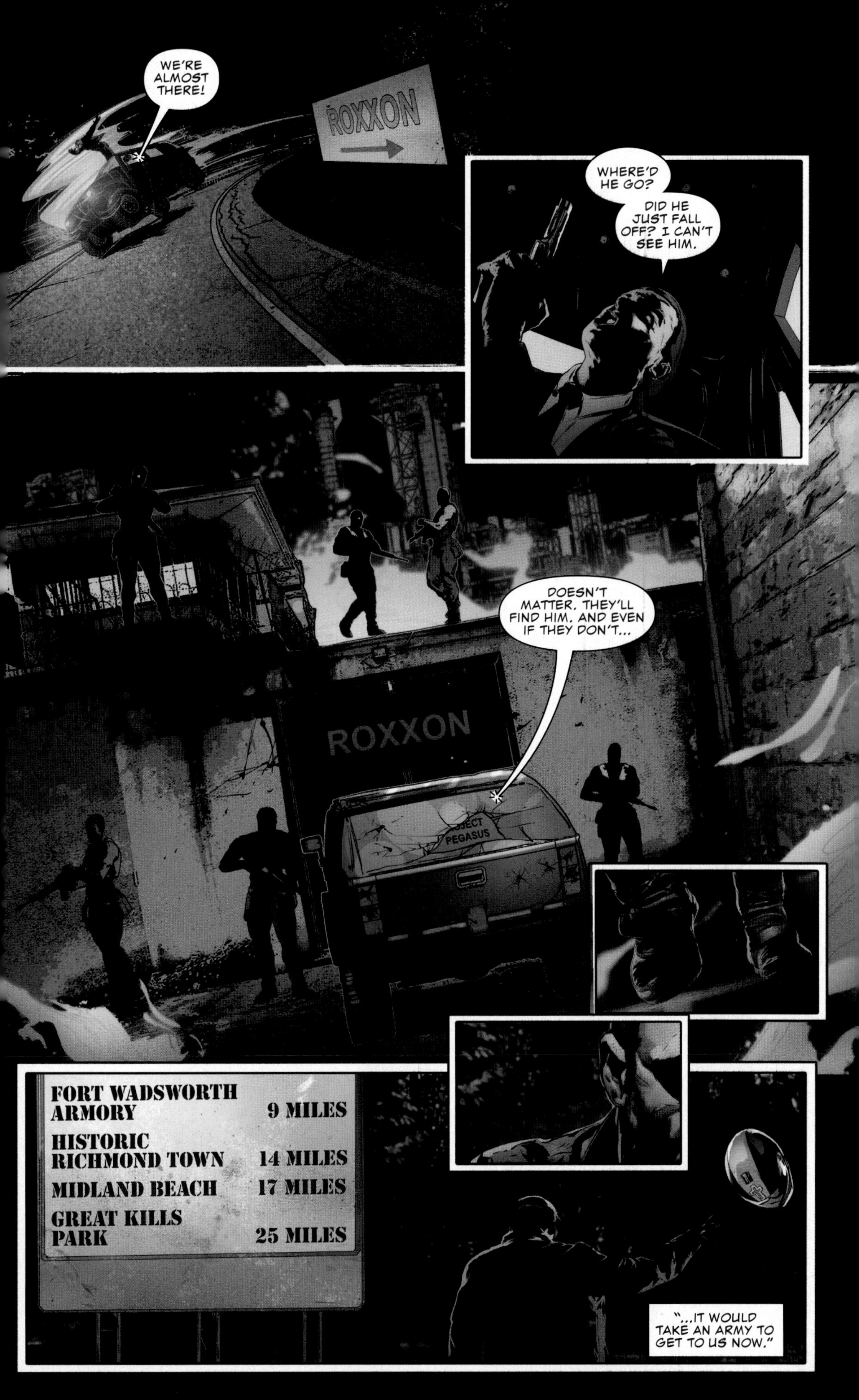
WE'RE ALMOST THERE!
ROXXON
WHERE'D HE GO?
DID HE JUST FALL OFF? I CAN'T SEE HIM.
DOESN'T MATTER. THEY'LL FIND HIM. AND EVEN IF THEY DON'T...
ROXXON
PEGASUS
FORT WADSWORTH ARMORY 9 MILES
HISTORIC RICHMOND TOWN 14 MILES
MIDLAND BEACH 17 MILES
GREAT KILLS PARK 25 MILES
"...IT WOULD TAKE AN ARMY TO GET TO US NOW."

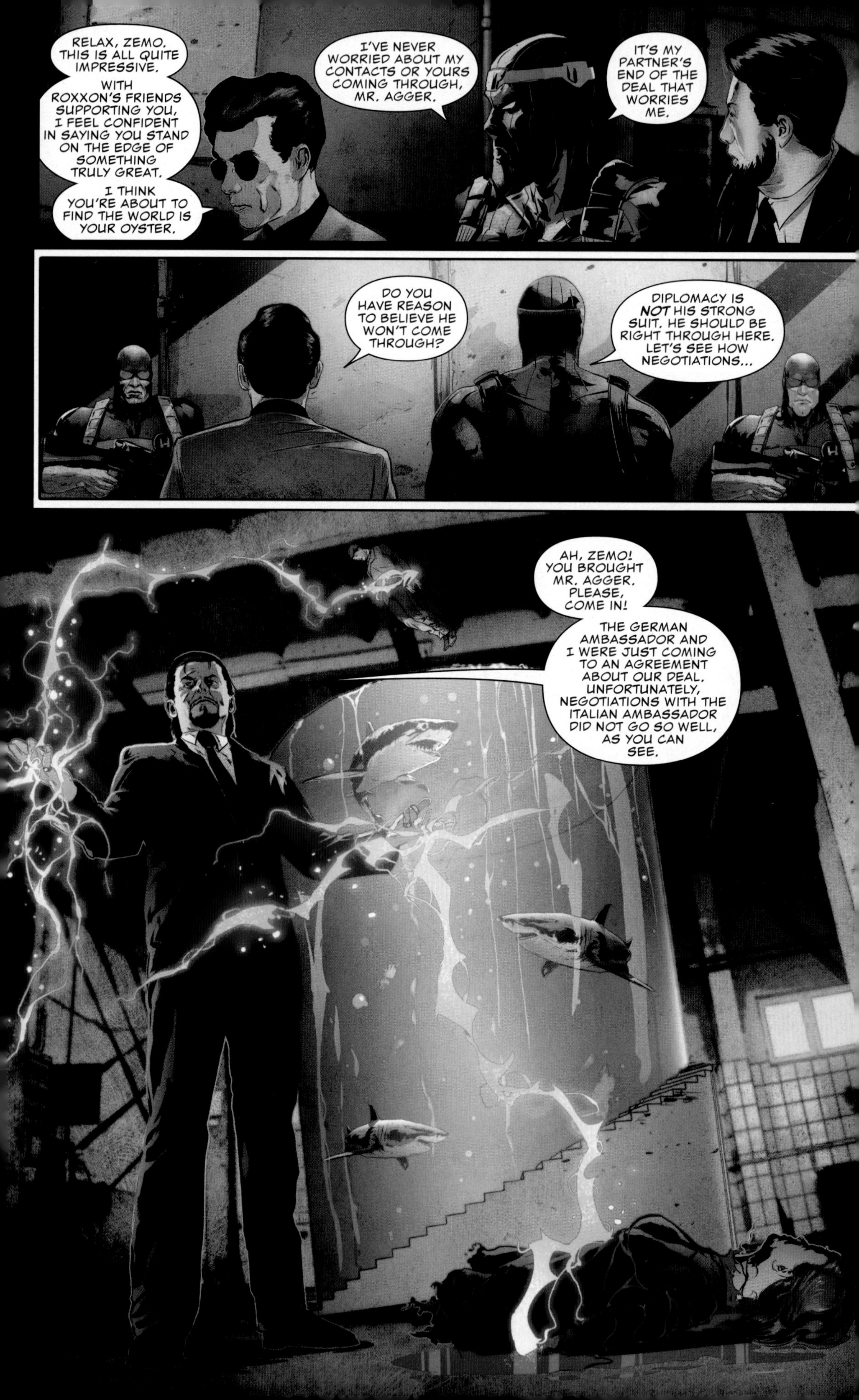
RELAX, ZEMO. THIS IS ALL QUITE IMPRESSIVE.
WITH ROXXON'S FRIENDS SUPPORTING YOU, I FEEL CONFIDENT IN SAYING YOU STAND ON THE EDGE OF SOMETHING TRULY GREAT.
I THINK YOU'RE ABOUT TO FIND THE WORLD IS YOUR OYSTER.
I'VE NEVER WORRIED ABOUT MY CONTACTS OR YOURS COMING THROUGH, MR. AGGER.
IT'S MY PARTNER'S END OF THE DEAL THAT WORRIES ME.
DO YOU HAVE REASON TO BELIEVE HE WON'T COME THROUGH?
DIPLOMACY IS **NOT** HIS STRONG SUIT. HE SHOULD BE RIGHT THROUGH HERE. LET'S SEE HOW NEGOTIATIONS...
AH, ZEMO! YOU BROUGHT MR. AGGER. PLEASE, COME IN!
THE GERMAN AMBASSADOR AND I WERE JUST COMING TO AN AGREEMENT ABOUT OUR DEAL. UNFORTUNATELY, NEGOTIATIONS WITH THE ITALIAN AMBASSADOR DID NOT GO SO WELL, AS YOU CAN SEE.

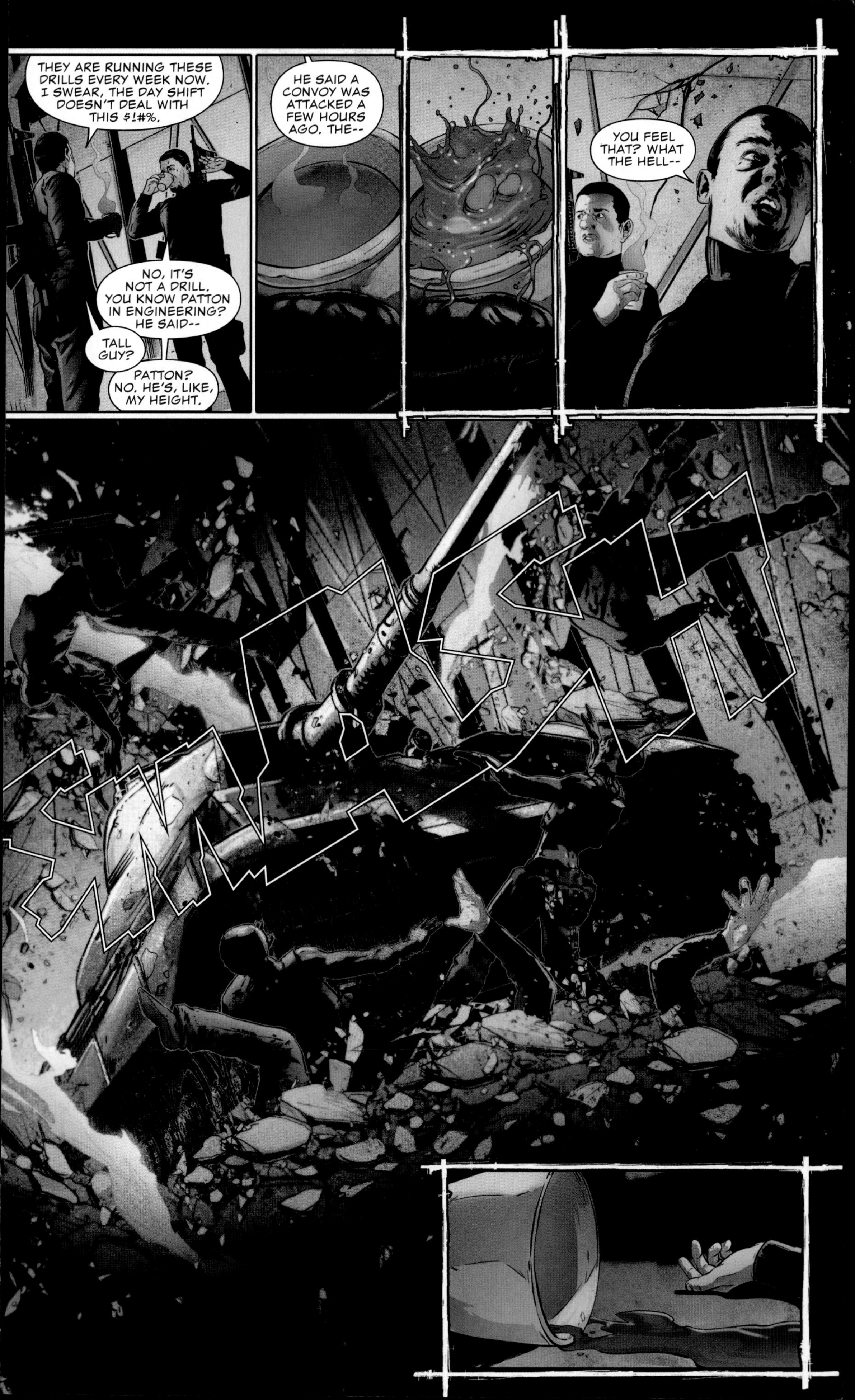
THEY ARE RUNNING THESE DRILLS EVERY WEEK NOW. I SWEAR, THE DAY SHIFT DOESN'T DEAL WITH THIS $!#%.
NO, IT'S NOT A DRILL. YOU KNOW PATTON IN ENGINEERING? HE SAID--
TALL GUY?
PATTON? NO. HE'S, LIKE, MY HEIGHT.
HE SAID A CONVOY WAS ATTACKED A FEW HOURS AGO. THE--
YOU FEEL THAT? WHAT THE HELL--

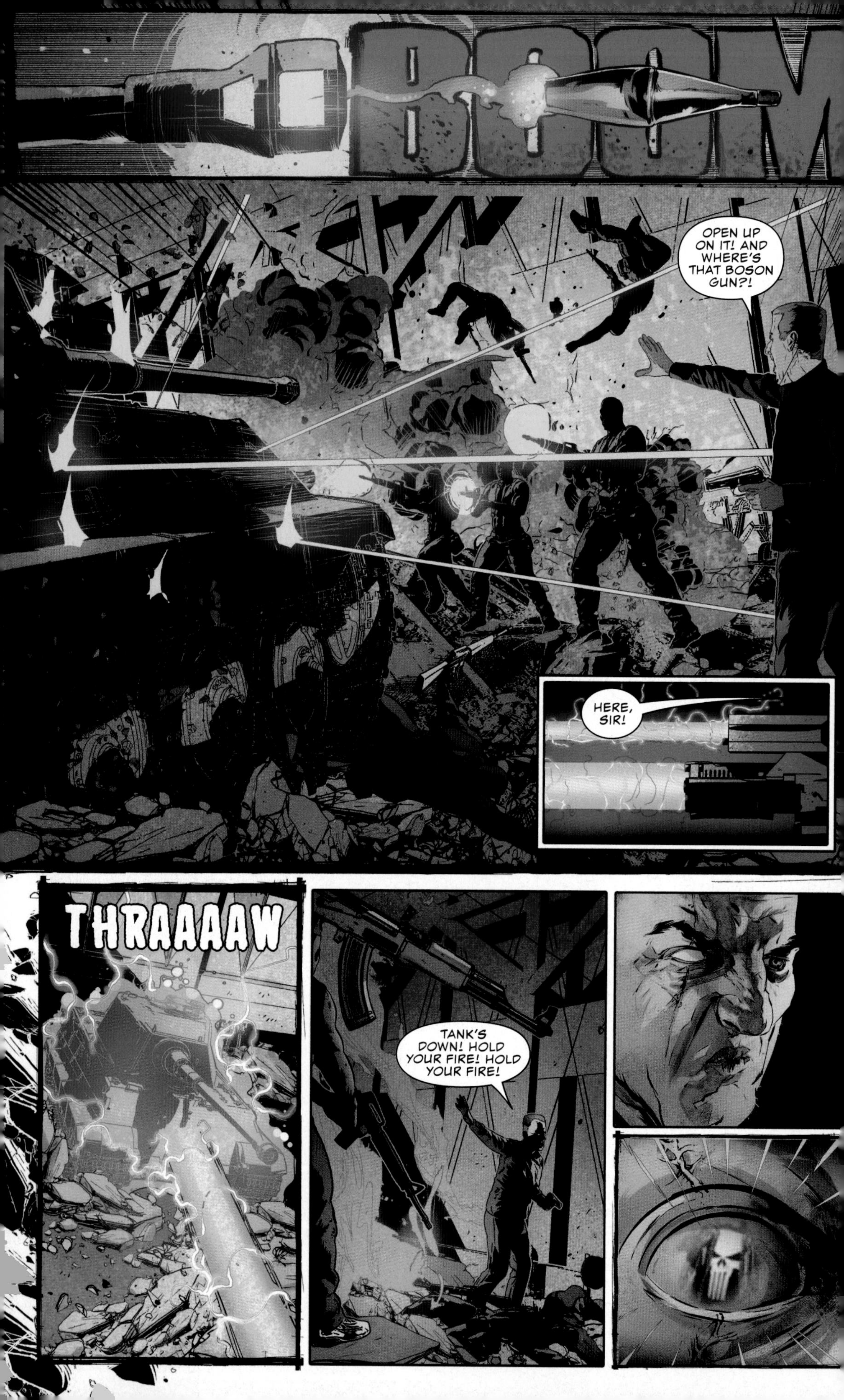
BOOM
OPEN UP ON IT! AND WHERE'S THAT BOSON GUN?!
HERE, SIR!
THRAAAAW
TANK'S DOWN! HOLD YOUR FIRE! HOLD YOUR FIRE!

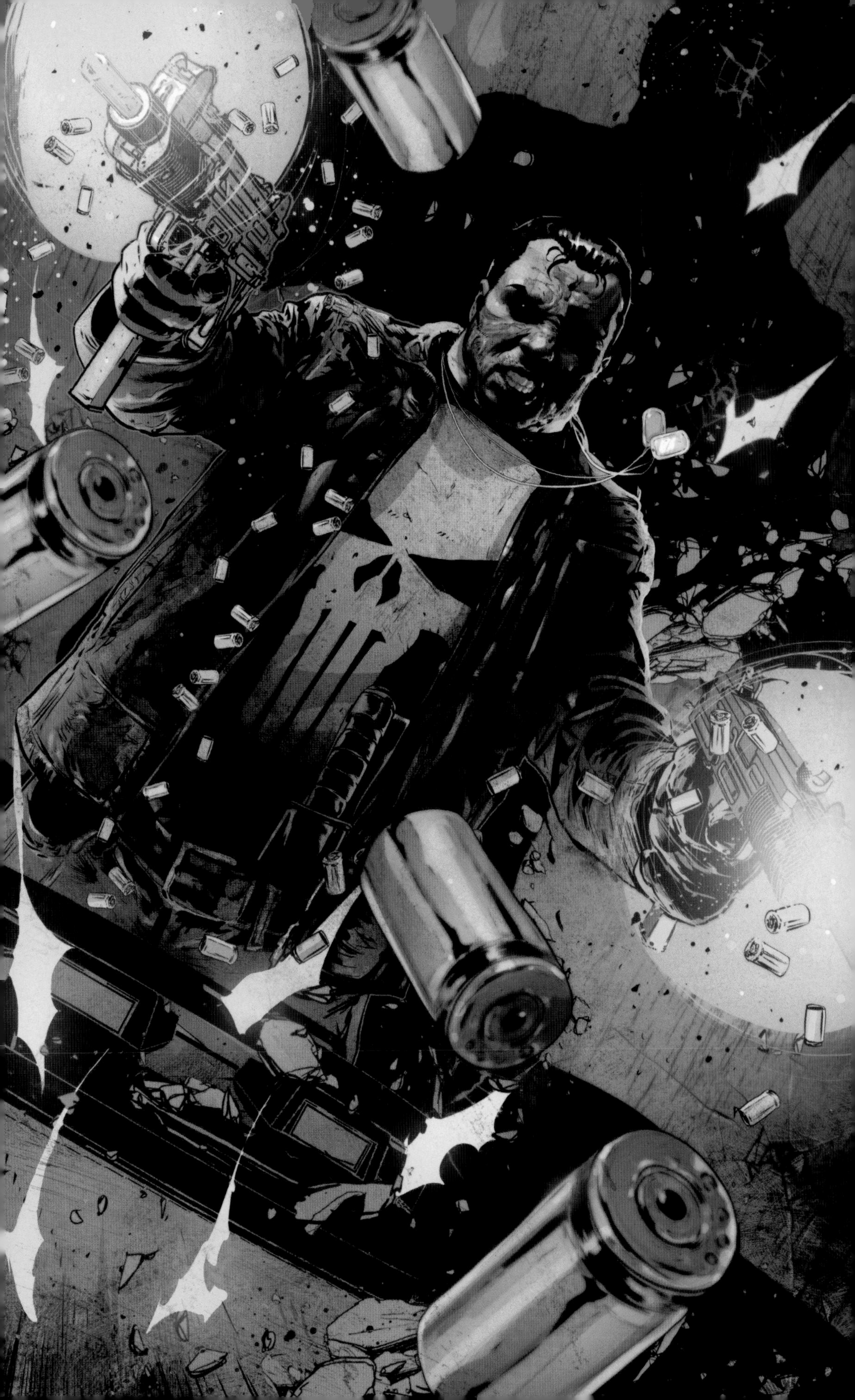

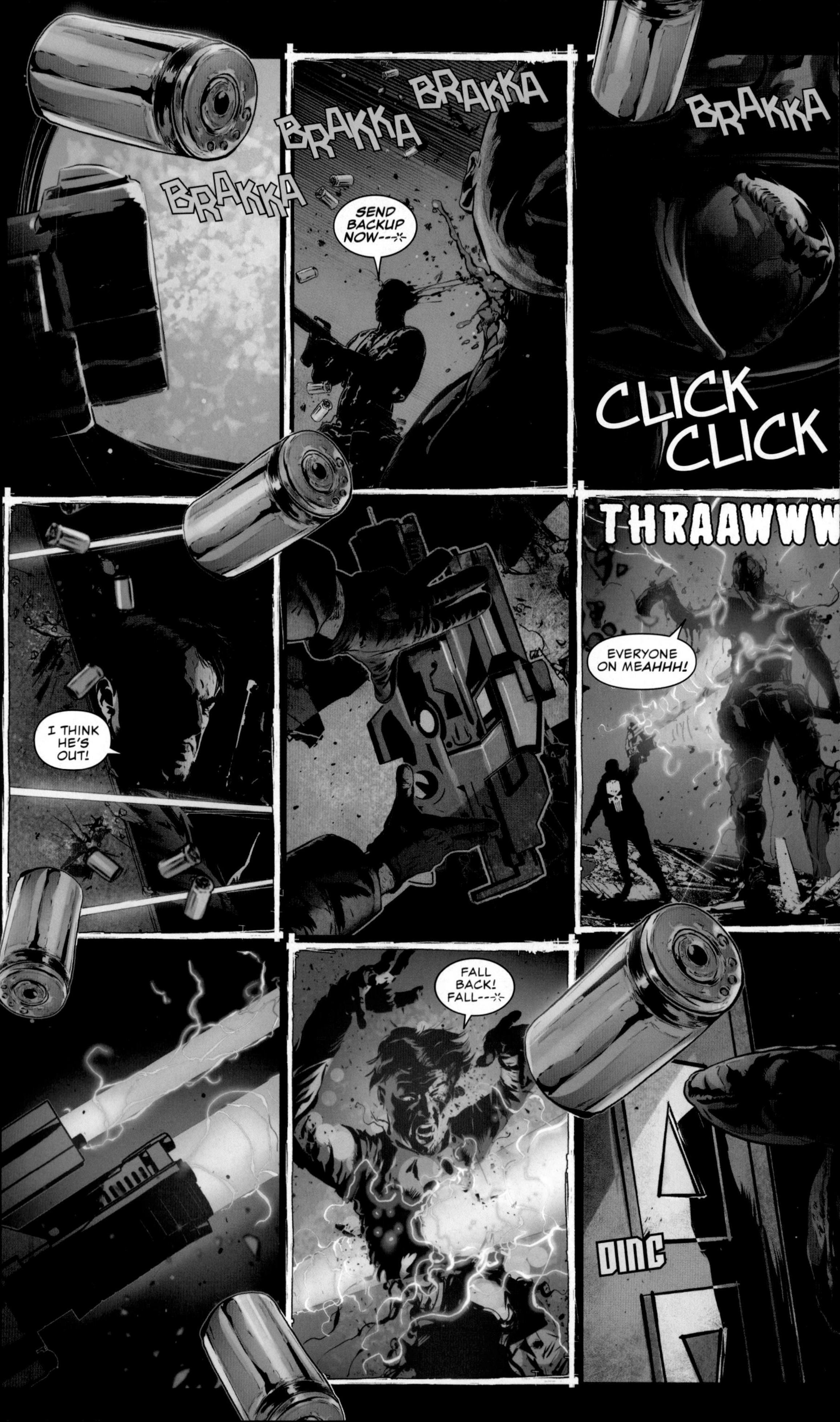
BRAKKA
BRAKKA
BRAKKA
SEND BACKUP NOW--
BRAKKA
CLICK CLICK
I THINK HE'S OUT!
THRAAWWW
EVERYONE ON MEAHHH!
FALL BACK! FALL--
DING

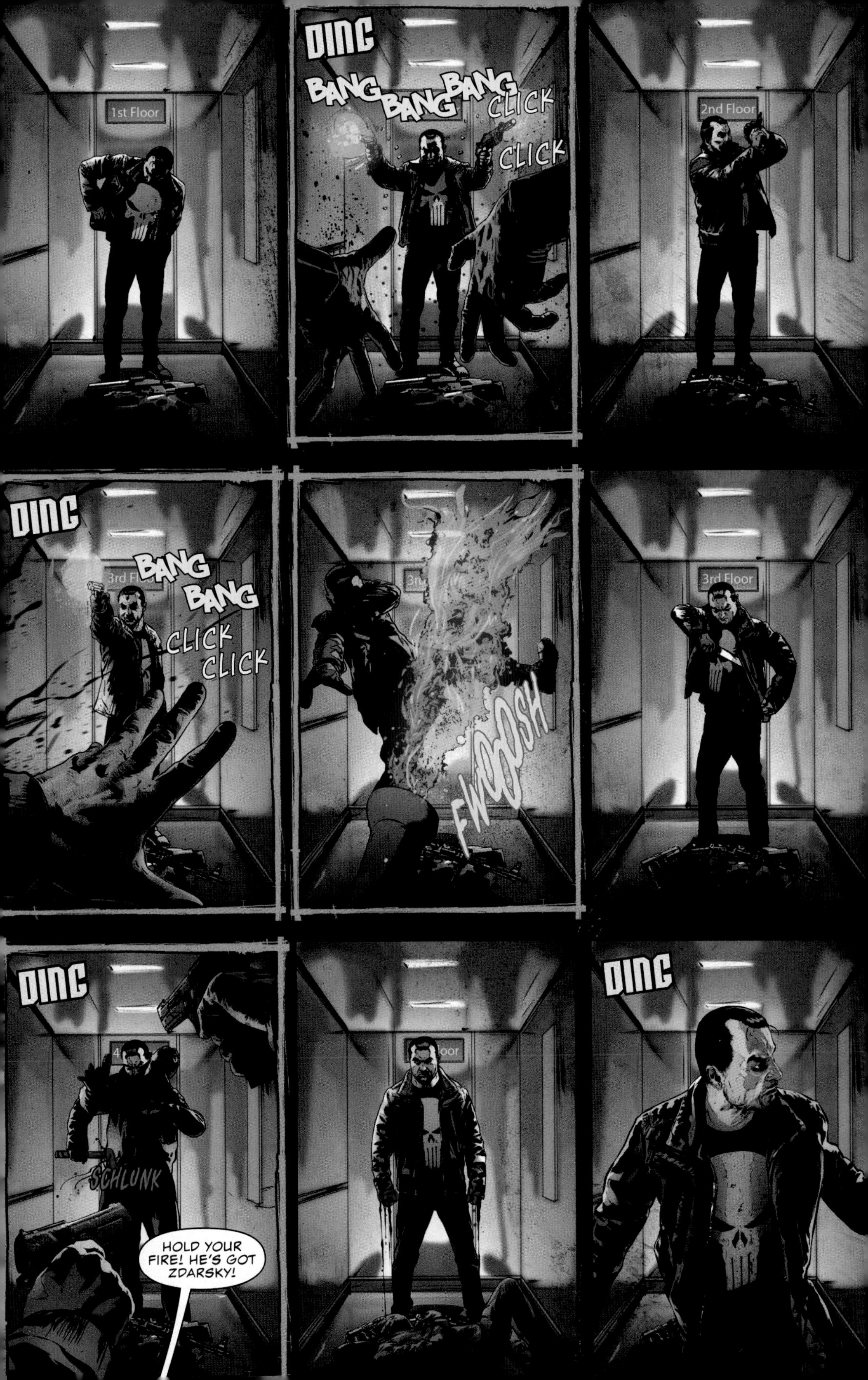
1st Floor
DING
BANG BANG BANG
CLICK
CLICK
2nd Floor
DING
3rd Floor
BANG
BANG
CLICK
CLICK
FWOOSH
3rd Floor
DING
SCHLUNK
HOLD YOUR FIRE! HE'S GOT ZDARSKY!
DING

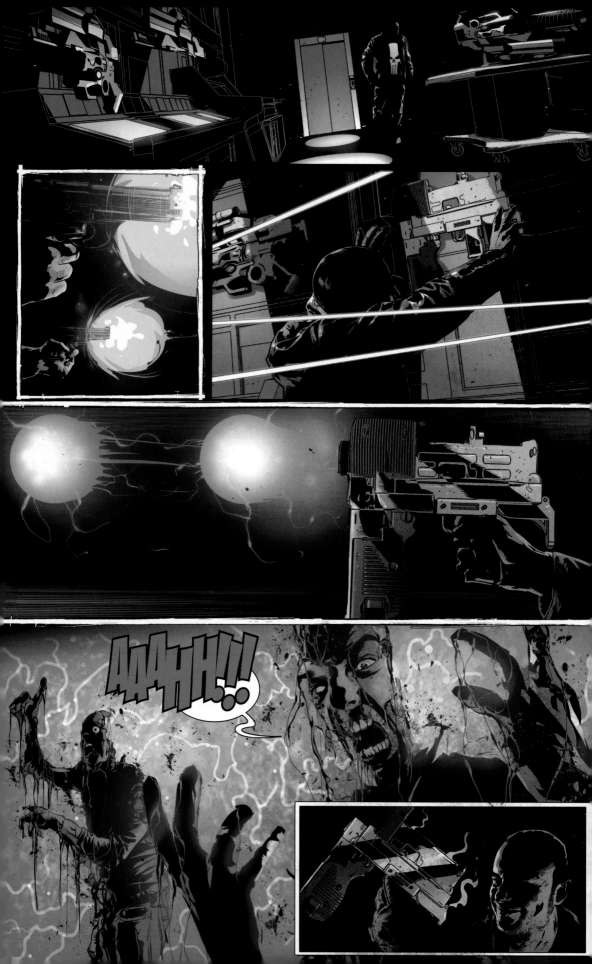

AAAHH!!!

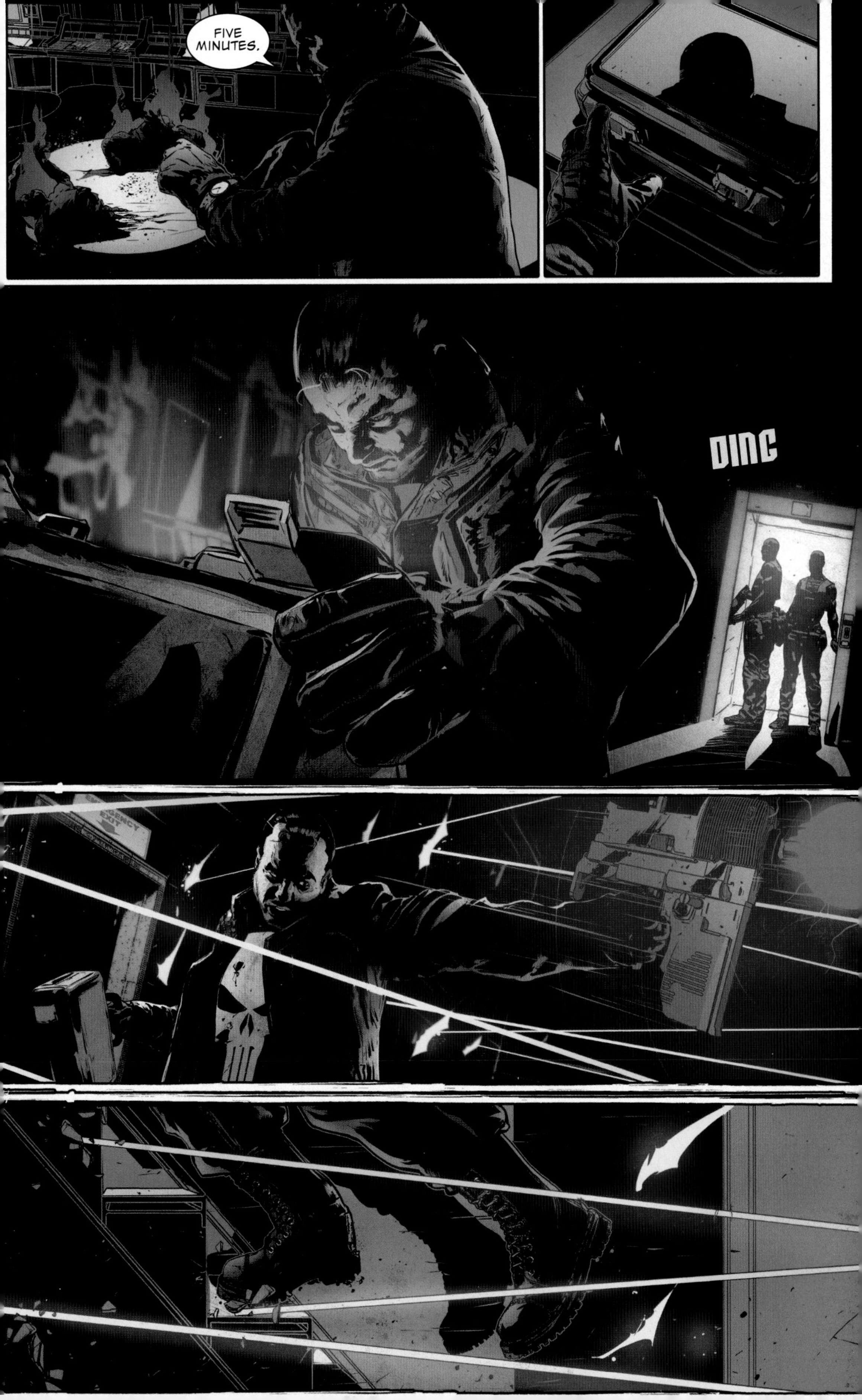
FIVE MINUTES.
DING
EMERGENCY EXIT

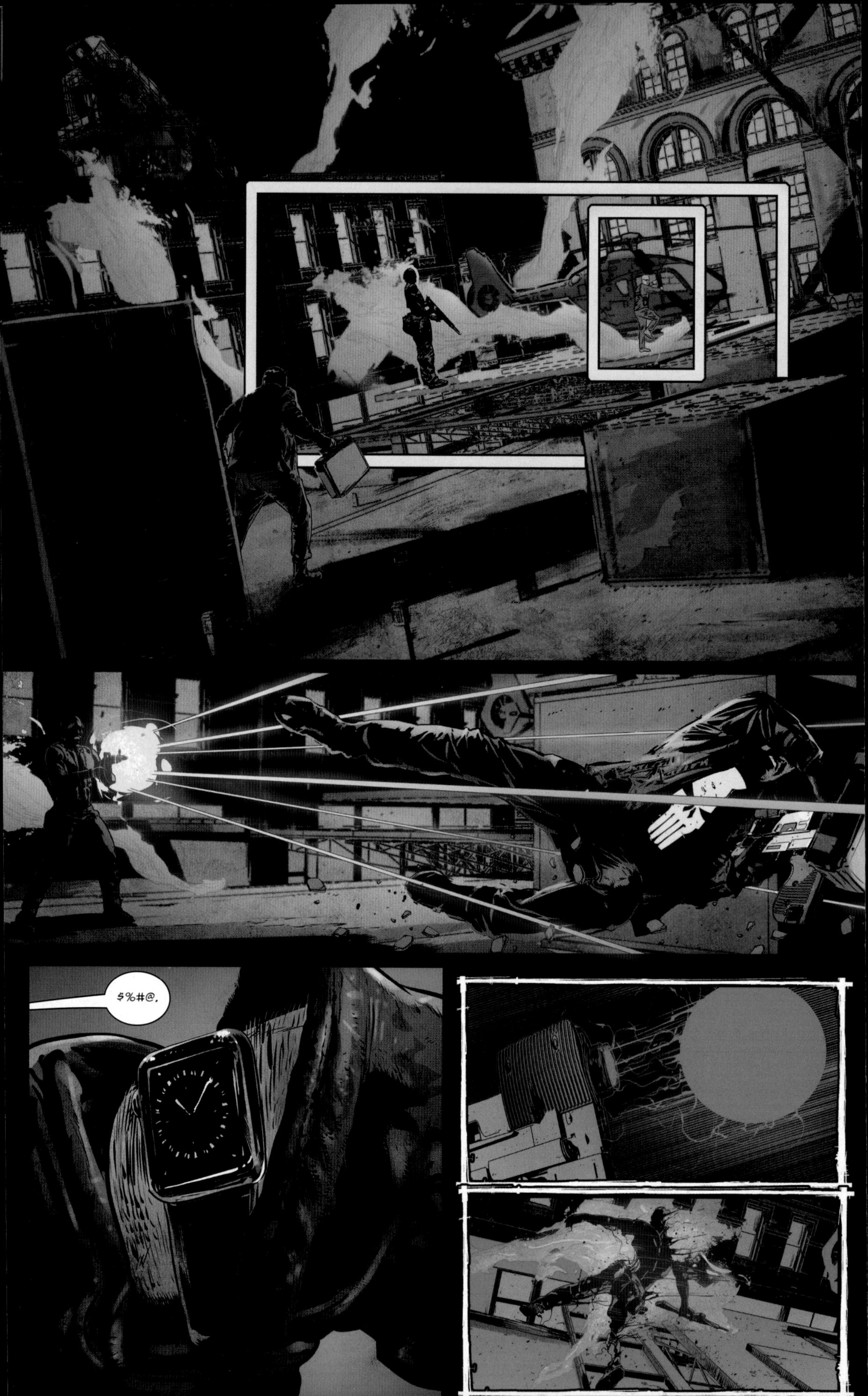
$%#@.

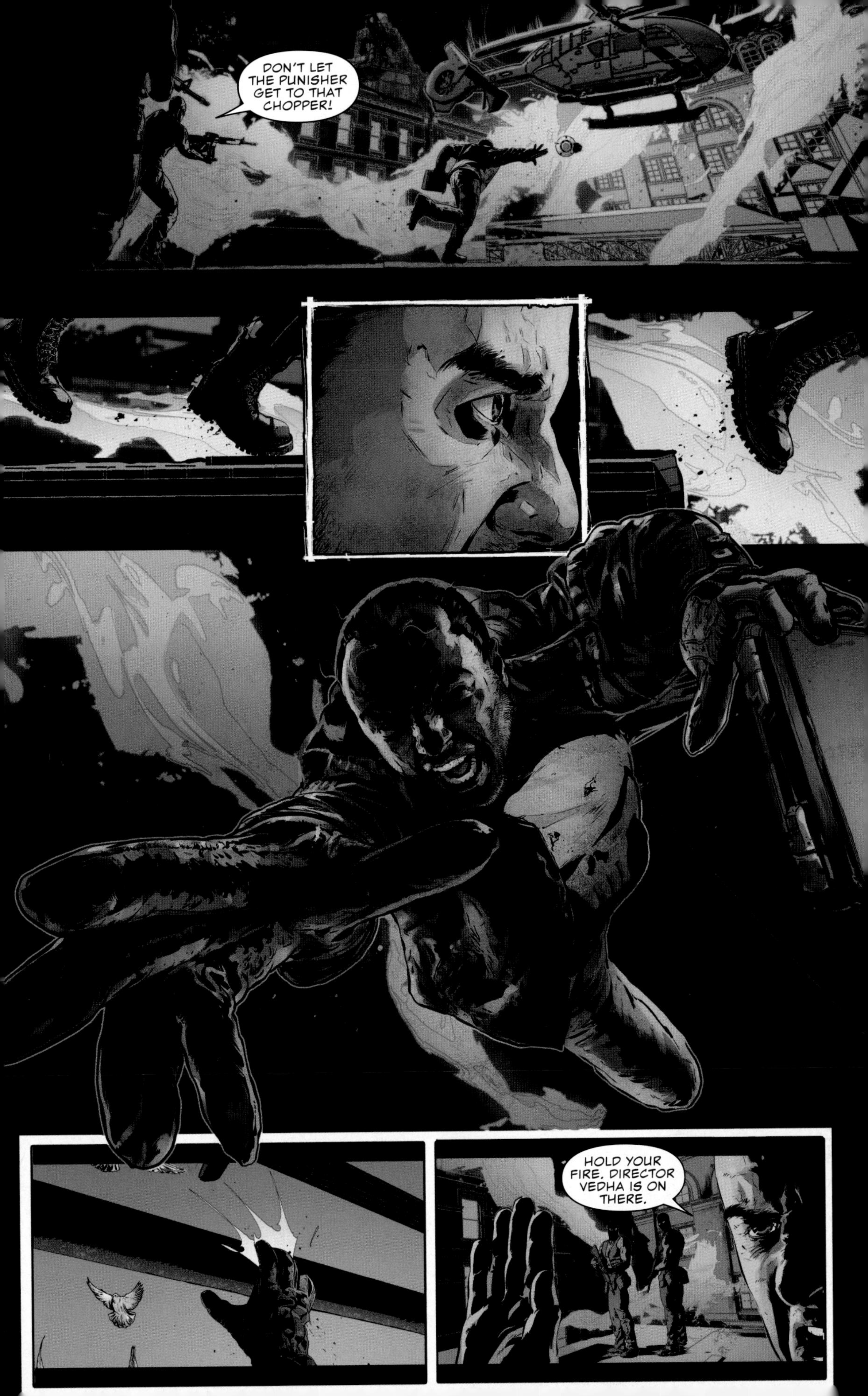
DON'T LET THE PUNISHER GET TO THAT CHOPPER!
HOLD YOUR FIRE. DIRECTOR VEDHA IS ON THERE.

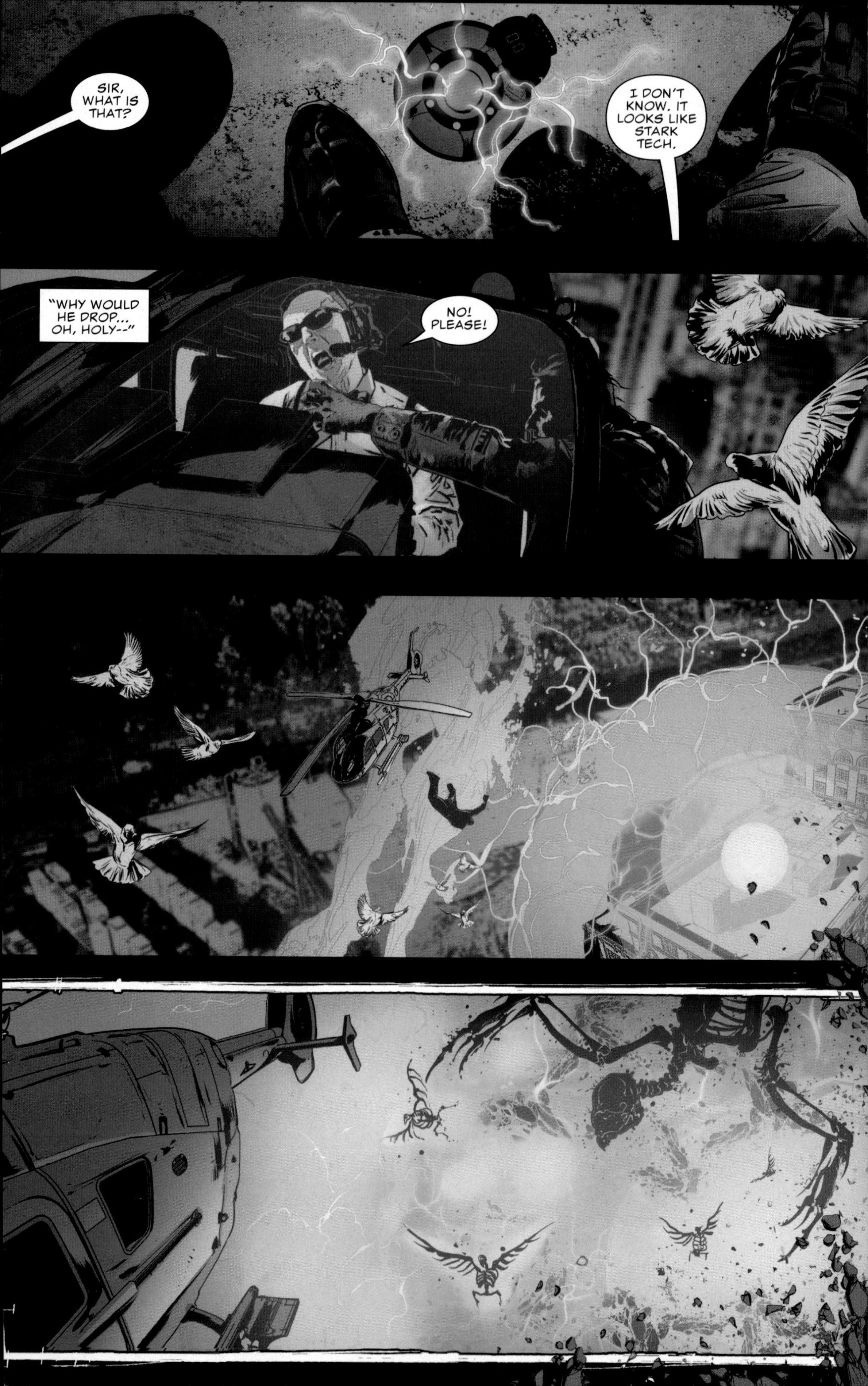
SIR, WHAT IS THAT?
I DON'T KNOW. IT LOOKS LIKE STARK TECH.
"WHY WOULD HE DROP... OH, HOLY--"
NO! PLEASE!

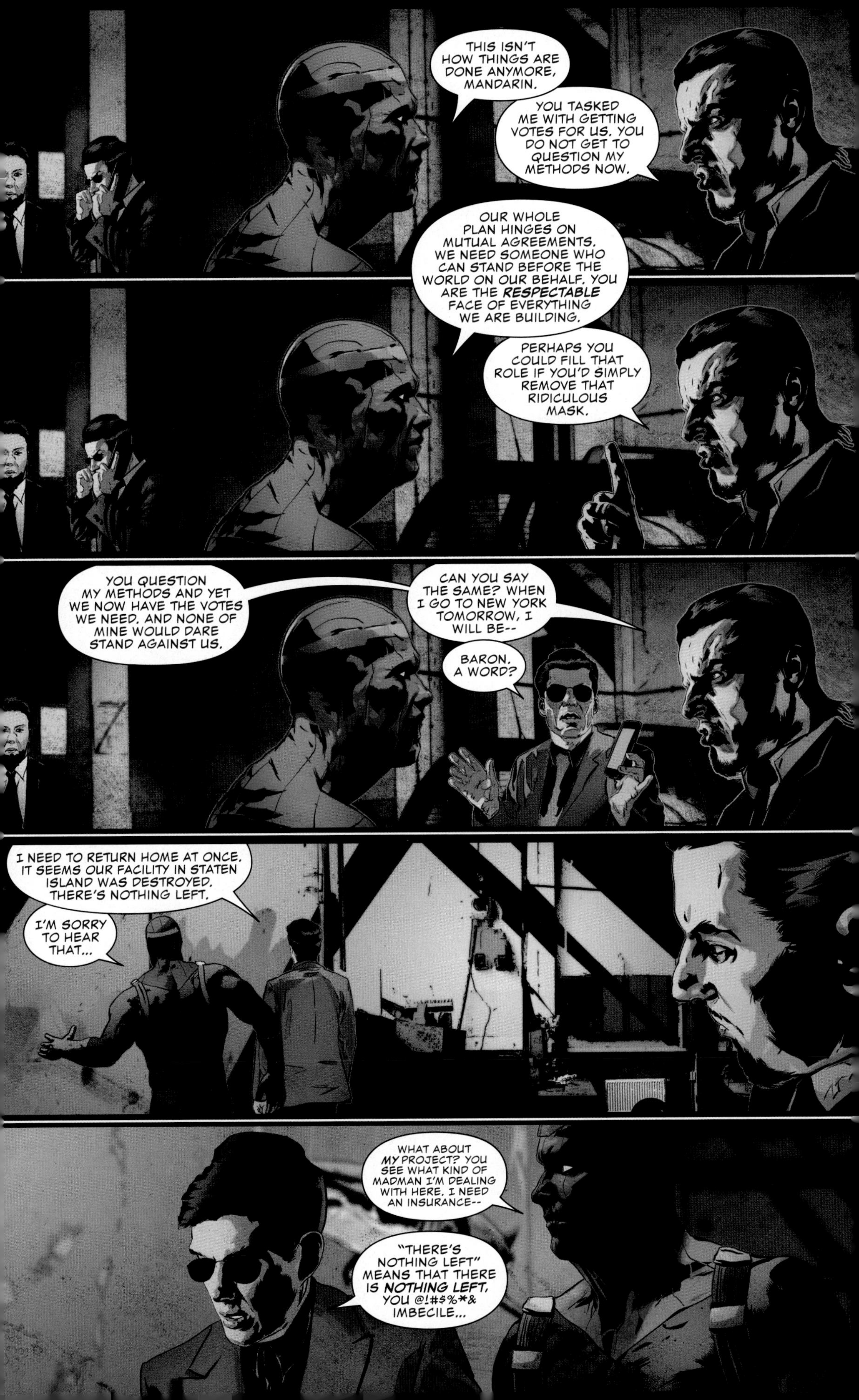
THIS ISN'T HOW THINGS ARE DONE ANYMORE, MANDARIN.
YOU TASKED ME WITH GETTING VOTES FOR US. YOU DO NOT GET TO QUESTION MY METHODS NOW.
OUR WHOLE PLAN HINGES ON MUTUAL AGREEMENTS. WE NEED SOMEONE WHO CAN STAND BEFORE THE WORLD ON OUR BEHALF. YOU ARE THE RESPECTABLE FACE OF EVERYTHING WE ARE BUILDING.
PERHAPS YOU COULD FILL THAT ROLE IF YOU'D SIMPLY REMOVE THAT RIDICULOUS MASK.
YOU QUESTION MY METHODS AND YET WE NOW HAVE THE VOTES WE NEED. AND NONE OF MINE WOULD DARE STAND AGAINST US.
CAN YOU SAY THE SAME? WHEN I GO TO NEW YORK TOMORROW, I WILL BE--
BARON, A WORD?
I NEED TO RETURN HOME AT ONCE. IT SEEMS OUR FACILITY IN STATEN ISLAND WAS DESTROYED. THERE'S NOTHING LEFT.
I'M SORRY TO HEAR THAT...
WHAT ABOUT MY PROJECT? YOU SEE WHAT KIND OF MADMAN I'M DEALING WITH HERE. I NEED AN INSURANCE--
"THERE'S NOTHING LEFT" MEANS THAT THERE IS NOTHING LEFT, YOU @!#$%*& IMBECILE...

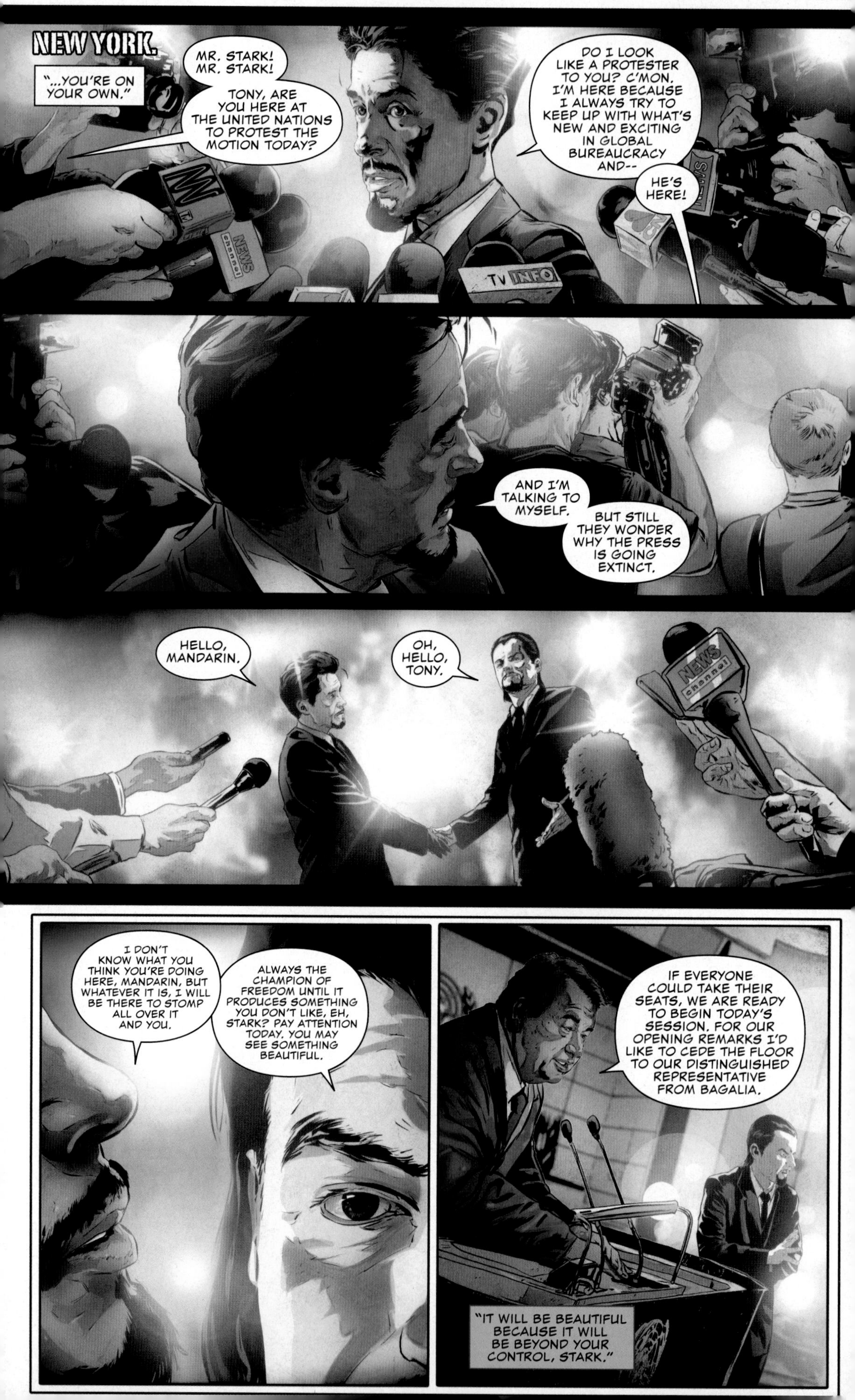

NEW YORK.
"...YOU'RE ON YOUR OWN."
MR. STARK! MR. STARK!
TONY, ARE YOU HERE AT THE UNITED NATIONS TO PROTEST THE MOTION TODAY?
DO I LOOK LIKE A PROTESTER TO YOU? C'MON. I'M HERE BECAUSE I ALWAYS TRY TO KEEP UP WITH WHAT'S NEW AND EXCITING IN GLOBAL BUREAUCRACY AND--
HE'S HERE!
TV INFO
NEWS channel
AND I'M TALKING TO MYSELF.
BUT STILL THEY WONDER WHY THE PRESS IS GOING EXTINCT.
HELLO, MANDARIN.
OH, HELLO, TONY.
NEWS channel
I DON'T KNOW WHAT YOU THINK YOU'RE DOING HERE, MANDARIN, BUT WHATEVER IT IS, I WILL BE THERE TO STOMP ALL OVER IT AND YOU.
ALWAYS THE CHAMPION OF FREEDOM UNTIL IT PRODUCES SOMETHING YOU DON'T LIKE, EH, STARK? PAY ATTENTION TODAY. YOU MAY SEE SOMETHING BEAUTIFUL.
IF EVERYONE COULD TAKE THEIR SEATS, WE ARE READY TO BEGIN TODAY'S SESSION. FOR OUR OPENING REMARKS I'D LIKE TO CEDE THE FLOOR TO OUR DISTINGUISHED REPRESENTATIVE FROM BAGALIA.
"IT WILL BE BEAUTIFUL BECAUSE IT WILL BE BEYOND YOUR CONTROL, STARK."

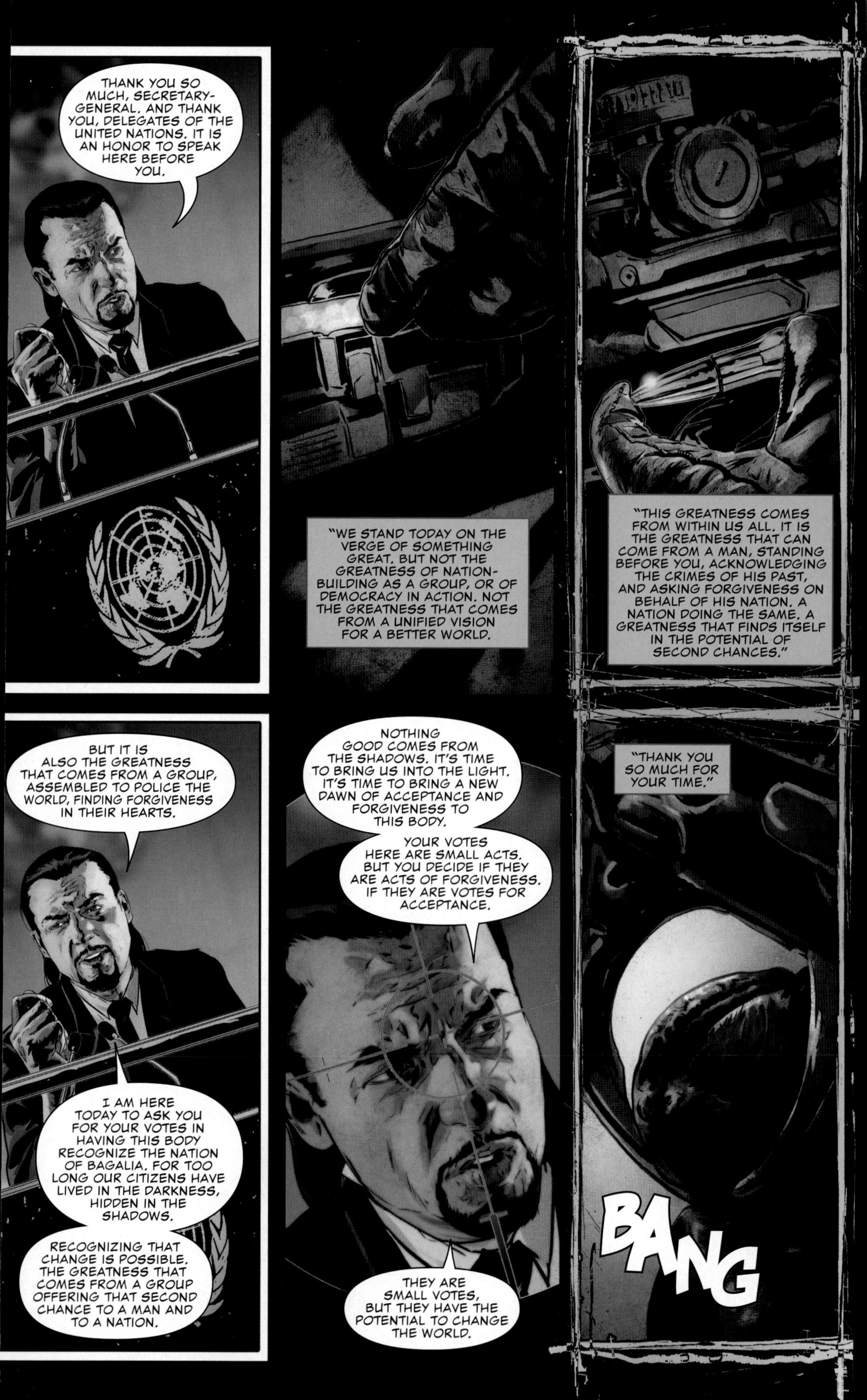
THANK YOU SO MUCH, SECRETARY-GENERAL, AND THANK YOU, DELEGATES OF THE UNITED NATIONS. IT IS AN HONOR TO SPEAK HERE BEFORE YOU.
"WE STAND TODAY ON THE VERGE OF SOMETHING GREAT. BUT NOT THE GREATNESS OF NATION-BUILDING AS A GROUP, OR OF DEMOCRACY IN ACTION. NOT THE GREATNESS THAT COMES FROM A UNIFIED VISION FOR A BETTER WORLD.
"THIS GREATNESS COMES FROM WITHIN US ALL. IT IS THE GREATNESS THAT CAN COME FROM A MAN, STANDING BEFORE YOU, ACKNOWLEDGING THE CRIMES OF HIS PAST, AND ASKING FORGIVENESS ON BEHALF OF HIS NATION. A NATION DOING THE SAME. A GREATNESS THAT FINDS ITSELF IN THE POTENTIAL OF SECOND CHANCES."
BUT IT IS ALSO THE GREATNESS THAT COMES FROM A GROUP, ASSEMBLED TO POLICE THE WORLD, FINDING FORGIVENESS IN THEIR HEARTS.
I AM HERE TODAY TO ASK YOU FOR YOUR VOTES IN HAVING THIS BODY RECOGNIZE THE NATION OF BAGALIA. FOR TOO LONG OUR CITIZENS HAVE LIVED IN THE DARKNESS, HIDDEN IN THE SHADOWS.
RECOGNIZING THAT CHANGE IS POSSIBLE. THE GREATNESS THAT COMES FROM A GROUP OFFERING THAT SECOND CHANCE TO A MAN AND TO A NATION.
NOTHING GOOD COMES FROM THE SHADOWS. IT'S TIME TO BRING US INTO THE LIGHT. IT'S TIME TO BRING A NEW DAWN OF ACCEPTANCE AND FORGIVENESS TO THIS BODY.
YOUR VOTES HERE ARE SMALL ACTS. BUT YOU DECIDE IF THEY ARE ACTS OF FORGIVENESS. IF THEY ARE VOTES FOR ACCEPTANCE.
THEY ARE SMALL VOTES, BUT THEY HAVE THE POTENTIAL TO CHANGE THE WORLD.
"THANK YOU SO MUCH FOR YOUR TIME."
BANG

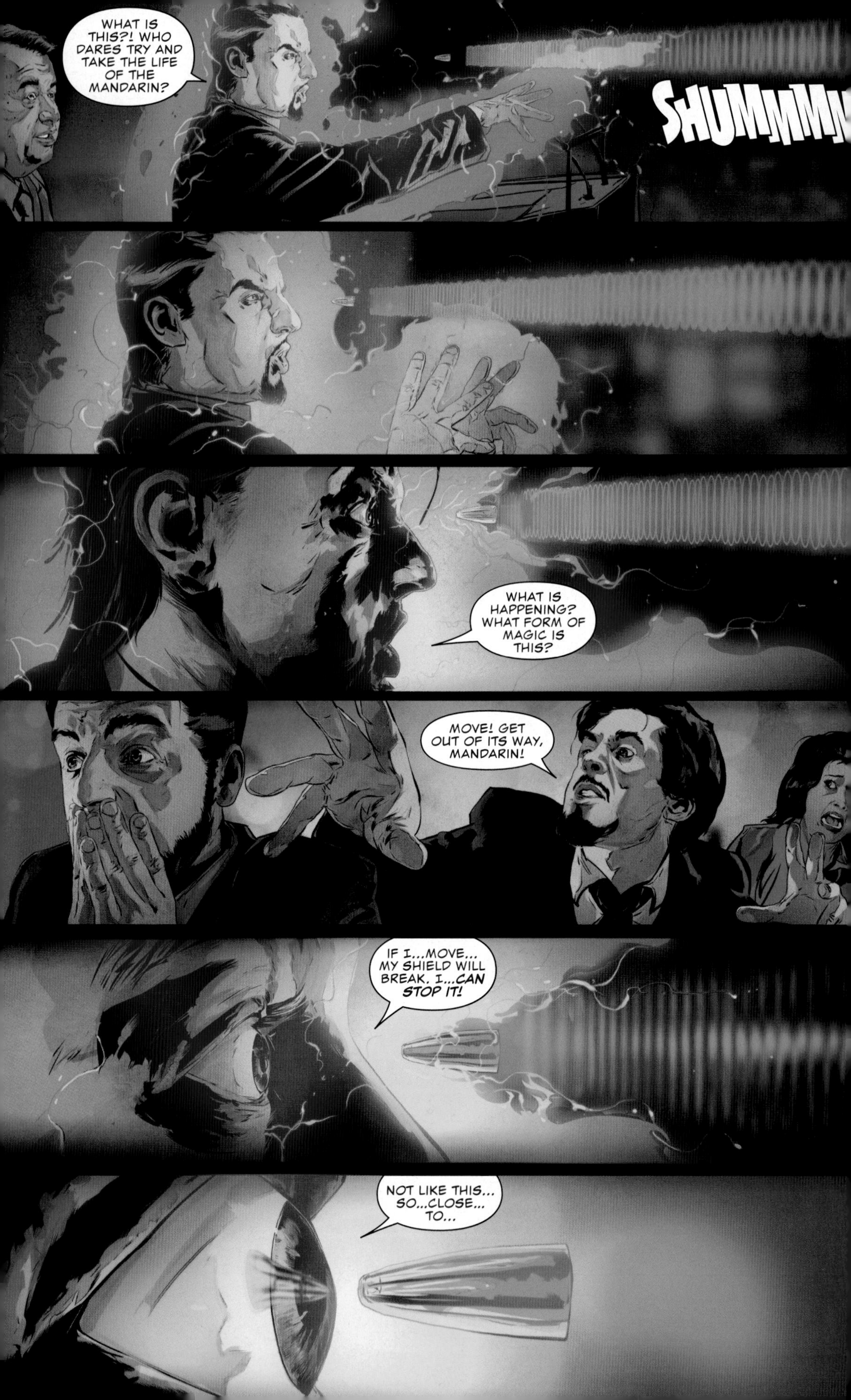
WHAT IS THIS?! WHO DARES TRY AND TAKE THE LIFE OF THE MANDARIN?
SHUMMMM
WHAT IS HAPPENING? WHAT FORM OF MAGIC IS THIS?
MOVE! GET OUT OF ITS WAY, MANDARIN!
IF I...MOVE... MY SHIELD WILL BREAK. I...CAN STOP IT!
NOT LIKE THIS... SO...CLOSE... TO...

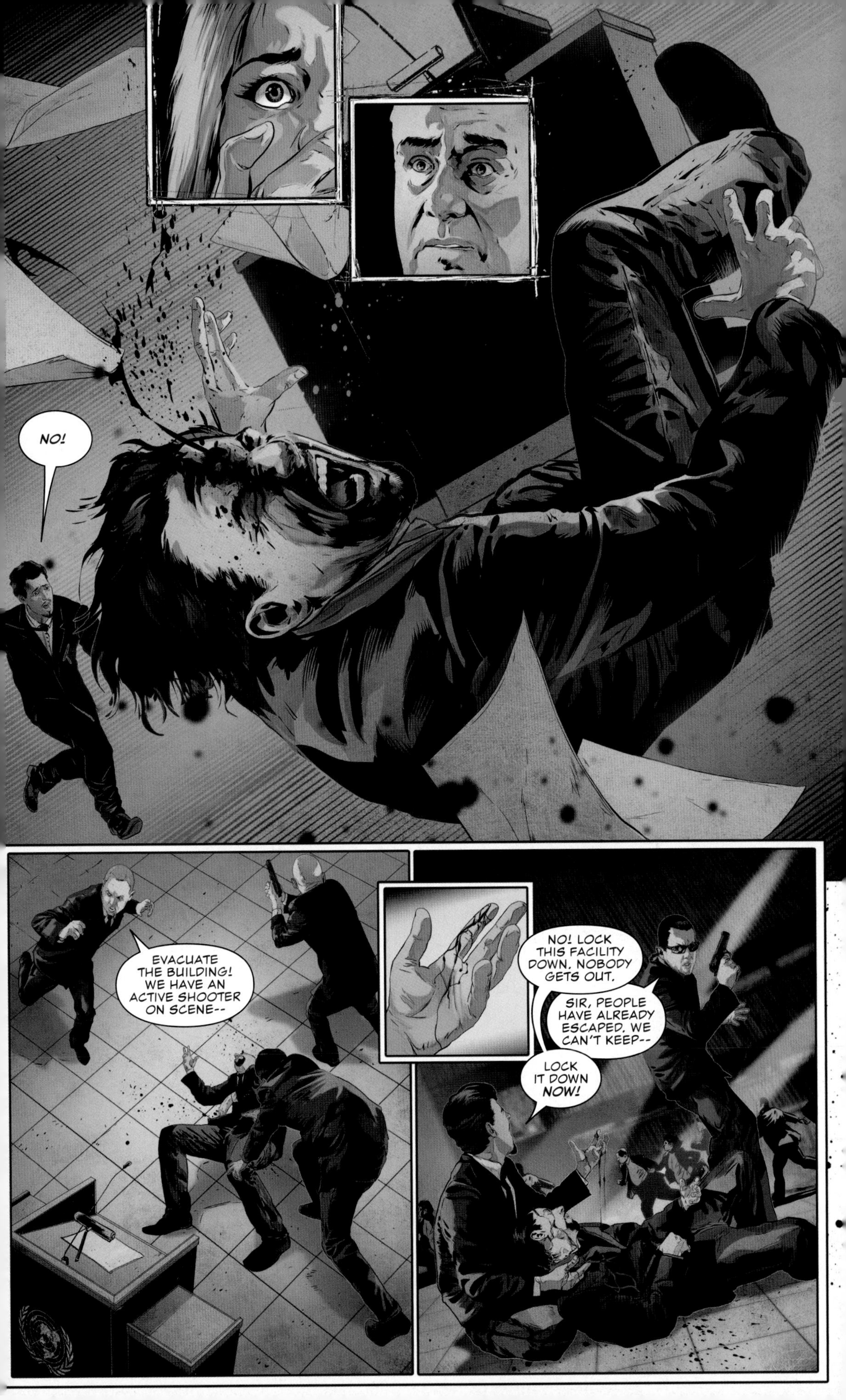
NO!
EVACUATE THE BUILDING! WE HAVE AN ACTIVE SHOOTER ON SCENE--
NO! LOCK THIS FACILITY DOWN. NOBODY GETS OUT.
SIR, PEOPLE HAVE ALREADY ESCAPED. WE CAN'T KEEP--
LOCK IT DOWN NOW!

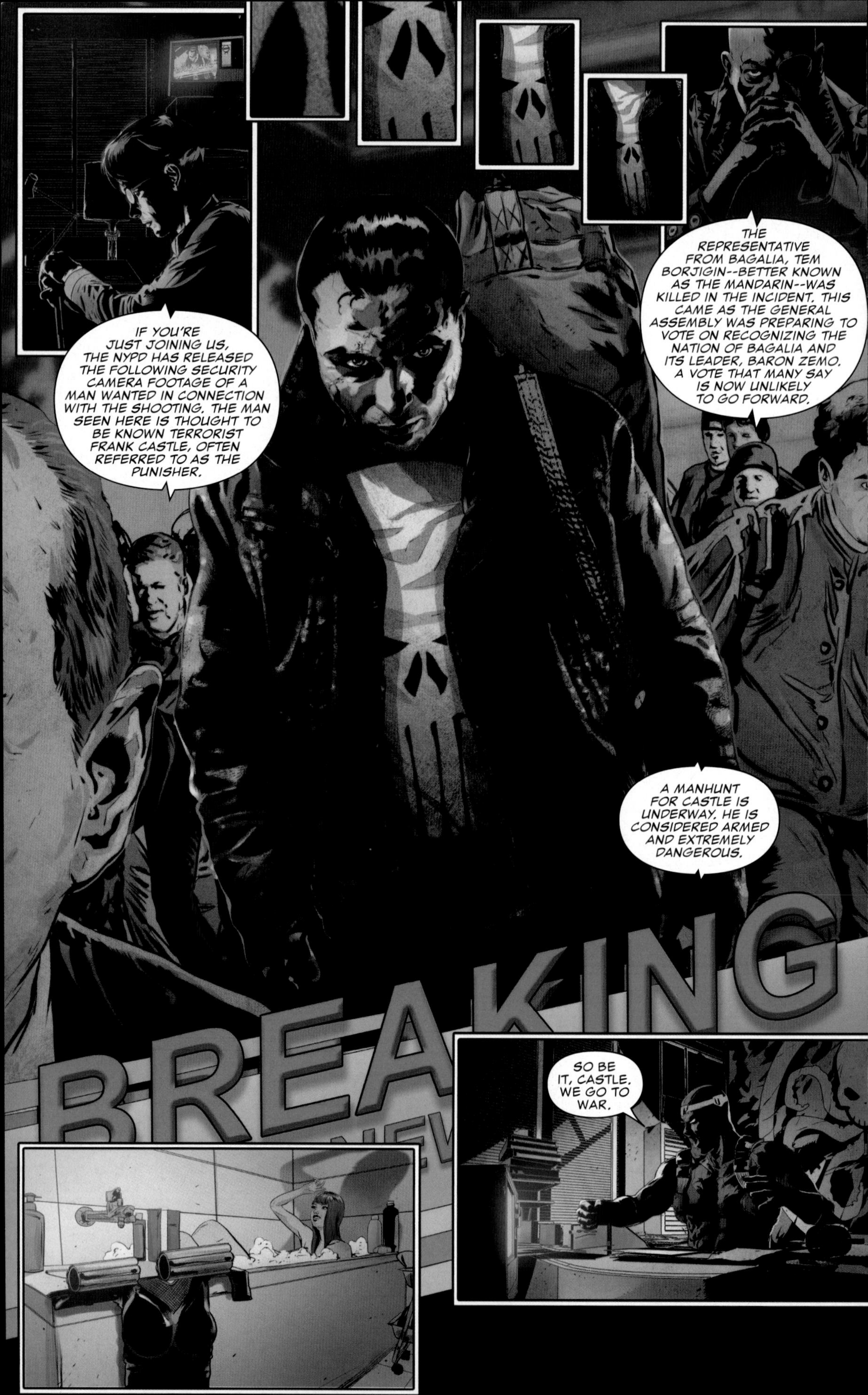
IF YOU'RE JUST JOINING US, THE NYPD HAS RELEASED THE FOLLOWING SECURITY CAMERA FOOTAGE OF A MAN WANTED IN CONNECTION WITH THE SHOOTING. THE MAN SEEN HERE IS THOUGHT TO BE KNOWN TERRORIST FRANK CASTLE, OFTEN REFERRED TO AS THE PUNISHER.
THE REPRESENTATIVE FROM BAGALIA, TEM BORJIGIN--BETTER KNOWN AS THE MANDARIN--WAS KILLED IN THE INCIDENT. THIS CAME AS THE GENERAL ASSEMBLY WAS PREPARING TO VOTE ON RECOGNIZING THE NATION OF BAGALIA AND ITS LEADER, BARON ZEMO. A VOTE THAT MANY SAY IS NOW UNLIKELY TO GO FORWARD.
A MANHUNT FOR CASTLE IS UNDERWAY. HE IS CONSIDERED ARMED AND EXTREMELY DANGEROUS.
BREAKING
SO BE IT, CASTLE. WE GO TO WAR.

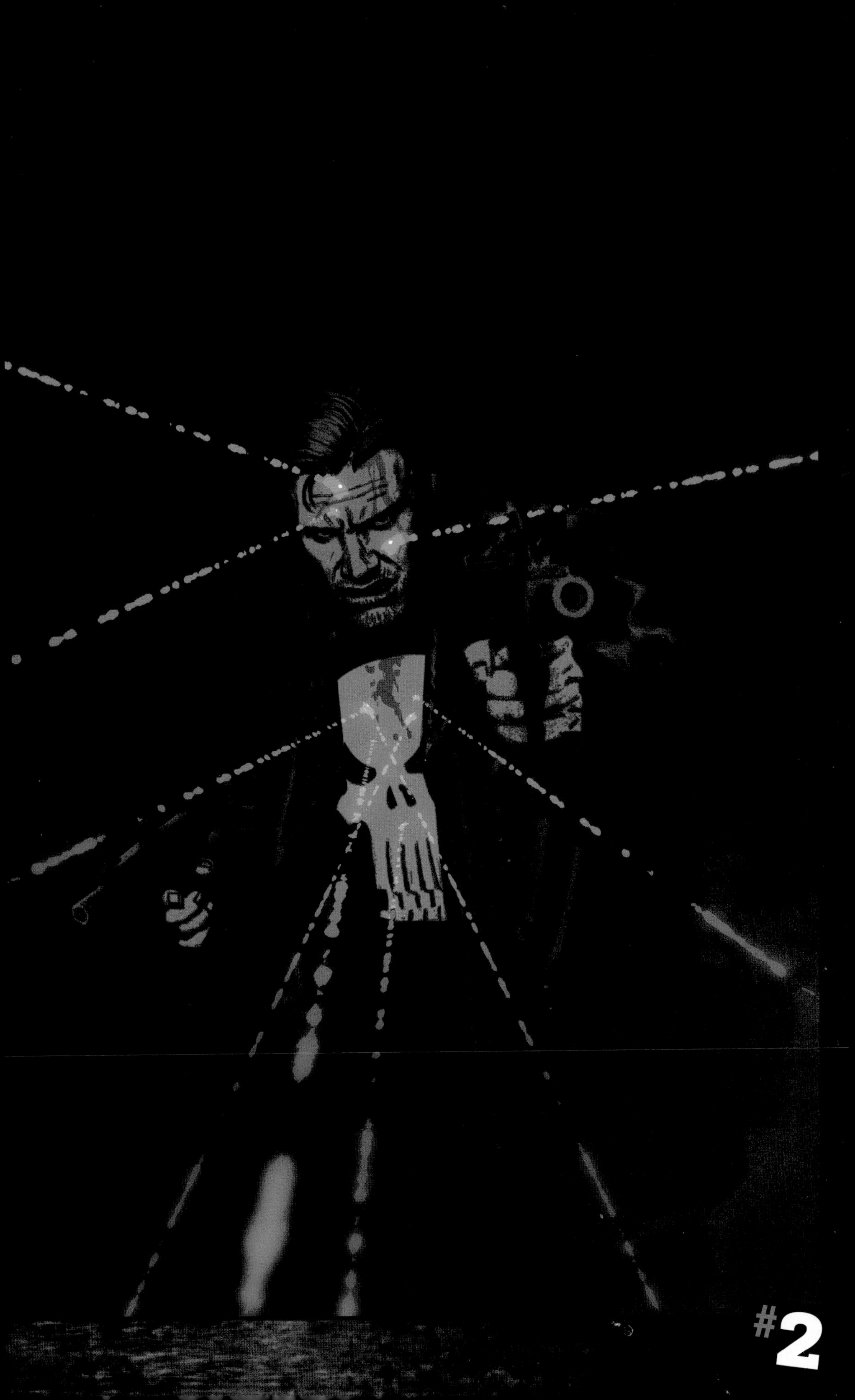
#2

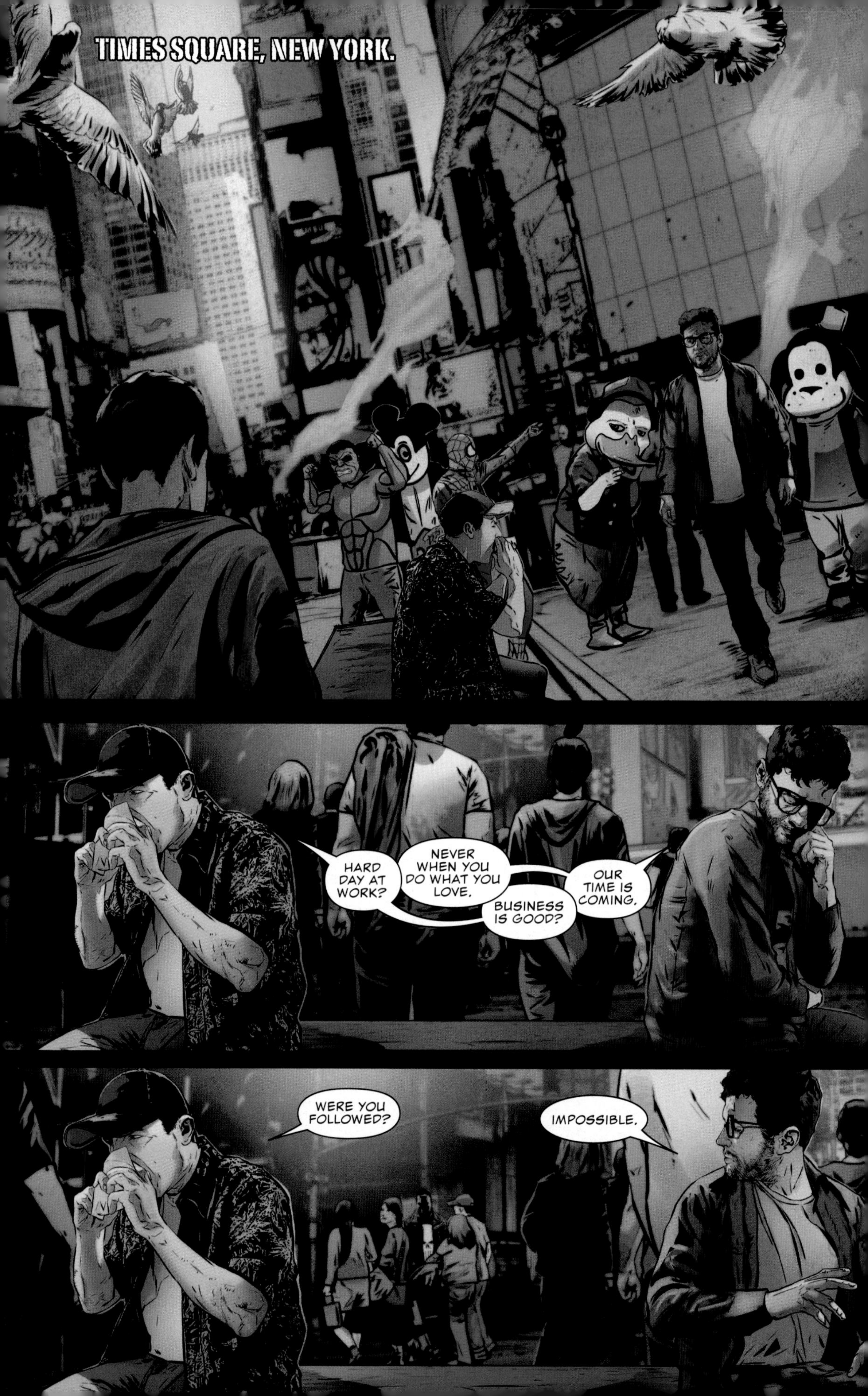
TIMES SQUARE, NEW YORK.
HARD DAY AT WORK?
NEVER WHEN YOU DO WHAT YOU LOVE.
BUSINESS IS GOOD?
OUR TIME IS COMING.
WERE YOU FOLLOWED?
IMPOSSIBLE.

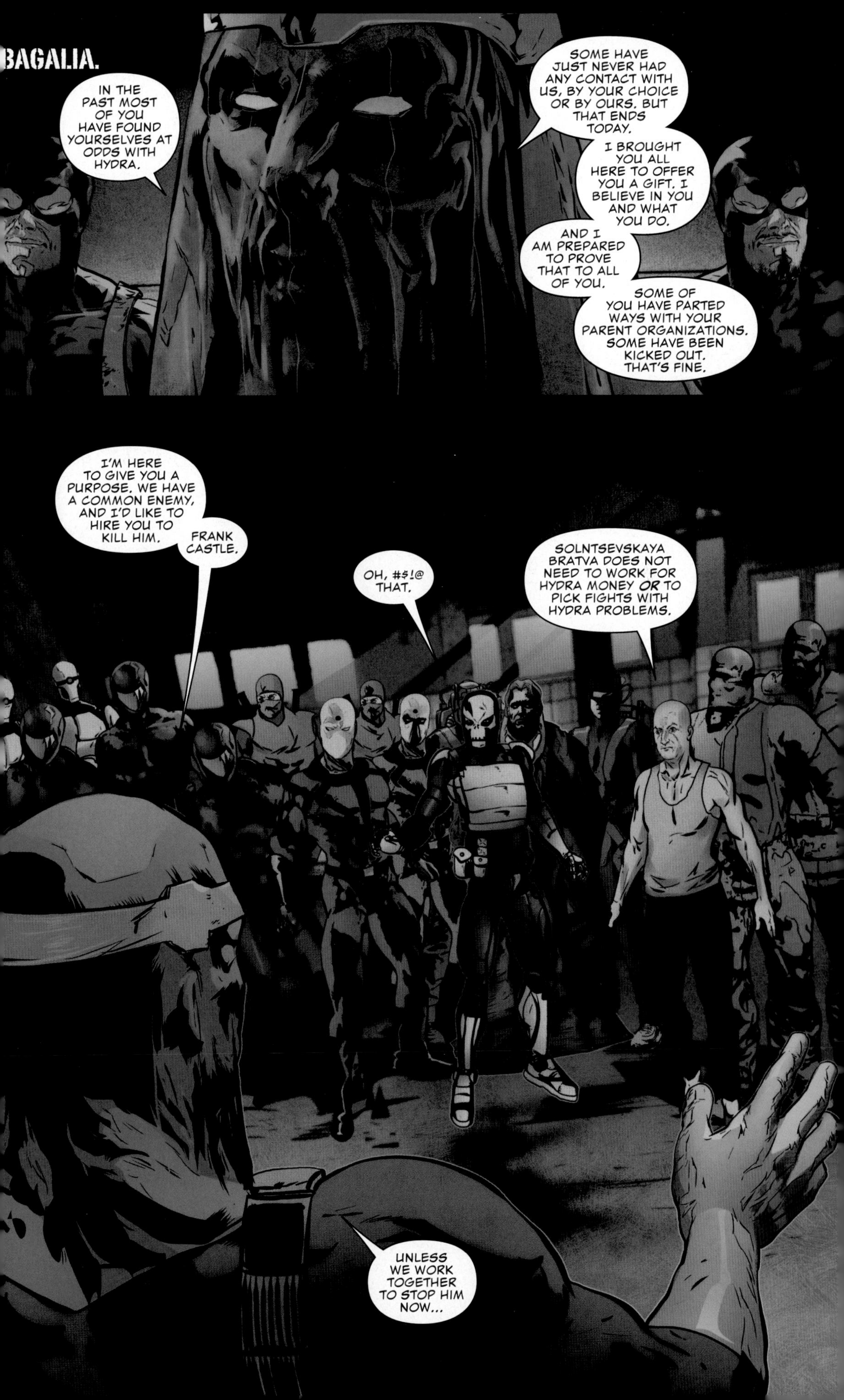
BAGALIA.
IN THE PAST MOST OF YOU HAVE FOUND YOURSELVES AT ODDS WITH HYDRA.
SOME HAVE JUST NEVER HAD ANY CONTACT WITH US, BY YOUR CHOICE OR BY OURS. BUT THAT ENDS TODAY.
I BROUGHT YOU ALL HERE TO OFFER YOU A GIFT. I BELIEVE IN YOU AND WHAT YOU DO.
AND I AM PREPARED TO PROVE THAT TO ALL OF YOU.
SOME OF YOU HAVE PARTED WAYS WITH YOUR PARENT ORGANIZATIONS. SOME HAVE BEEN KICKED OUT. THAT'S FINE.
I'M HERE TO GIVE YOU A PURPOSE. WE HAVE A COMMON ENEMY, AND I'D LIKE TO HIRE YOU TO KILL HIM.
FRANK CASTLE.
OH, #$!@ THAT.
SOLNTSEVSKAYA BRATVA DOES NOT NEED TO WORK FOR HYDRA MONEY *OR* TO PICK FIGHTS WITH HYDRA PROBLEMS.
UNLESS WE WORK TOGETHER TO STOP HIM NOW...

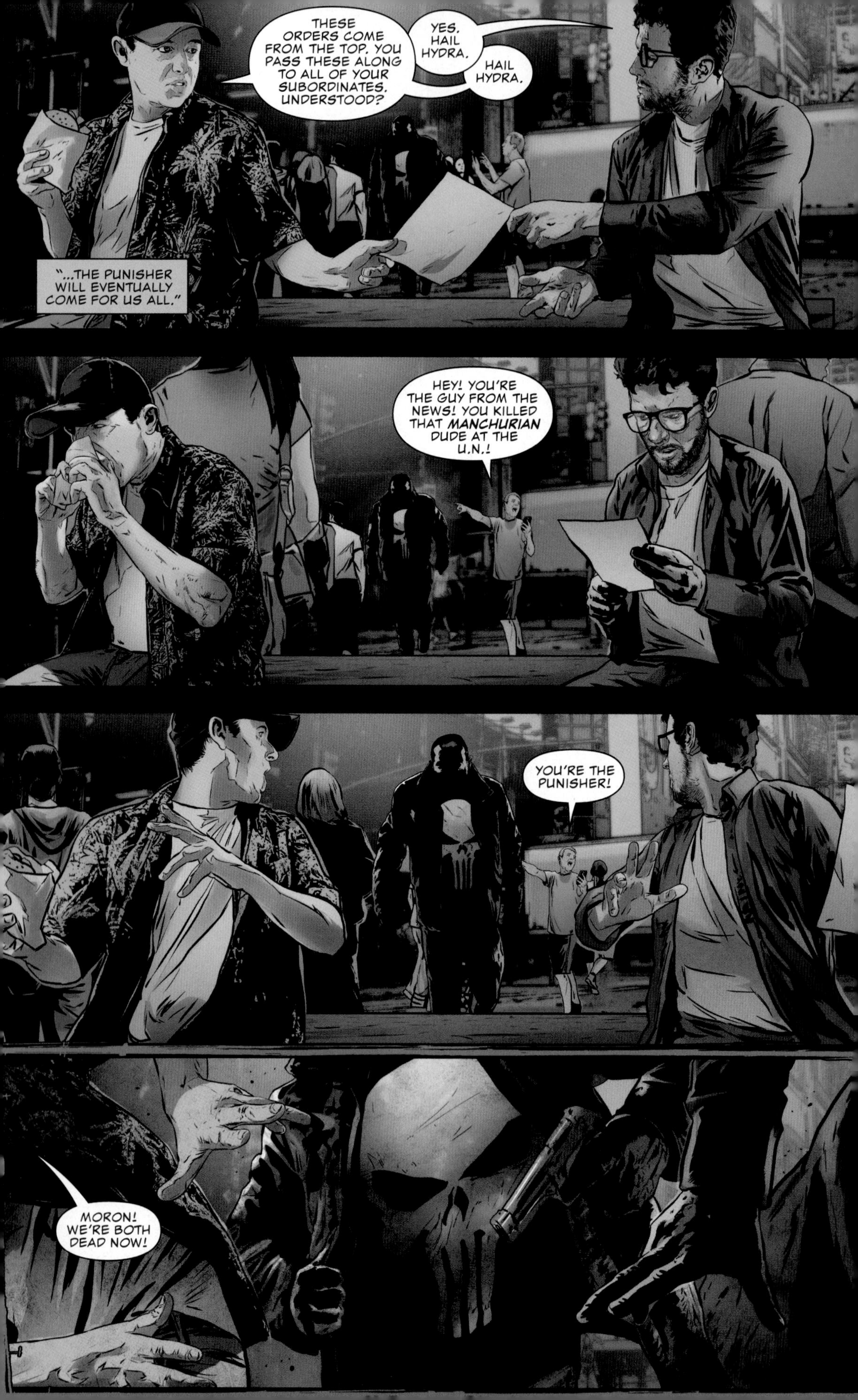
THESE ORDERS COME FROM THE TOP. YOU PASS THESE ALONG TO ALL OF YOUR SUBORDINATES. UNDERSTOOD?
YES. HAIL HYDRA.
HAIL HYDRA.
"...THE PUNISHER WILL EVENTUALLY COME FOR US ALL."
HEY! YOU'RE THE GUY FROM THE NEWS! YOU KILLED THAT MANCHURIAN DUDE AT THE U.N.!
YOU'RE THE PUNISHER!
MORON! WE'RE BOTH DEAD NOW!

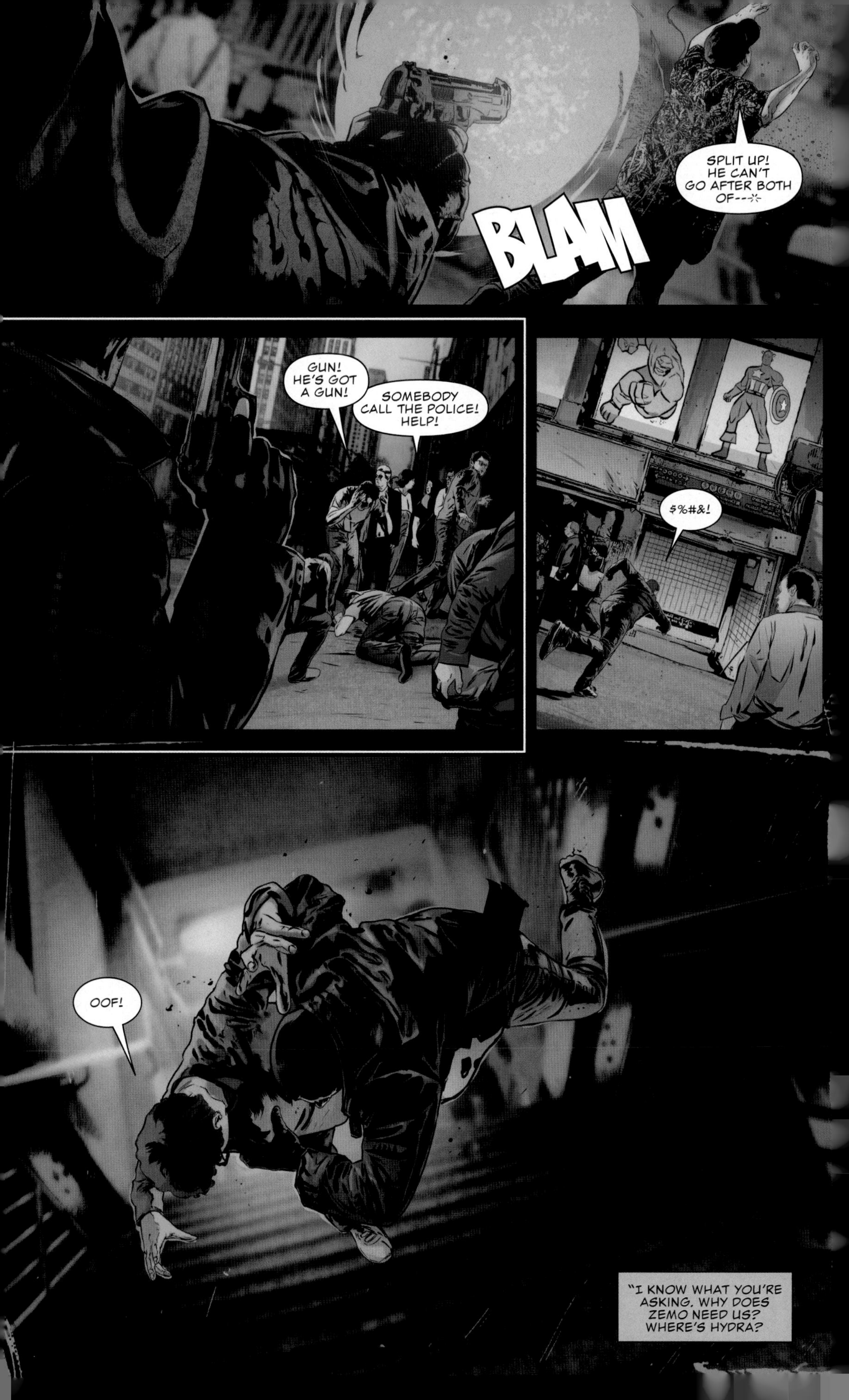
SPLIT UP! HE CAN'T GO AFTER BOTH OF--
BLAM
GUN! HE'S GOT A GUN!
SOMEBODY CALL THE POLICE! HELP!
$%#&!
OOF!
"I KNOW WHAT YOU'RE ASKING. WHY DOES ZEMO NEED US? WHERE'S HYDRA?

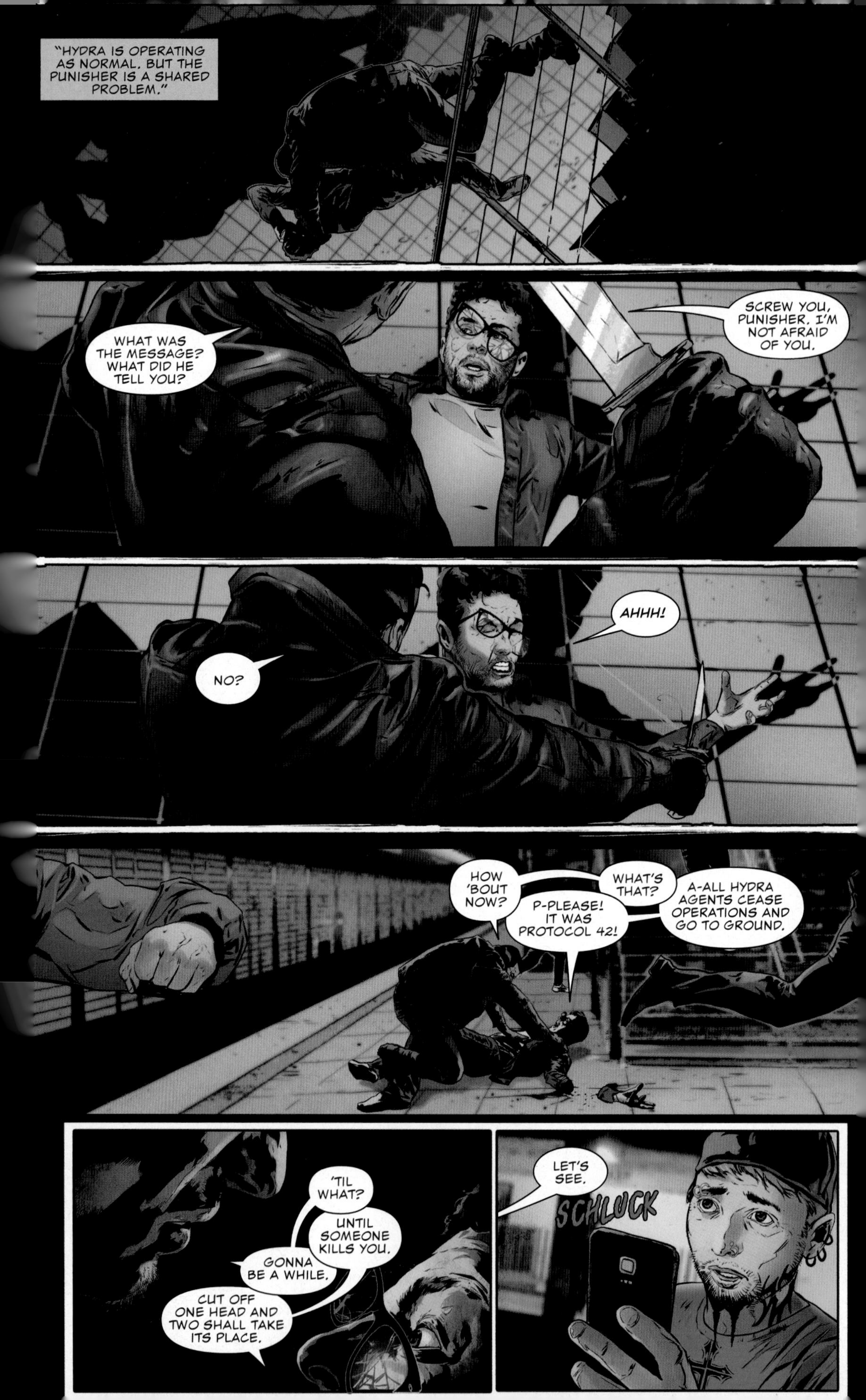
"HYDRA IS OPERATING AS NORMAL. BUT THE PUNISHER IS A SHARED PROBLEM."
WHAT WAS THE MESSAGE? WHAT DID HE TELL YOU?
SCREW YOU, PUNISHER. I'M NOT AFRAID OF YOU.
NO?
AHHH!
HOW 'BOUT NOW?
WHAT'S THAT?
P-PLEASE! IT WAS PROTOCOL 42!
A-ALL HYDRA AGENTS CEASE OPERATIONS AND GO TO GROUND.
'TIL WHAT?
UNTIL SOMEONE KILLS YOU.
GONNA BE A WHILE.
CUT OFF ONE HEAD AND TWO SHALL TAKE ITS PLACE.
LET'S SEE.
SCHLUCK

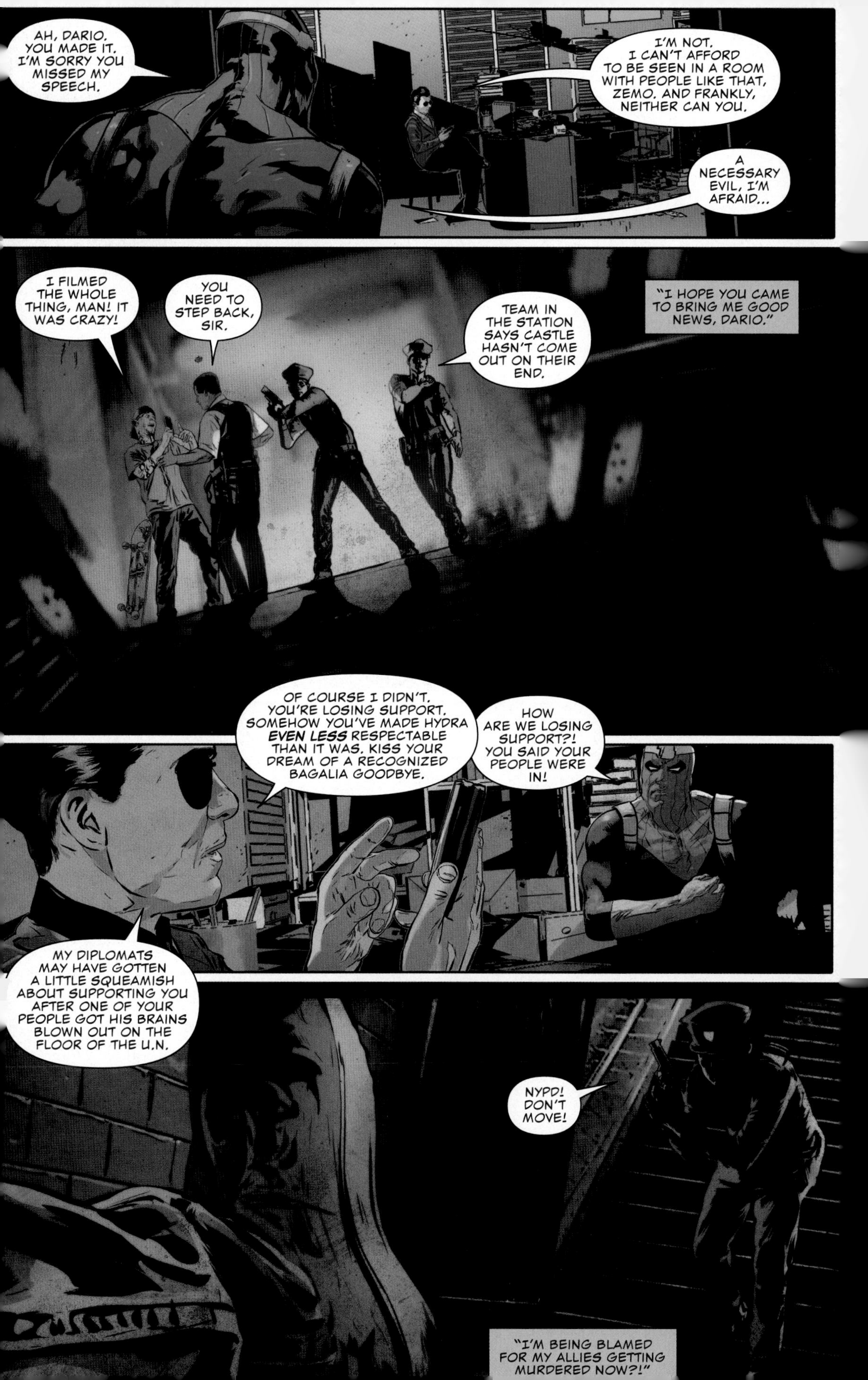
AH, DARIO. YOU MADE IT. I'M SORRY YOU MISSED MY SPEECH.
I'M NOT. I CAN'T AFFORD TO BE SEEN IN A ROOM WITH PEOPLE LIKE THAT, ZEMO. AND FRANKLY, NEITHER CAN YOU.
A NECESSARY EVIL, I'M AFRAID...
I FILMED THE WHOLE THING, MAN! IT WAS CRAZY!
YOU NEED TO STEP BACK, SIR.
TEAM IN THE STATION SAYS CASTLE HASN'T COME OUT ON THEIR END.
"I HOPE YOU CAME TO BRING ME GOOD NEWS, DARIO."
OF COURSE I DIDN'T. YOU'RE LOSING SUPPORT. SOMEHOW YOU'VE MADE HYDRA EVEN LESS RESPECTABLE THAN IT WAS. KISS YOUR DREAM OF A RECOGNIZED BAGALIA GOODBYE.
HOW ARE WE LOSING SUPPORT?! YOU SAID YOUR PEOPLE WERE IN!
MY DIPLOMATS MAY HAVE GOTTEN A LITTLE SQUEAMISH ABOUT SUPPORTING YOU AFTER ONE OF YOUR PEOPLE GOT HIS BRAINS BLOWN OUT ON THE FLOOR OF THE U.N.
NYPD! DON'T MOVE!
"I'M BEING BLAMED FOR MY ALLIES GETTING MURDERED NOW?!"

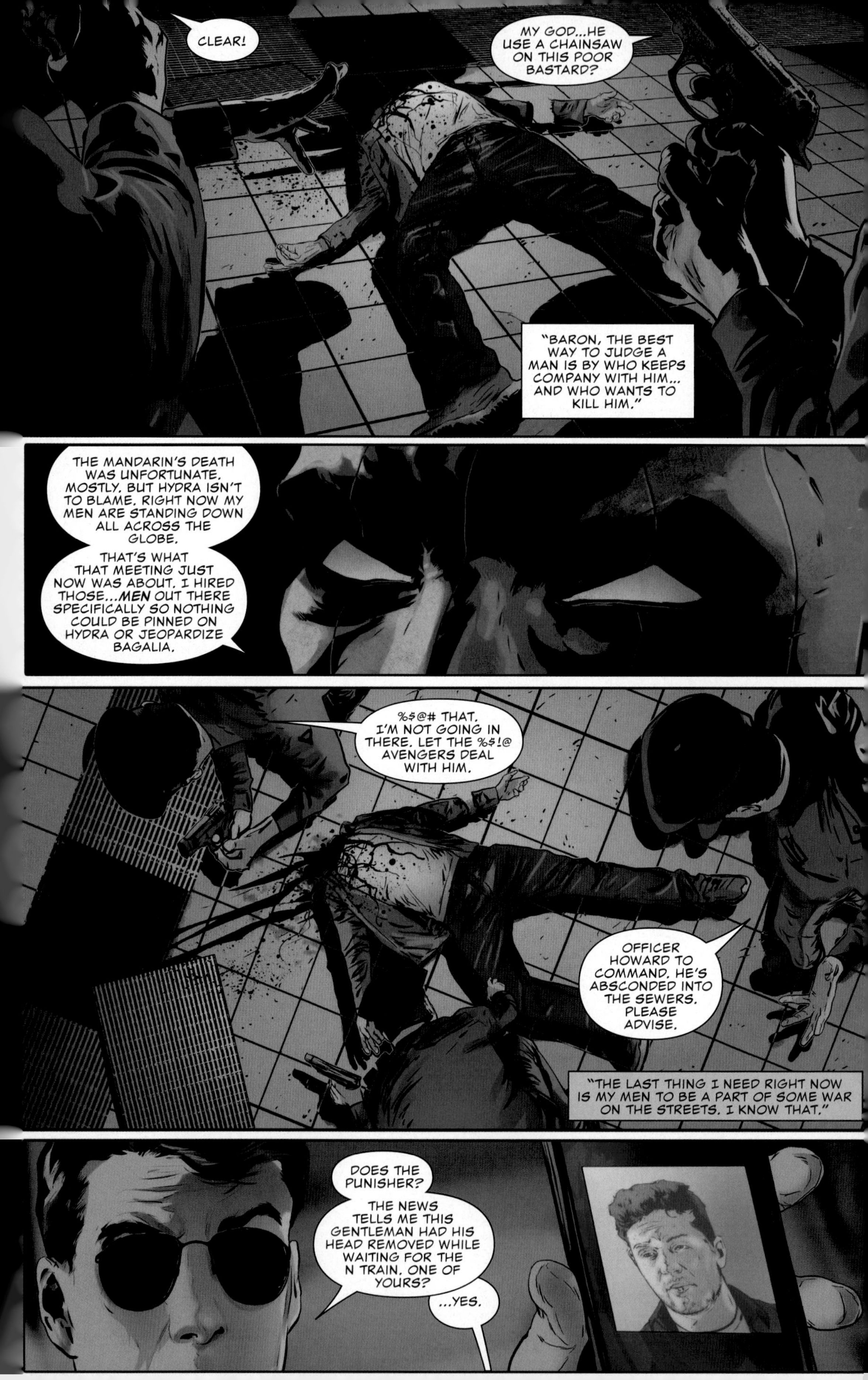
CLEAR!
MY GOD...HE USE A CHAINSAW ON THIS POOR BASTARD?
"BARON, THE BEST WAY TO JUDGE A MAN IS BY WHO KEEPS COMPANY WITH HIM... AND WHO WANTS TO KILL HIM."
THE MANDARIN'S DEATH WAS UNFORTUNATE. MOSTLY. BUT HYDRA ISN'T TO BLAME. RIGHT NOW MY MEN ARE STANDING DOWN ALL ACROSS THE GLOBE.
THAT'S WHAT THAT MEETING JUST NOW WAS ABOUT. I HIRED THOSE...MEN OUT THERE SPECIFICALLY SO NOTHING COULD BE PINNED ON HYDRA OR JEOPARDIZE BAGALIA.
%$@# THAT. I'M NOT GOING IN THERE. LET THE %$!@ AVENGERS DEAL WITH HIM.
OFFICER HOWARD TO COMMAND. HE'S ABSCONDED INTO THE SEWERS. PLEASE ADVISE.
"THE LAST THING I NEED RIGHT NOW IS MY MEN TO BE A PART OF SOME WAR ON THE STREETS. I KNOW THAT."
DOES THE PUNISHER?
THE NEWS TELLS ME THIS GENTLEMAN HAD HIS HEAD REMOVED WHILE WAITING FOR THE N TRAIN. ONE OF YOURS?
...YES.

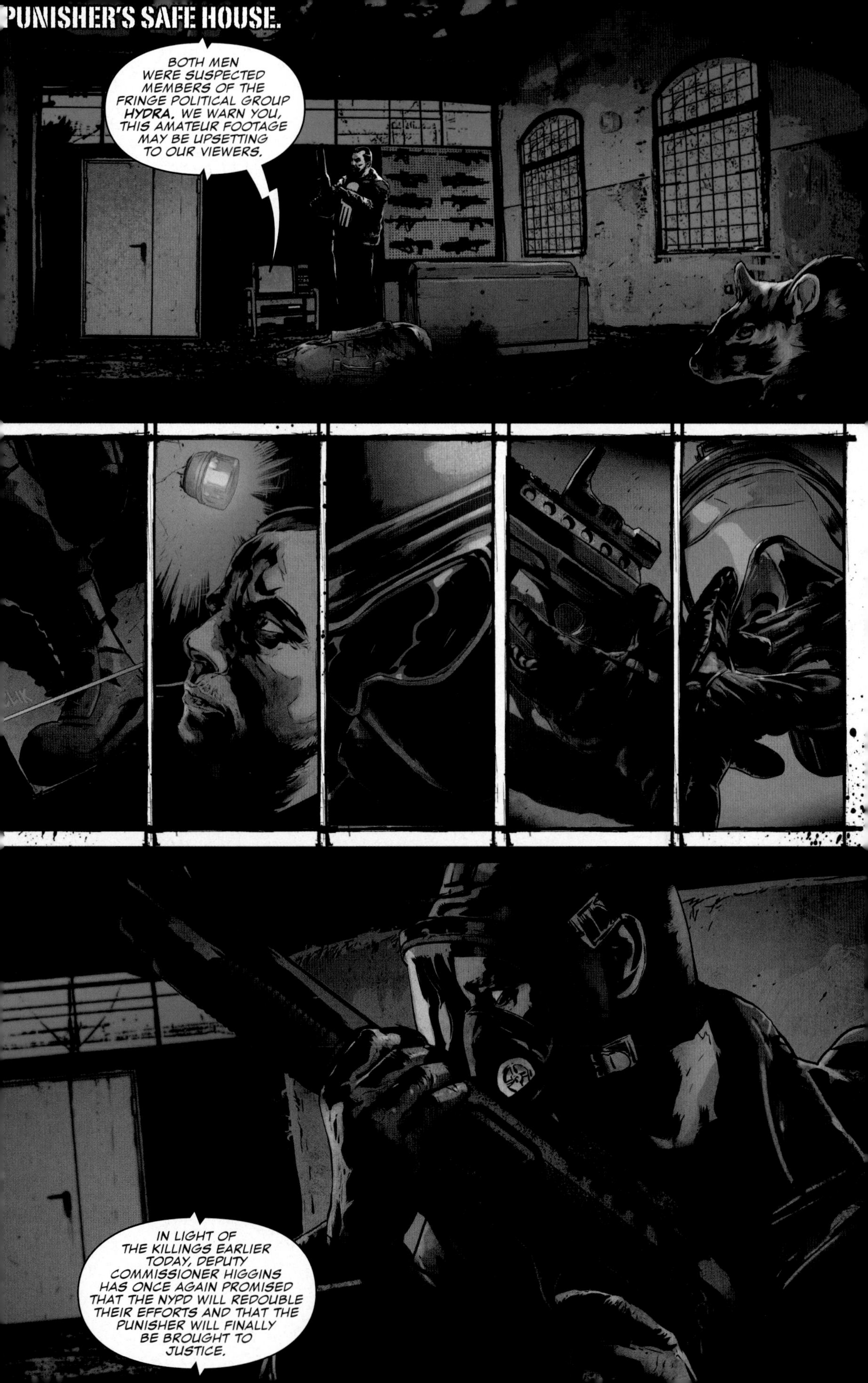
PUNISHER'S SAFE HOUSE.
BOTH MEN WERE SUSPECTED MEMBERS OF THE FRINGE POLITICAL GROUP HYDRA. WE WARN YOU, THIS AMATEUR FOOTAGE MAY BE UPSETTING TO OUR VIEWERS.
IN LIGHT OF THE KILLINGS EARLIER TODAY, DEPUTY COMMISSIONER HIGGINS HAS ONCE AGAIN PROMISED THAT THE NYPD WILL REDOUBLE THEIR EFFORTS AND THAT THE PUNISHER WILL FINALLY BE BROUGHT TO JUSTICE.

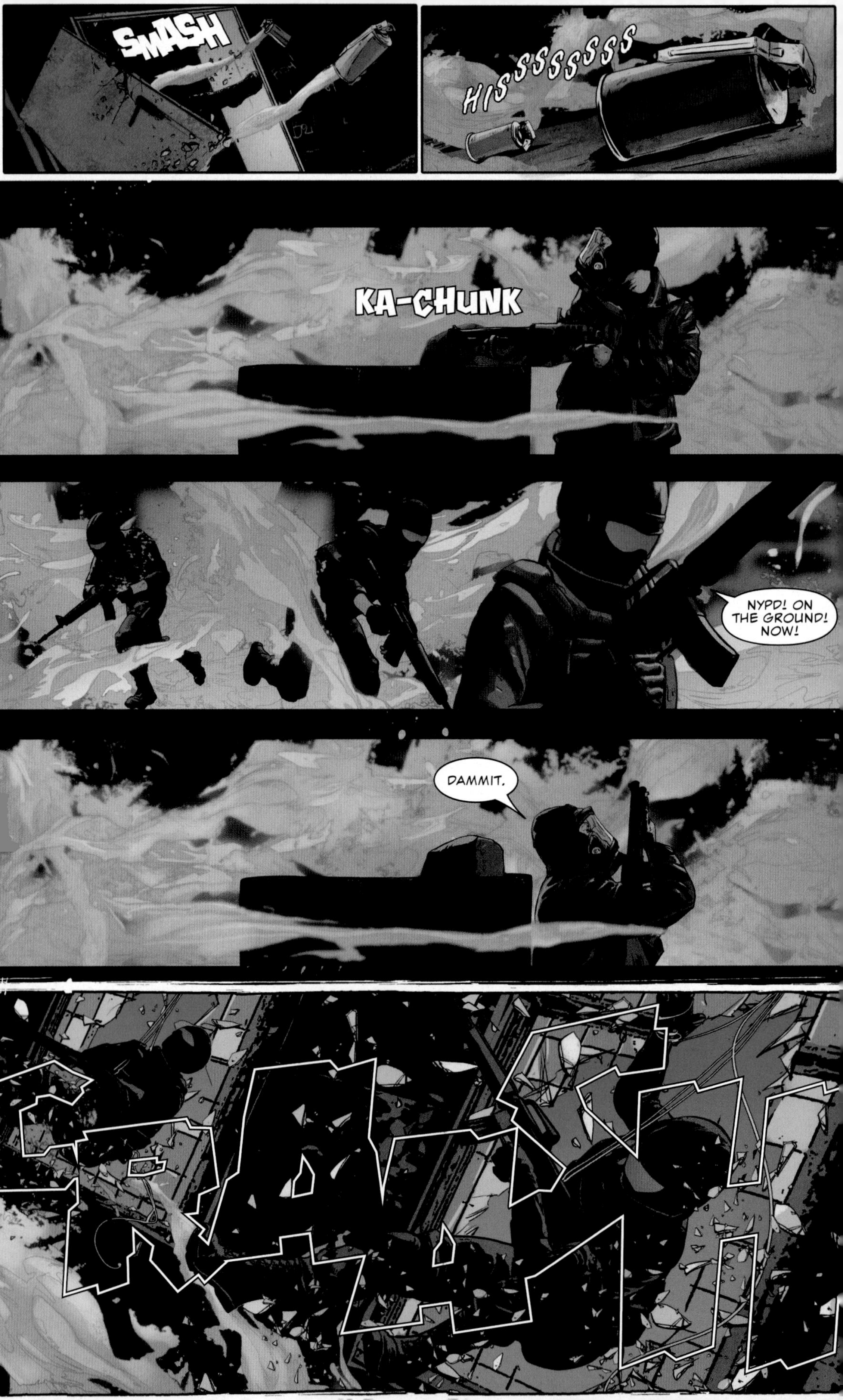
SMASH
HISSSSSSSSS
KA-CHUNK
NYPD! ON THE GROUND! NOW!
DAMMIT.

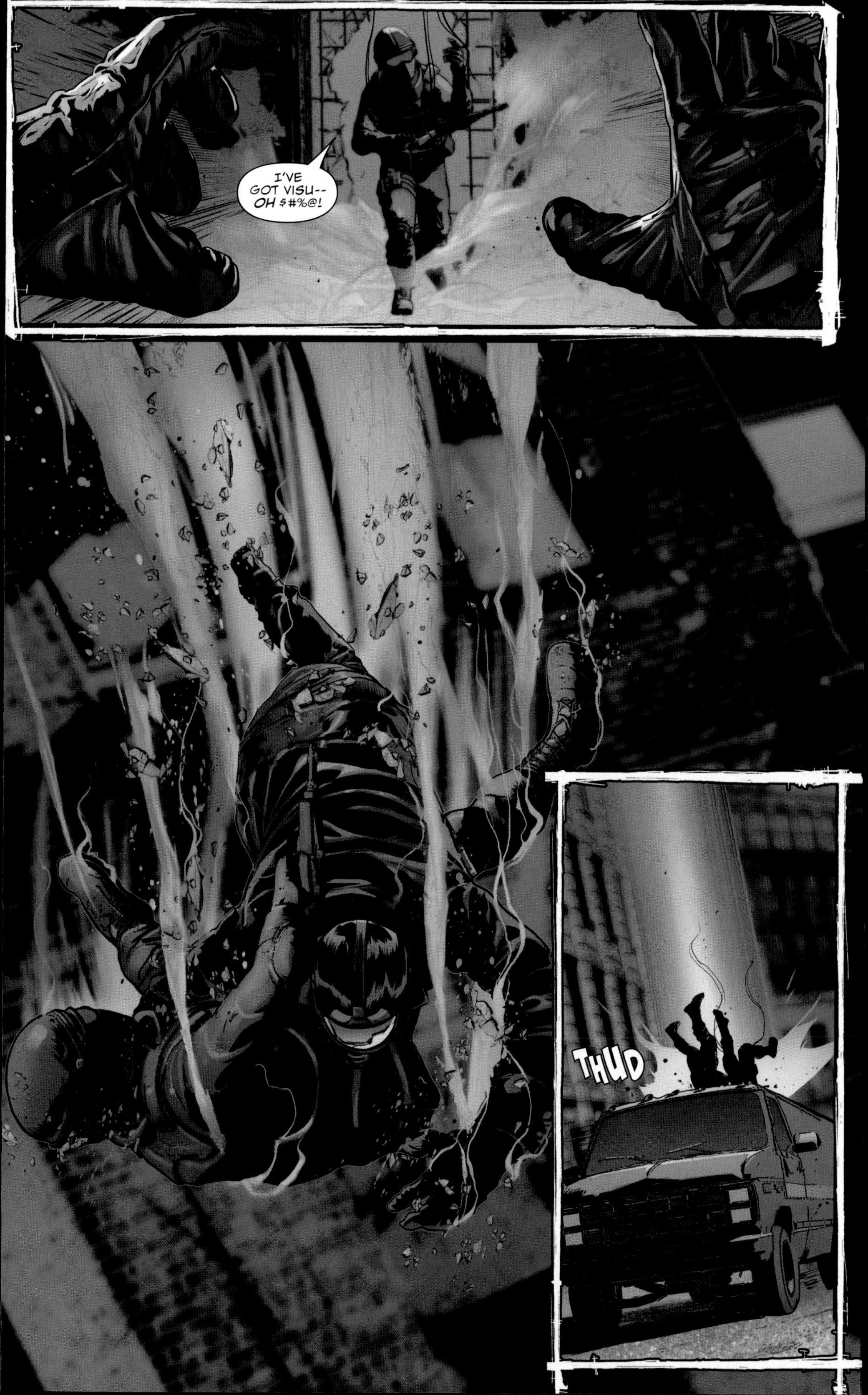
I'VE GOT VISU-- OH $#%@!
THUD

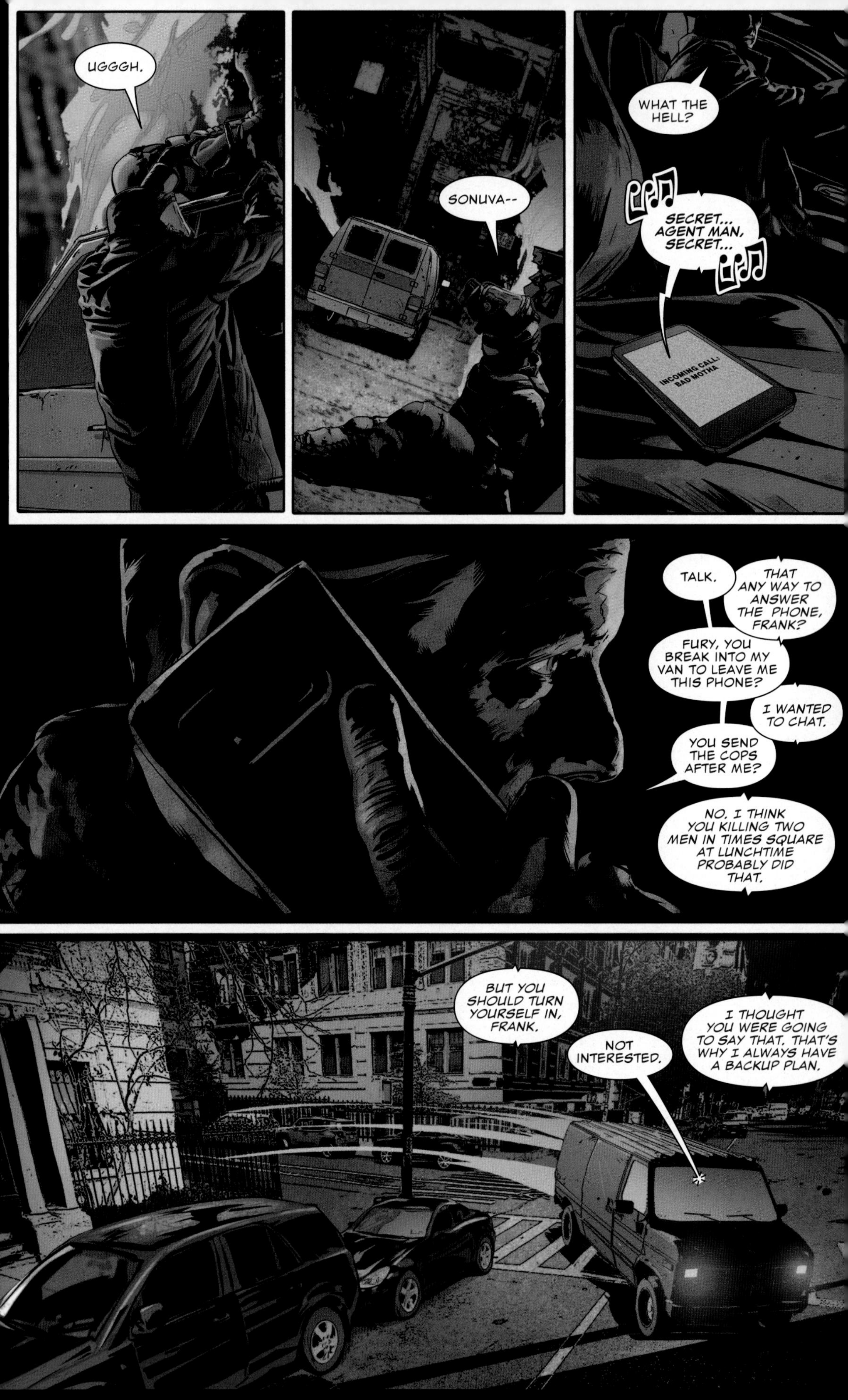
UGGGH.
SONUVA--
WHAT THE HELL?
SECRET... AGENT MAN, SECRET...
INCOMING CALL: BAD MOTHA
TALK.
THAT ANY WAY TO ANSWER THE PHONE, FRANK?
FURY, YOU BREAK INTO MY VAN TO LEAVE ME THIS PHONE?
I WANTED TO CHAT.
YOU SEND THE COPS AFTER ME?
NO. I THINK YOU KILLING TWO MEN IN TIMES SQUARE AT LUNCHTIME PROBABLY DID THAT.
BUT YOU SHOULD TURN YOURSELF IN, FRANK.
NOT INTERESTED.
I THOUGHT YOU WERE GOING TO SAY THAT. THAT'S WHY I ALWAYS HAVE A BACKUP PLAN.

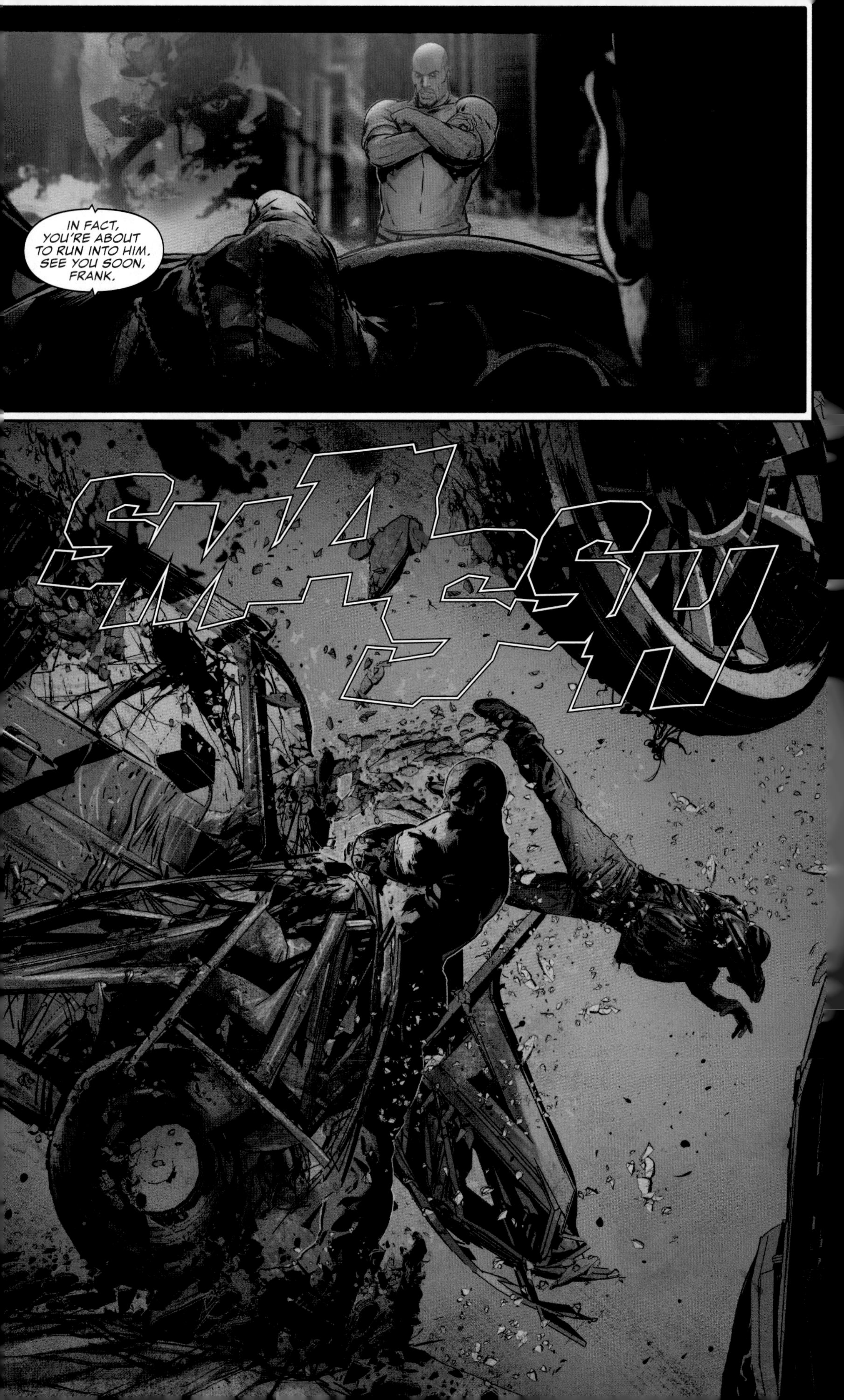
IN FACT, YOU'RE ABOUT TO RUN INTO HIM. SEE YOU SOON, FRANK.
SMASH

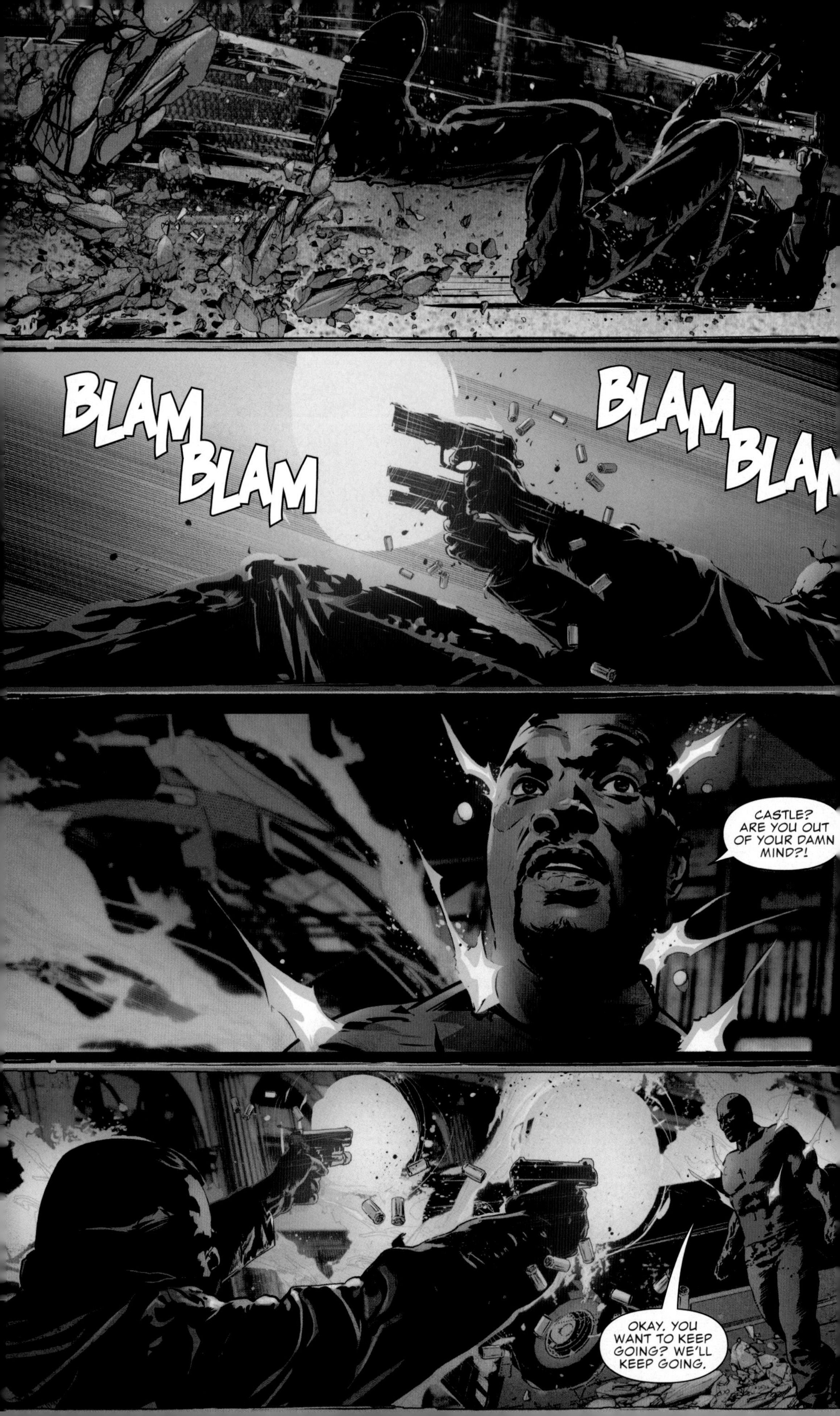
BLAM
BLAM
BLAM
BLAM
CASTLE? ARE YOU OUT OF YOUR DAMN MIND?!
OKAY. YOU WANT TO KEEP GOING? WE'LL KEEP GOING.

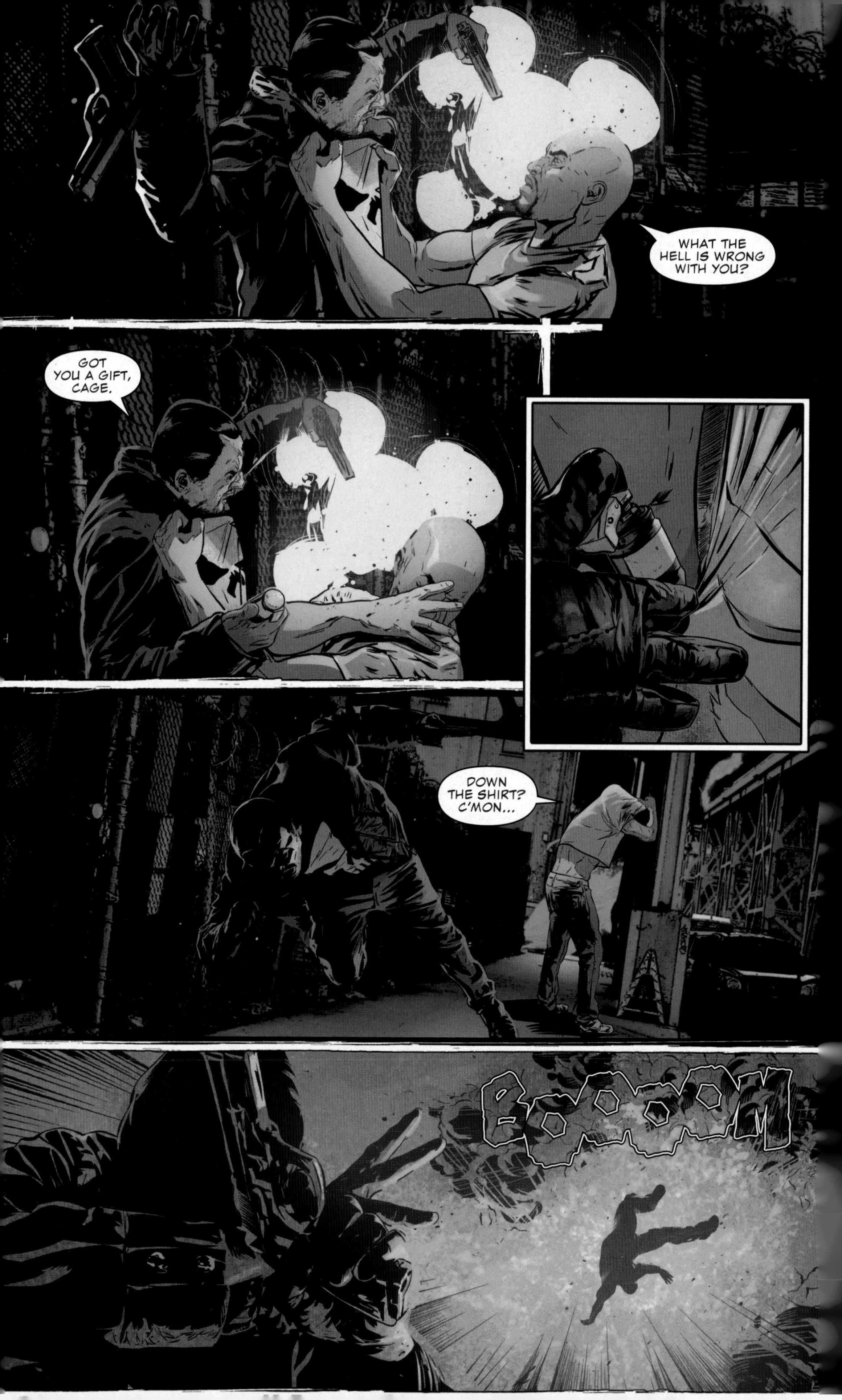
WHAT THE HELL IS WRONG WITH YOU?
GOT YOU A GIFT, CAGE.
DOWN THE SHIRT? C'MON...
BOOOOOM

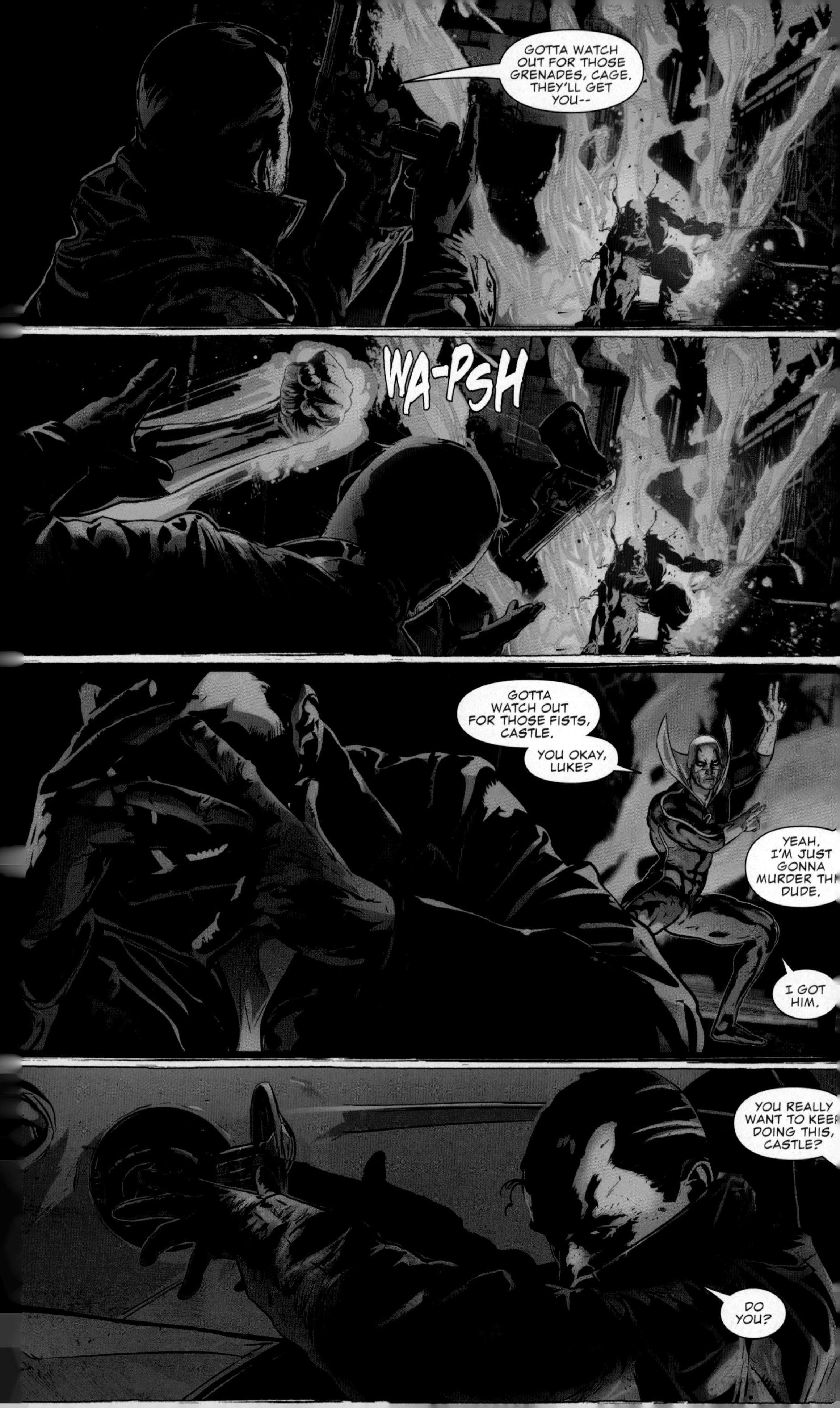
GOTTA WATCH OUT FOR THOSE GRENADES, CAGE. THEY'LL GET YOU--
WA-PSH
GOTTA WATCH OUT FOR THOSE FISTS, CASTLE.
YOU OKAY, LUKE?
YEAH. I'M JUST GONNA MURDER THI DUDE.
I GOT HIM.
YOU REALLY WANT TO KEE DOING THIS, CASTLE?
DO YOU?

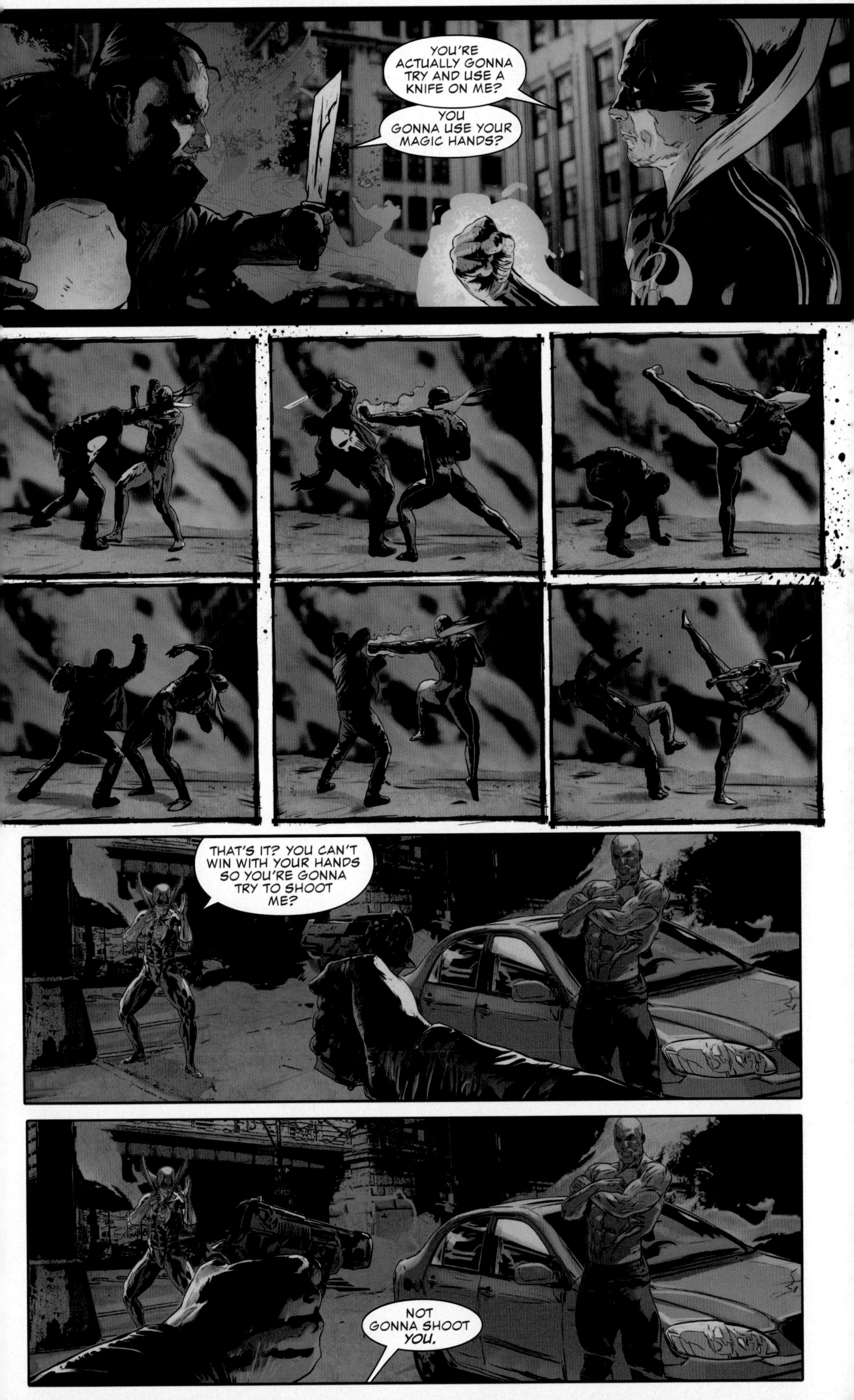

YOU'RE ACTUALLY GONNA TRY AND USE A KNIFE ON ME?
YOU GONNA USE YOUR MAGIC HANDS?
THAT'S IT? YOU CAN'T WIN WITH YOUR HANDS SO YOU'RE GONNA TRY TO SHOOT ME?
NOT GONNA SHOOT *YOU.*

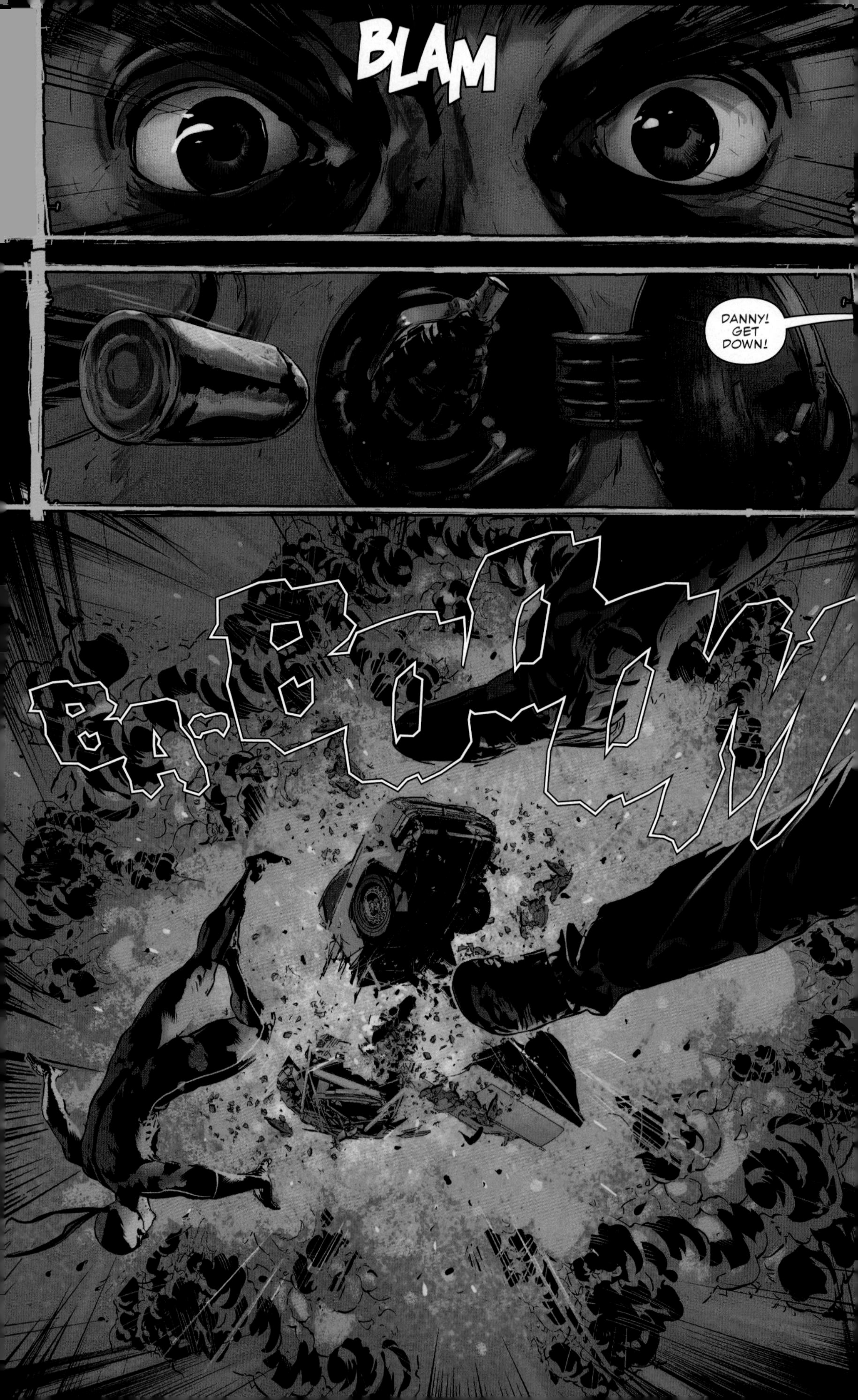
BLAM
DANNY! GET DOWN!
BA-BOOOM

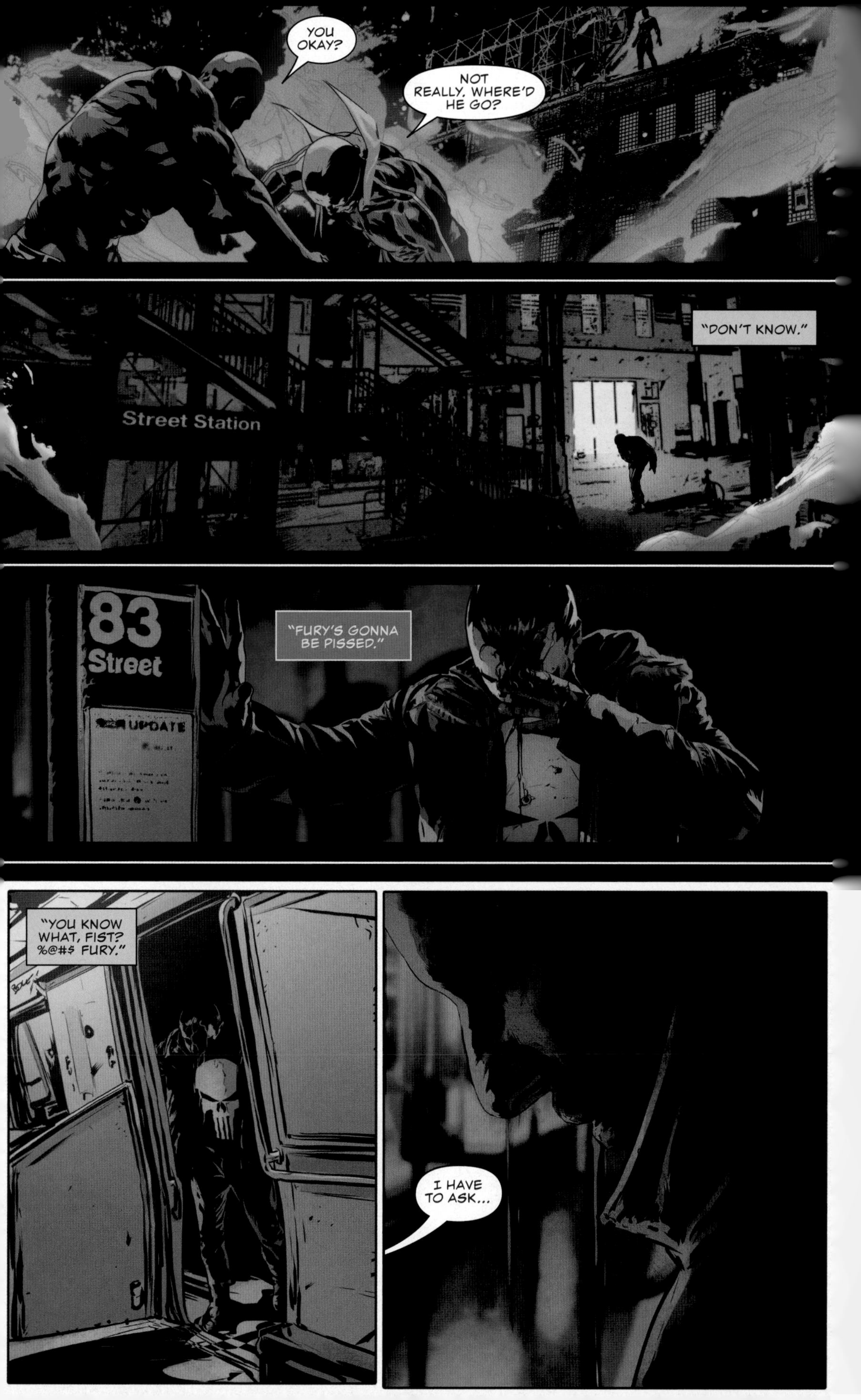
YOU OKAY?
NOT REALLY. WHERE'D HE GO?
"DON'T KNOW."
Street Station
83 Street
UPDATE
"FURY'S GONNA BE PISSED."
"YOU KNOW WHAT, FIST? %@#$ FURY."
I HAVE TO ASK...

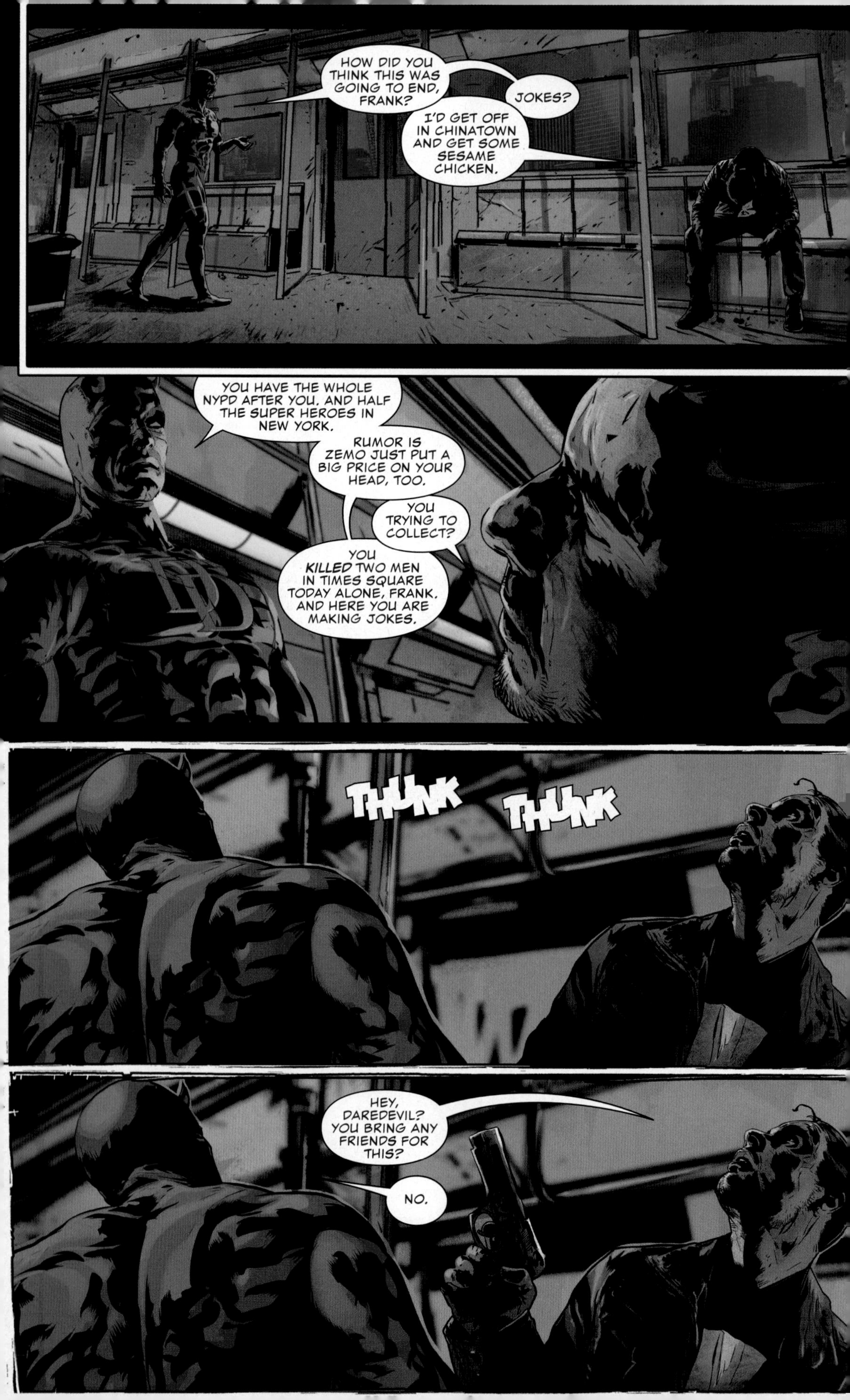
HOW DID YOU THINK THIS WAS GOING TO END, FRANK?
JOKES?
I'D GET OFF IN CHINATOWN AND GET SOME SESAME CHICKEN.
YOU HAVE THE WHOLE NYPD AFTER YOU. AND HALF THE SUPER HEROES IN NEW YORK.
RUMOR IS ZEMO JUST PUT A BIG PRICE ON YOUR HEAD, TOO.
YOU TRYING TO COLLECT?
YOU *KILLED* TWO MEN IN TIMES SQUARE TODAY ALONE, FRANK, AND HERE YOU ARE MAKING JOKES.
THUNK
THUNK
HEY, DAREDEVIL? YOU BRING ANY FRIENDS FOR THIS?
NO.

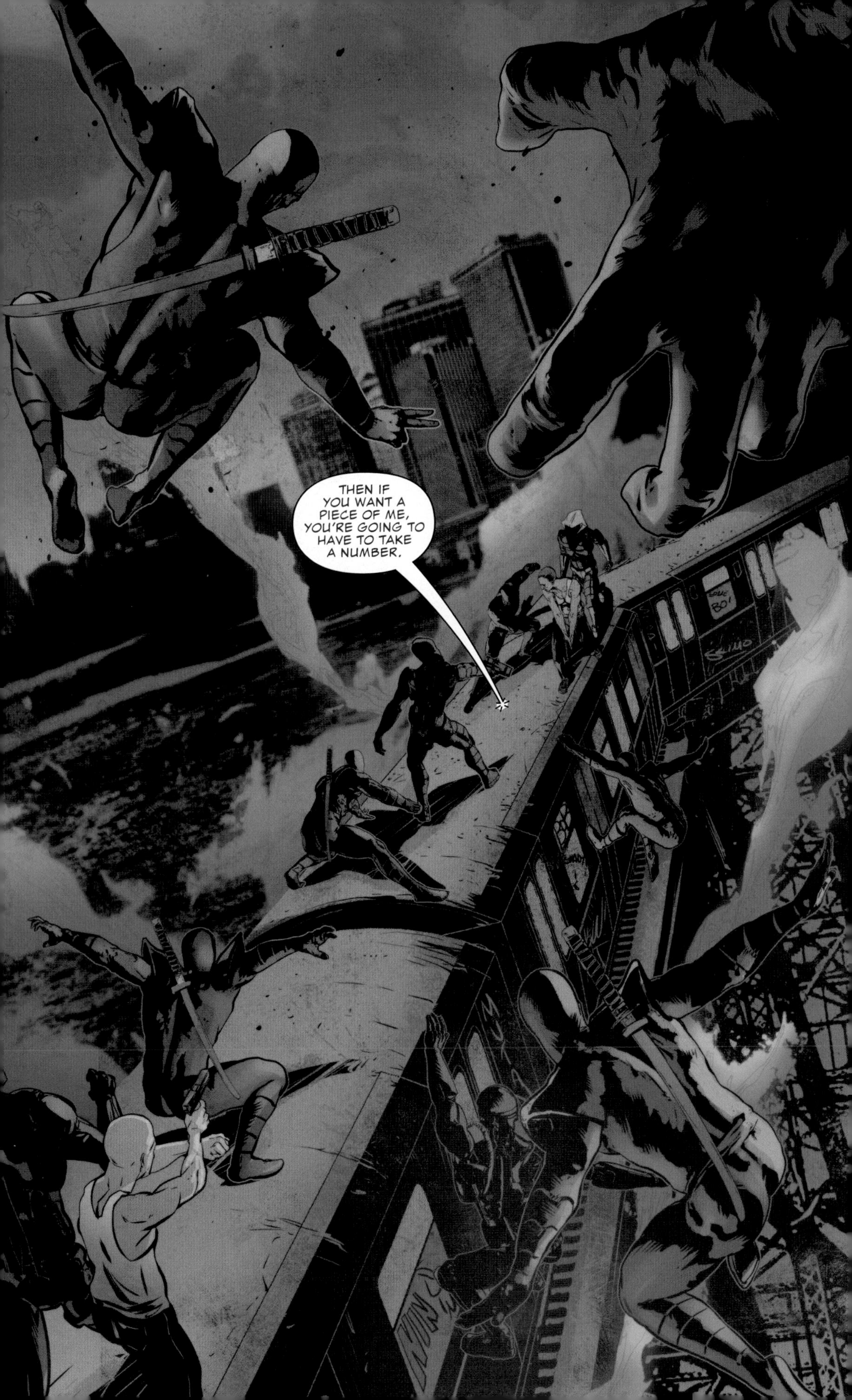
THEN IF YOU WANT A PIECE OF ME, YOU'RE GOING TO HAVE TO TAKE A NUMBER.

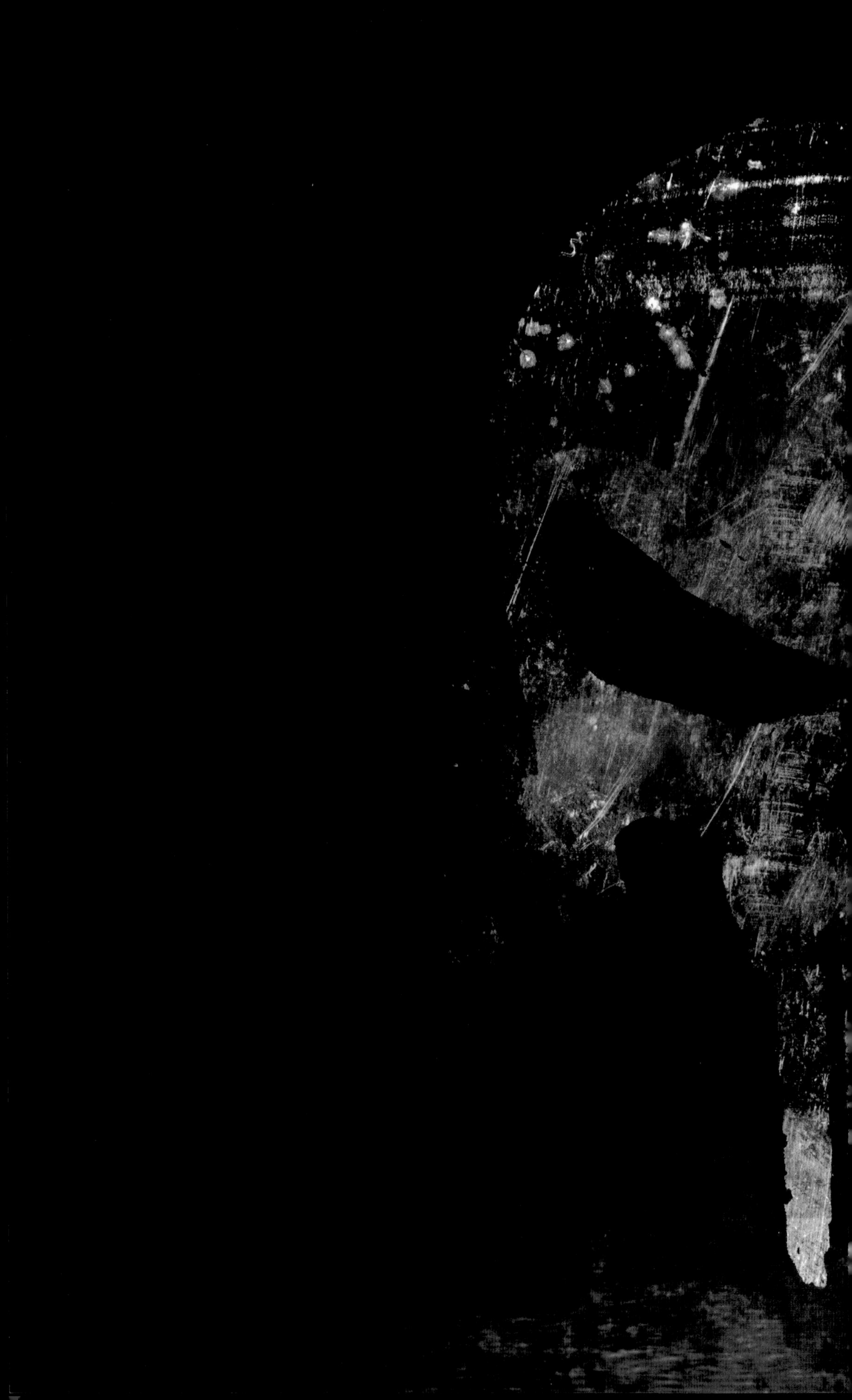

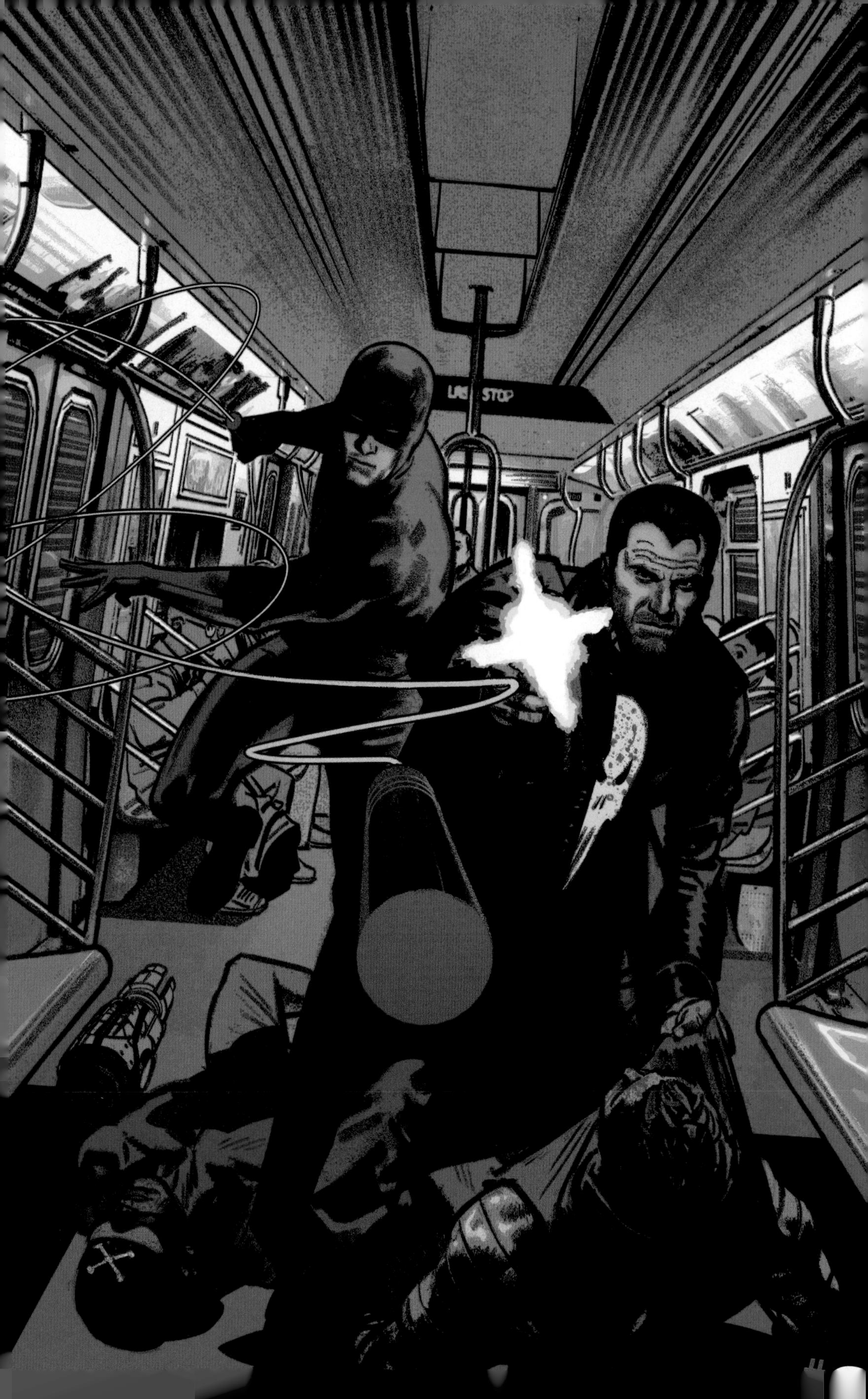
LAS STOP

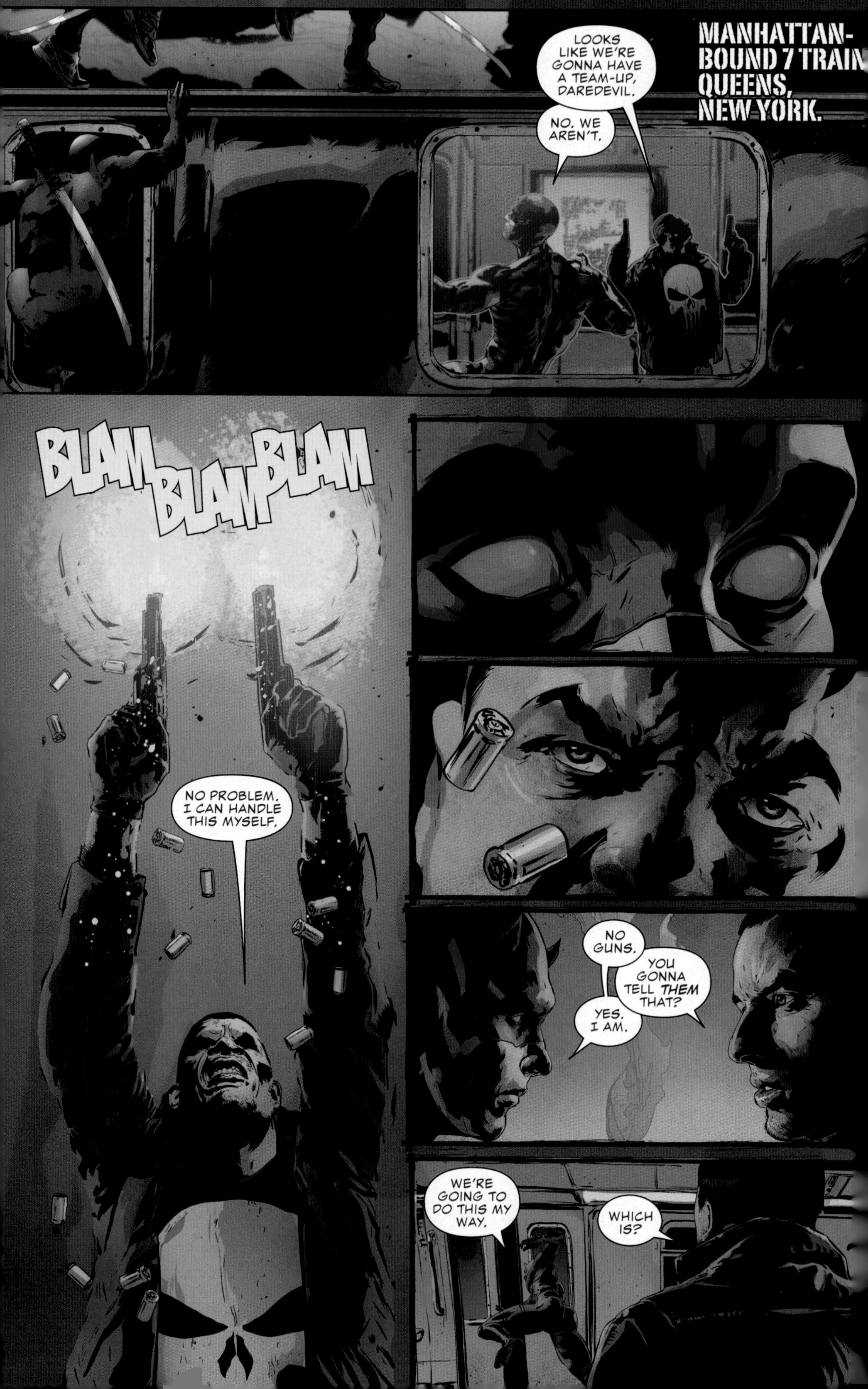
MANHATTAN-BOUND 7 TRAIN QUEENS, NEW YORK.
LOOKS LIKE WE'RE GONNA HAVE A TEAM-UP, DAREDEVIL.
NO. WE AREN'T.
BLAM BLAM BLAM BLAM
NO PROBLEM. I CAN HANDLE THIS MYSELF.
NO GUNS.
YOU GONNA TELL THEM THAT?
YES, I AM.
WE'RE GOING TO DO THIS MY WAY.
WHICH IS?

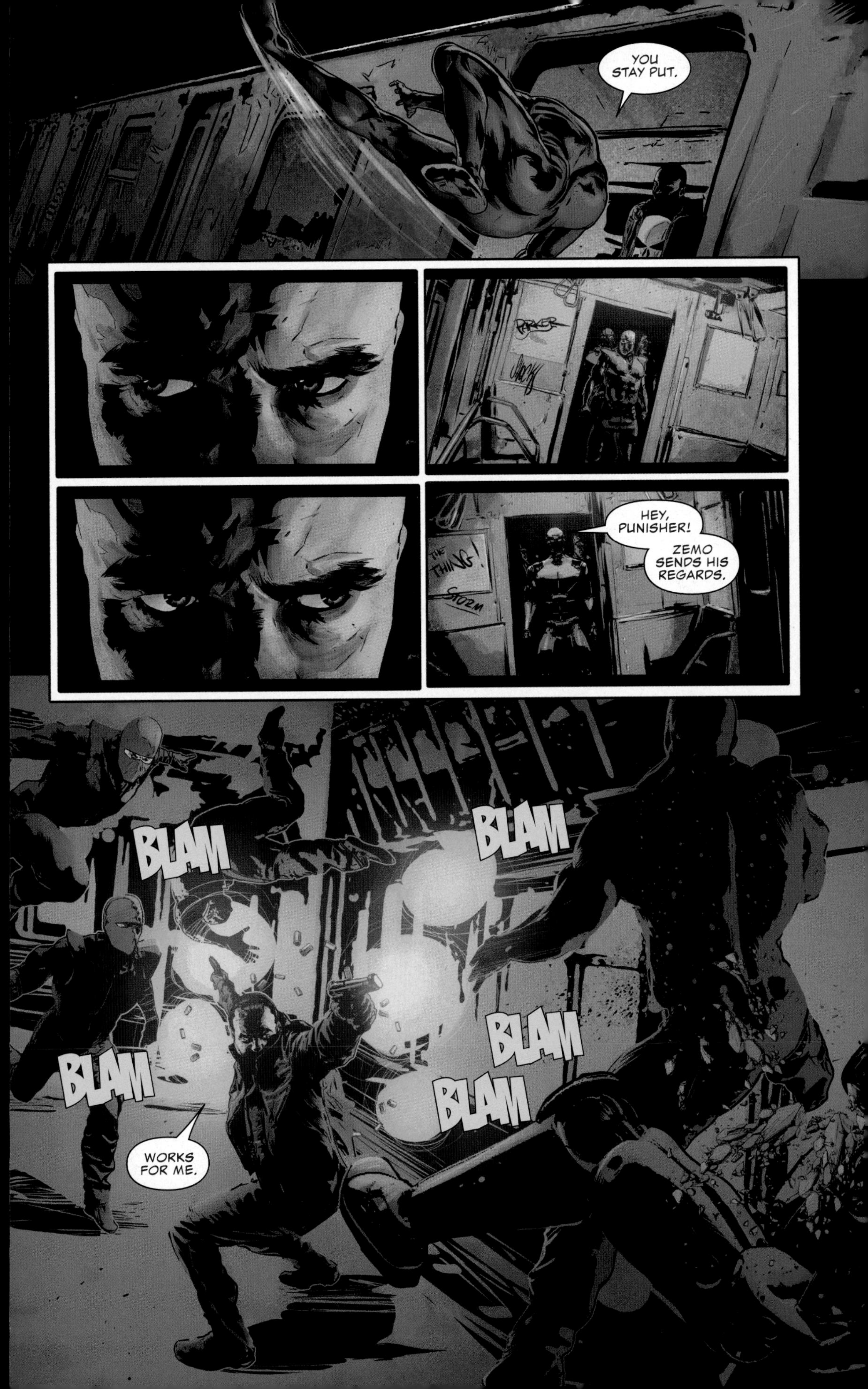
YOU STAY PUT.
PARKER
THE THING!
STORM
HEY, PUNISHER!
ZEMO SENDS HIS REGARDS.
BLAM
BLAM
BLAM
BLAM
BLAM
WORKS FOR ME.

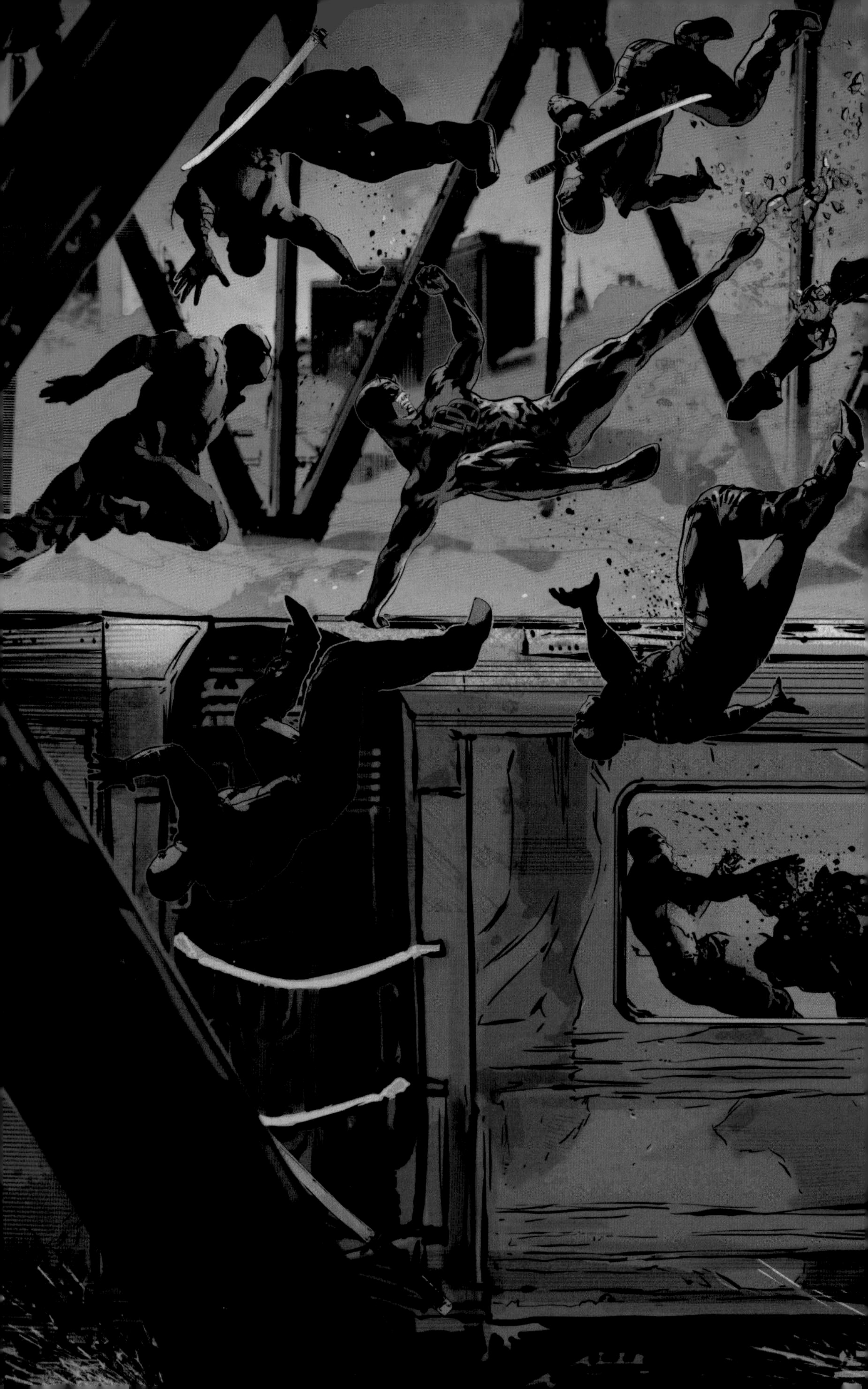

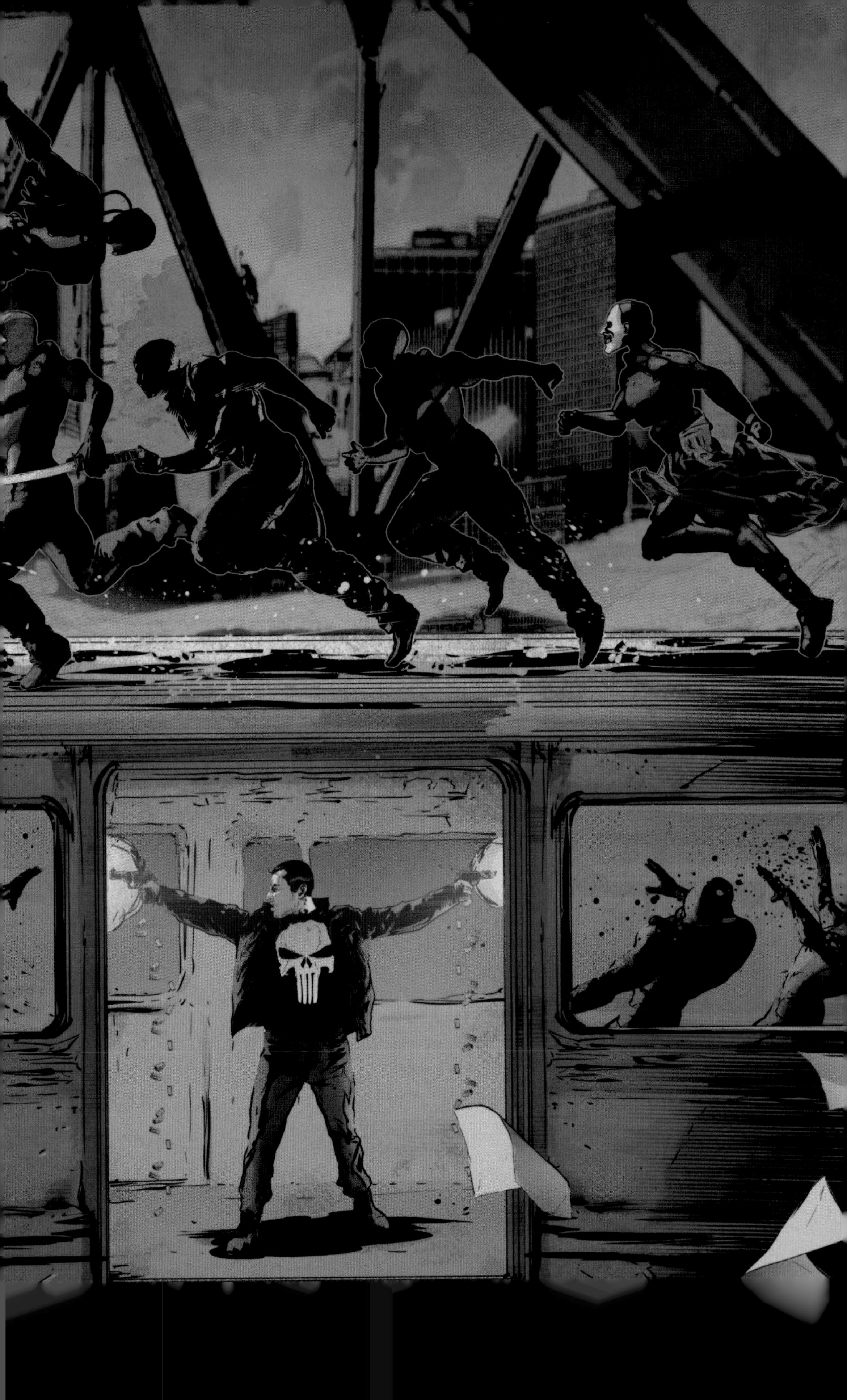

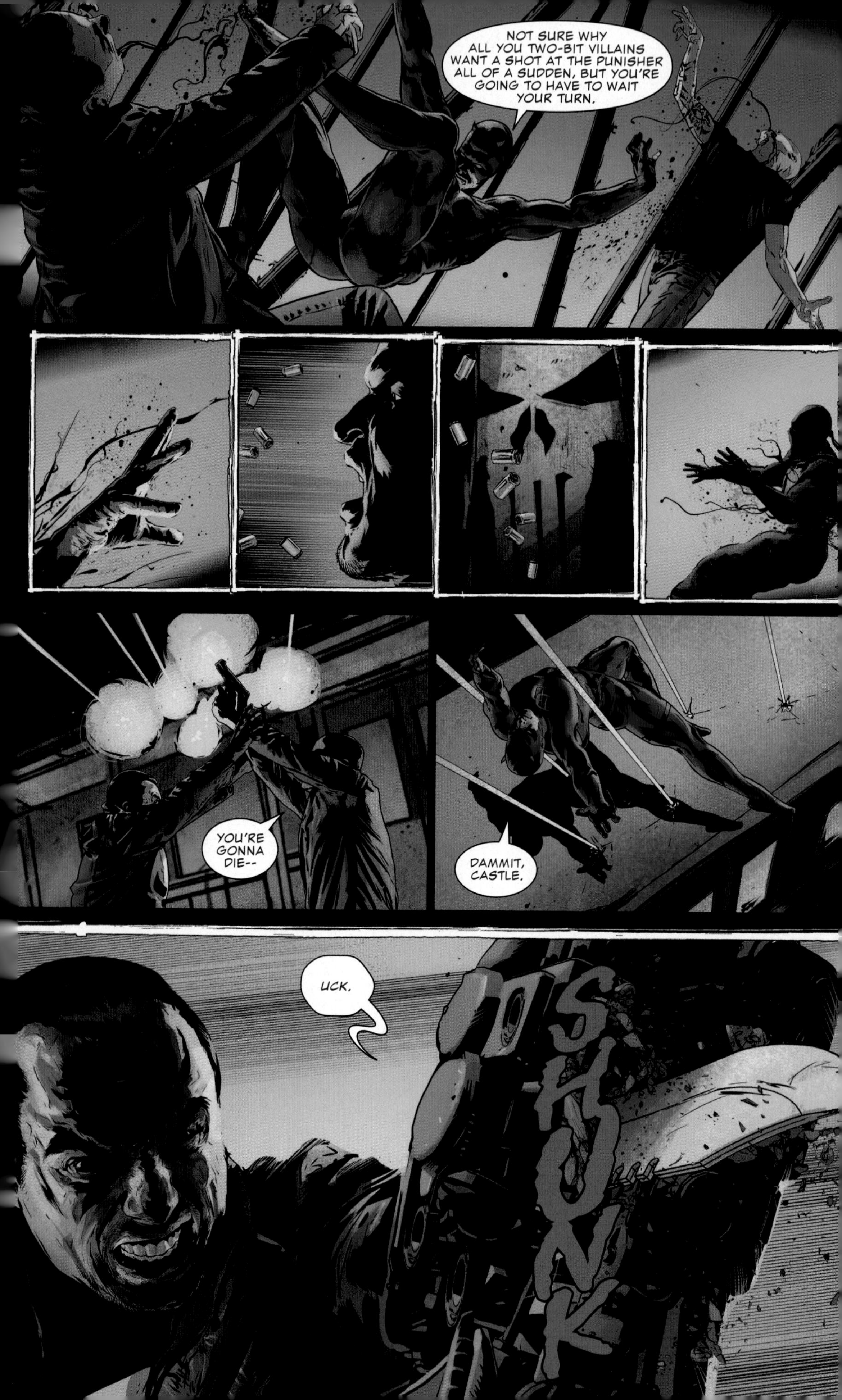
NOT SURE WHY ALL YOU TWO-BIT VILLAINS WANT A SHOT AT THE PUNISHER ALL OF A SUDDEN, BUT YOU'RE GOING TO HAVE TO WAIT YOUR TURN.
YOU'RE GONNA DIE--
DAMMIT, CASTLE.
UCK.
SHUNK

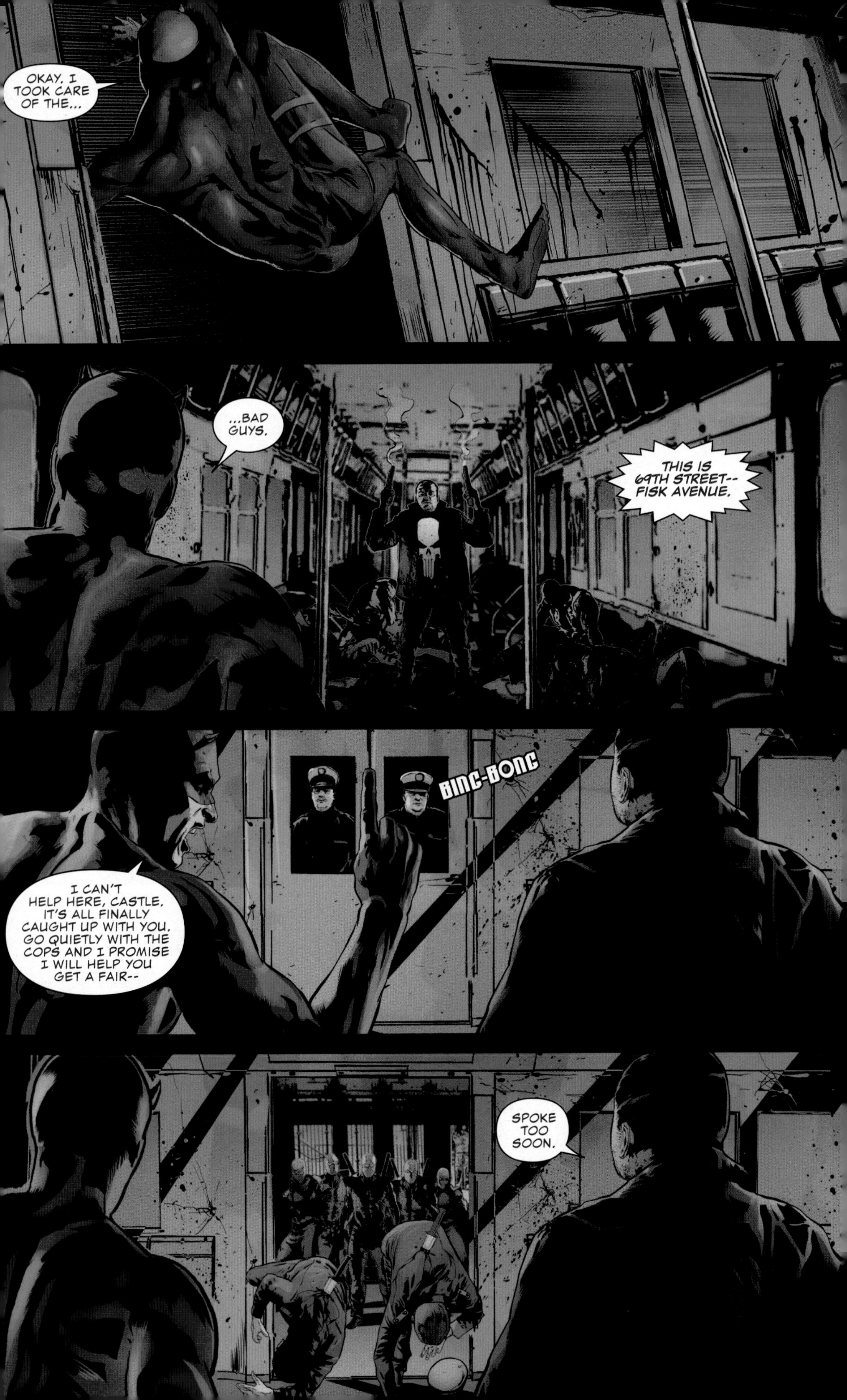
OKAY, I TOOK CARE OF THE...
...BAD GUYS.
THIS IS 69TH STREET-- FISK AVENUE.
BING-BONG
I CAN'T HELP HERE, CASTLE. IT'S ALL FINALLY CAUGHT UP WITH YOU. GO QUIETLY WITH THE COPS AND I PROMISE I WILL HELP YOU GET A FAIR--
SPOKE TOO SOON.

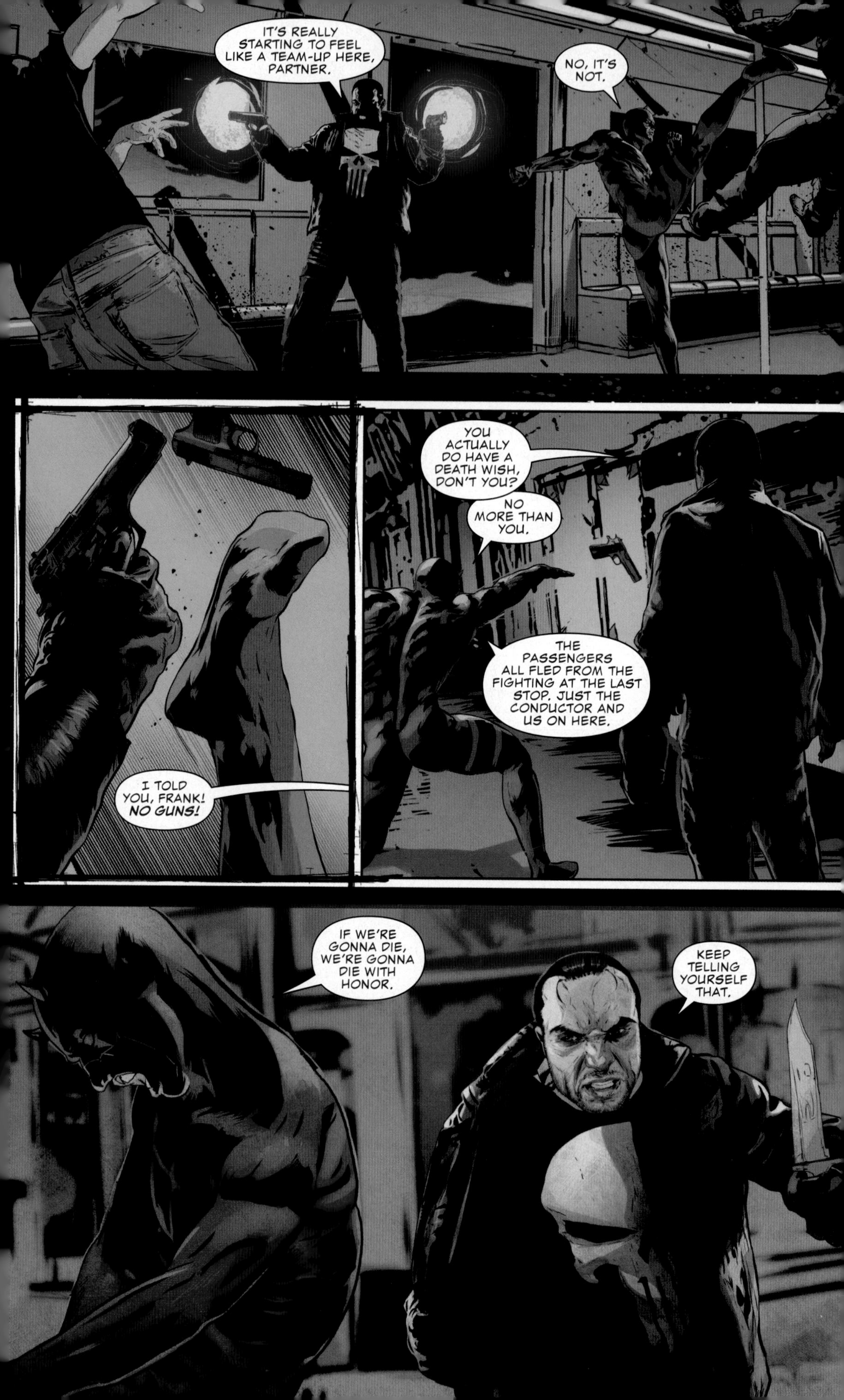
IT'S REALLY STARTING TO FEEL LIKE A TEAM-UP HERE, PARTNER.
NO, IT'S NOT.
I TOLD YOU, FRANK! *NO GUNS!*
YOU ACTUALLY DO HAVE A DEATH WISH, DON'T YOU?
NO MORE THAN YOU.
THE PASSENGERS ALL FLED FROM THE FIGHTING AT THE LAST STOP. JUST THE CONDUCTOR AND US ON HERE.
IF WE'RE GONNA DIE, WE'RE GONNA DIE WITH HONOR.
KEEP TELLING YOURSELF THAT.

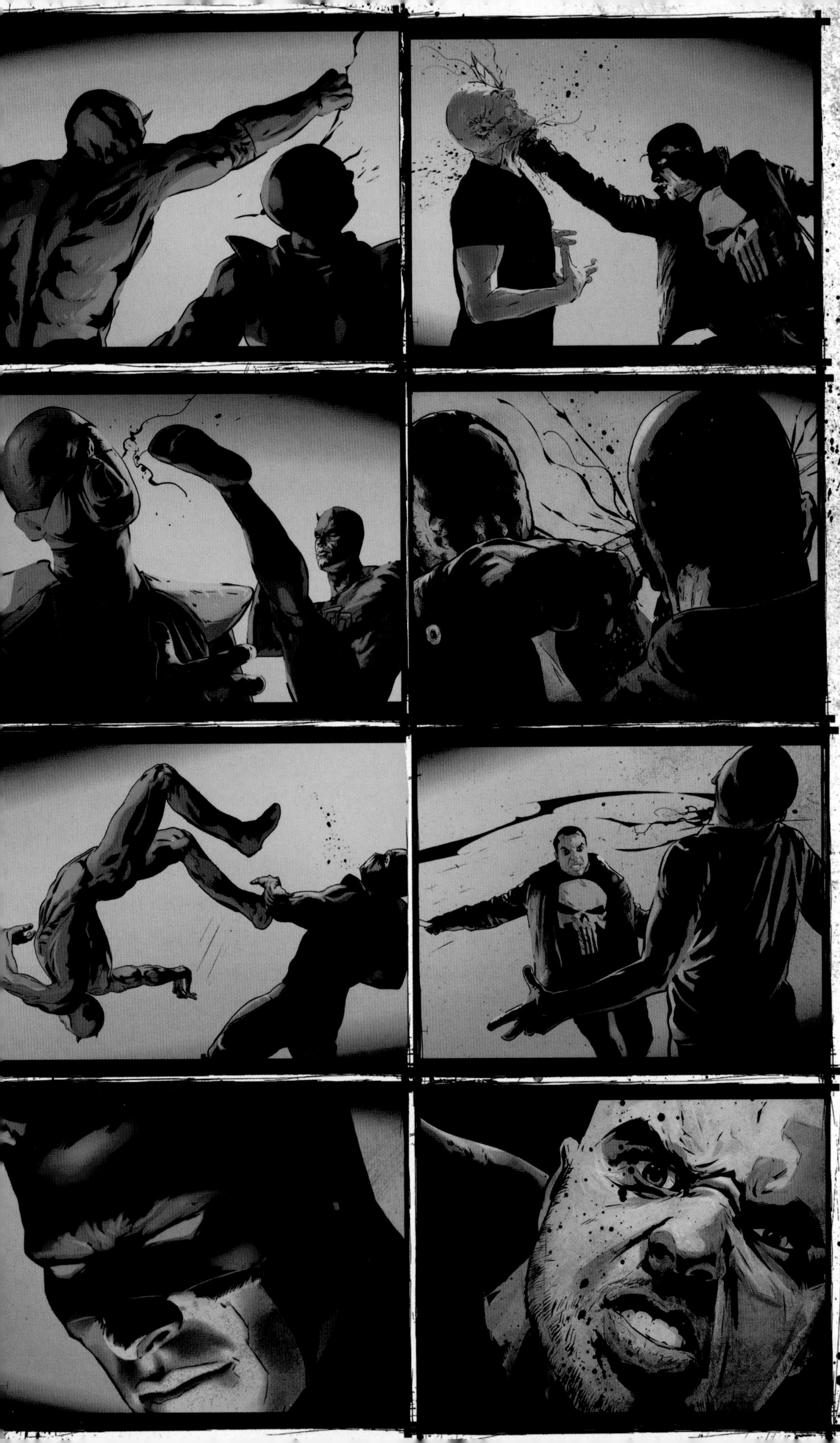

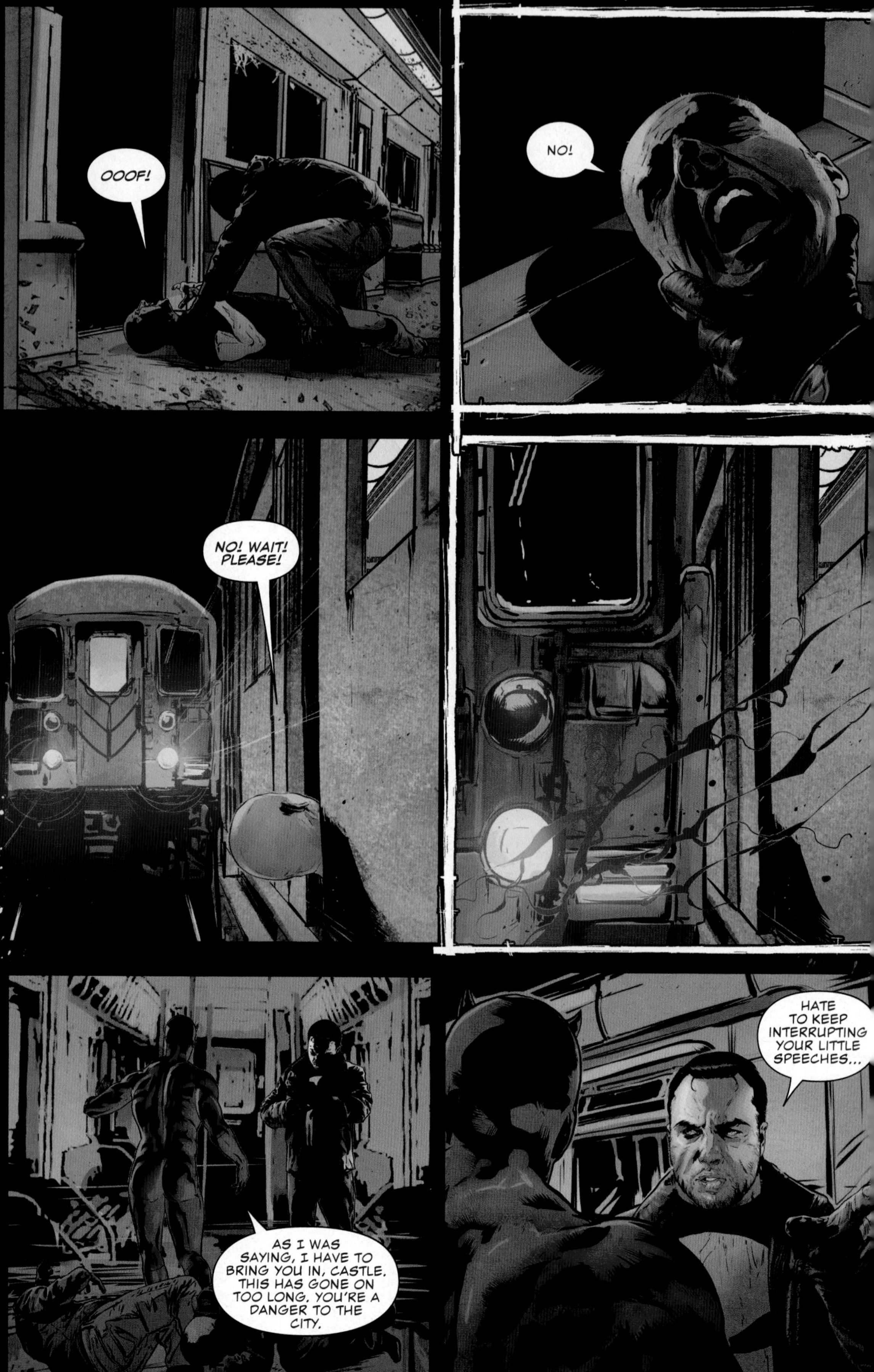
OOOF!
NO!
NO! WAIT! PLEASE!
AS I WAS SAYING, I HAVE TO BRING YOU IN, CASTLE. THIS HAS GONE ON TOO LONG. YOU'RE A DANGER TO THE CITY.
HATE TO KEEP INTERRUPTING YOUR LITTLE SPEECHES...

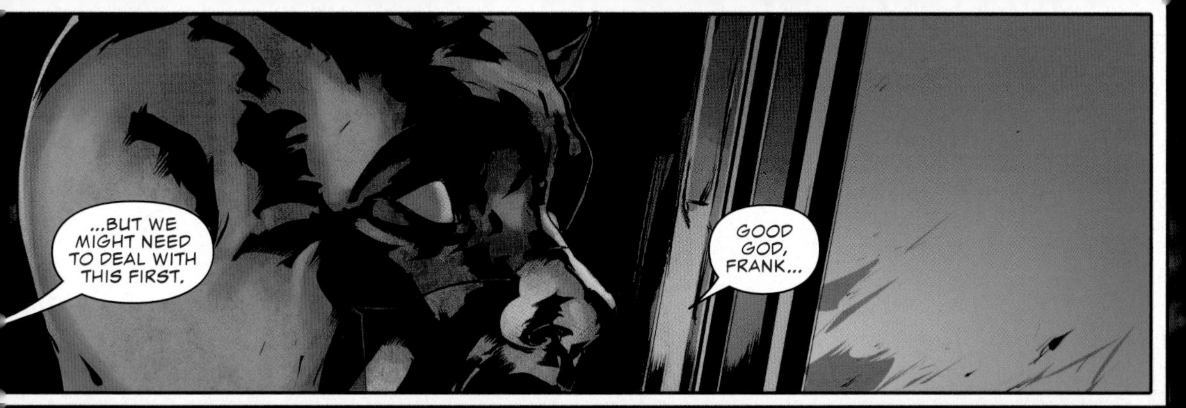
...BUT WE MIGHT NEED TO DEAL WITH THIS FIRST.
GOOD GOD, FRANK...

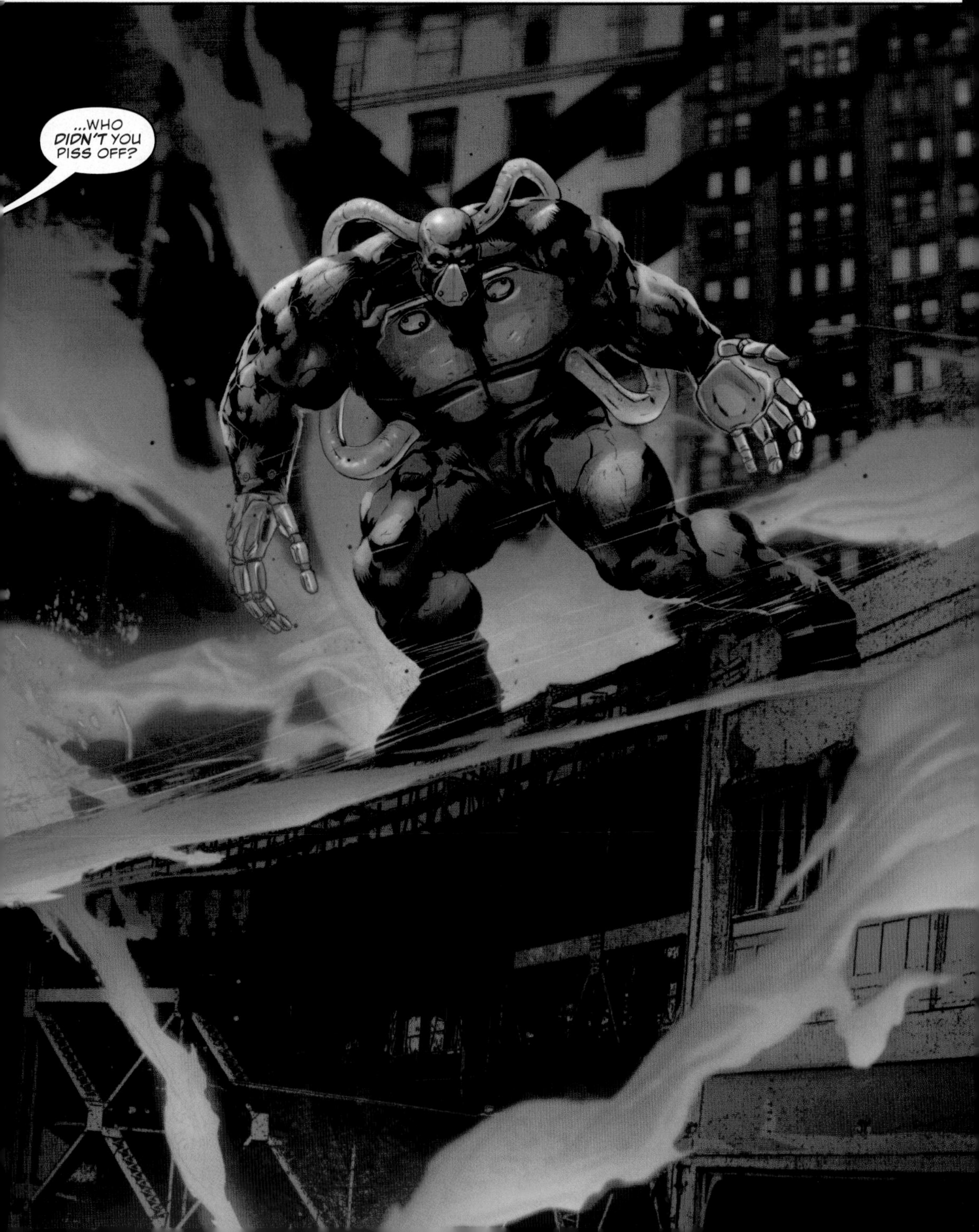
...WHO *DIDN'T* YOU PISS OFF?

LET'S GO! WE JUMP, MAYBE HE WON'T CRUSH THE TRAIN!
FRANK?
LET'S DO THIS, YOU GIANT PIECE OF--

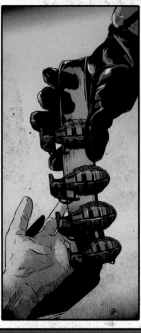

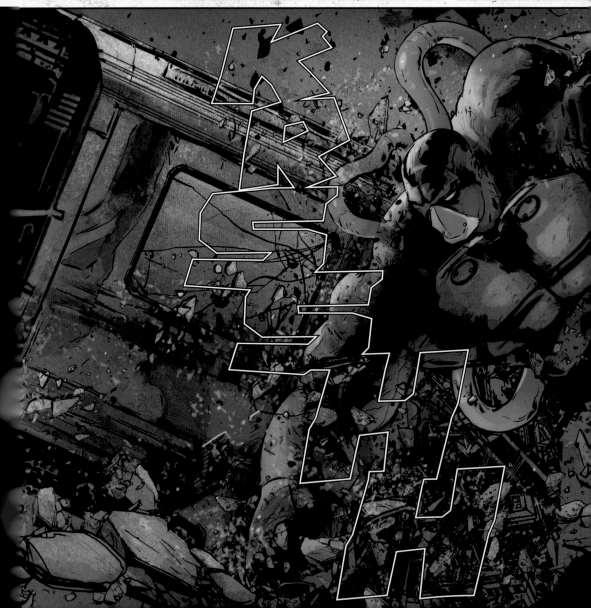

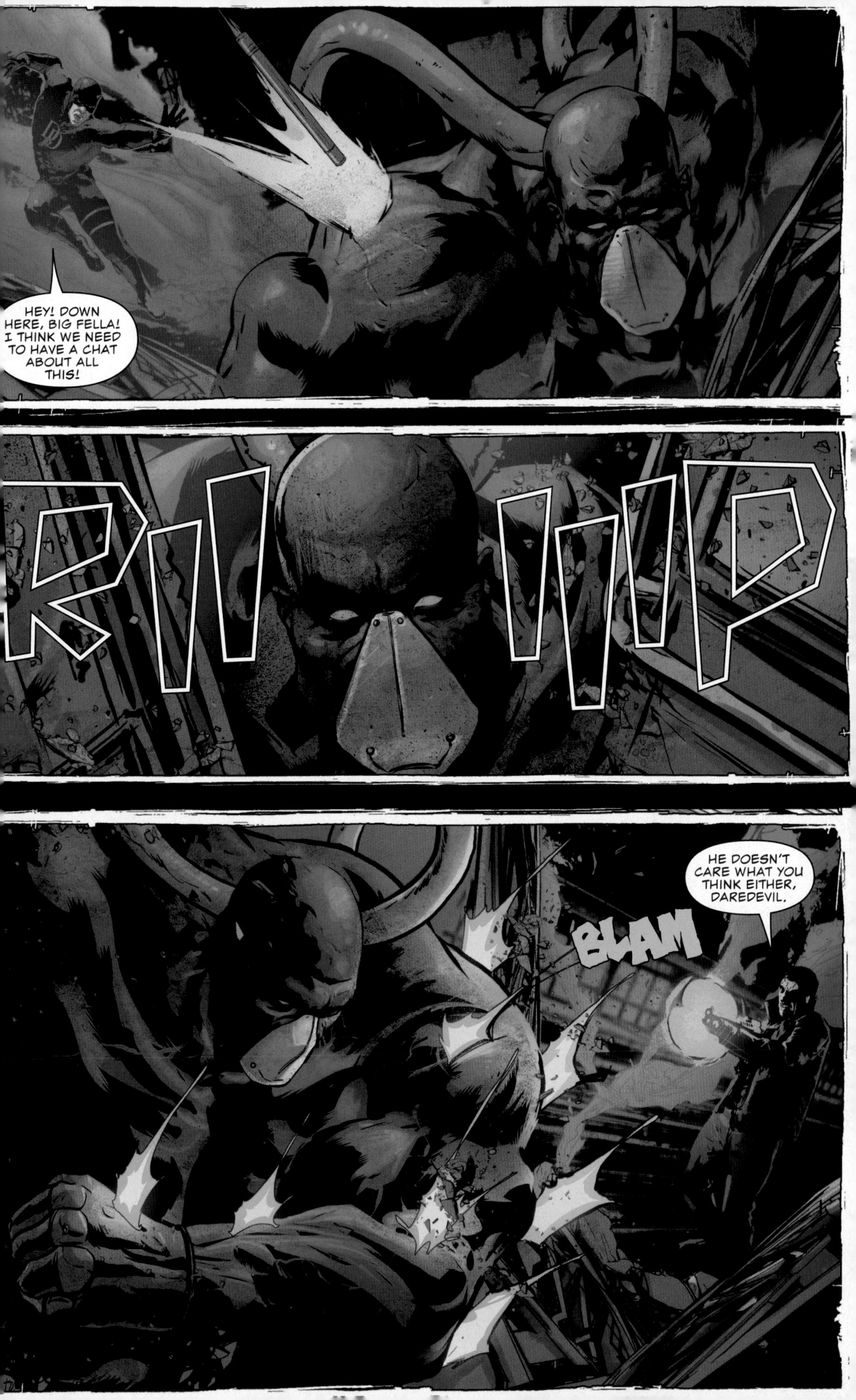
HEY! DOWN HERE, BIG FELLA! I THINK WE NEED TO HAVE A CHAT ABOUT ALL THIS!
RIIIIIP
HE DOESN'T CARE WHAT YOU THINK EITHER, DAREDEVIL.
BLAM

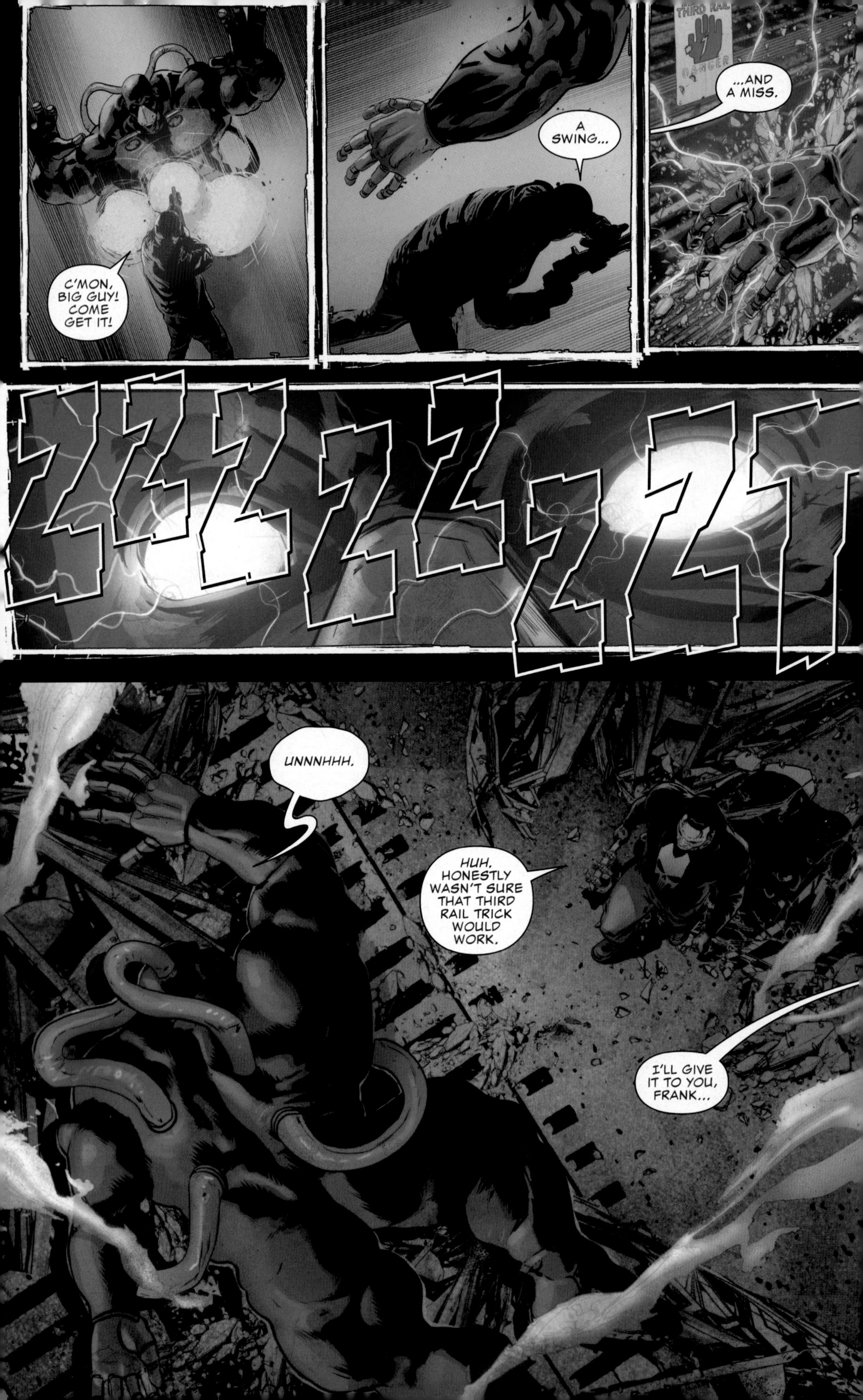
C'MON, BIG GUY! COME GET IT!
A SWING...
THIRD RAIL
DANGER
...AND A MISS.
ZZZZZZZZT
UNNNHHH.
HUH. HONESTLY WASN'T SURE THAT THIRD RAIL TRICK WOULD WORK.
I'LL GIVE IT TO YOU, FRANK...

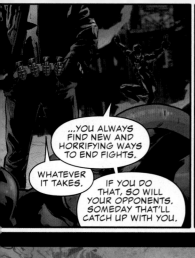

...YOU ALWAYS FIND NEW AND HORRIFYING WAYS TO END FIGHTS.

WHATEVER IT TAKES.

IF YOU DO THAT, SO WILL YOUR OPPONENTS. SOMEDAY THAT'LL CATCH UP WITH YOU.

NOT TODAY.

WELL, I'M JUST GLAD YOU REALIZED YOU DIDN'T HAVE TO KILL HIM.

NO, I DID.

YOU SICK @#$%! HOW DARE YOU--

HE PUT THE LIVES OF EVERYONE IN THIS NEIGHBORHOOD IN JEOPARDY, FOR MONEY.

HE'S A BIG BOY WHO MADE HIS OWN LIFE CHOICES. HE JUST CHOSE WRONG.

YOU'RE A MURDERING PIECE OF FILTH, CASTLE, AND THIS...

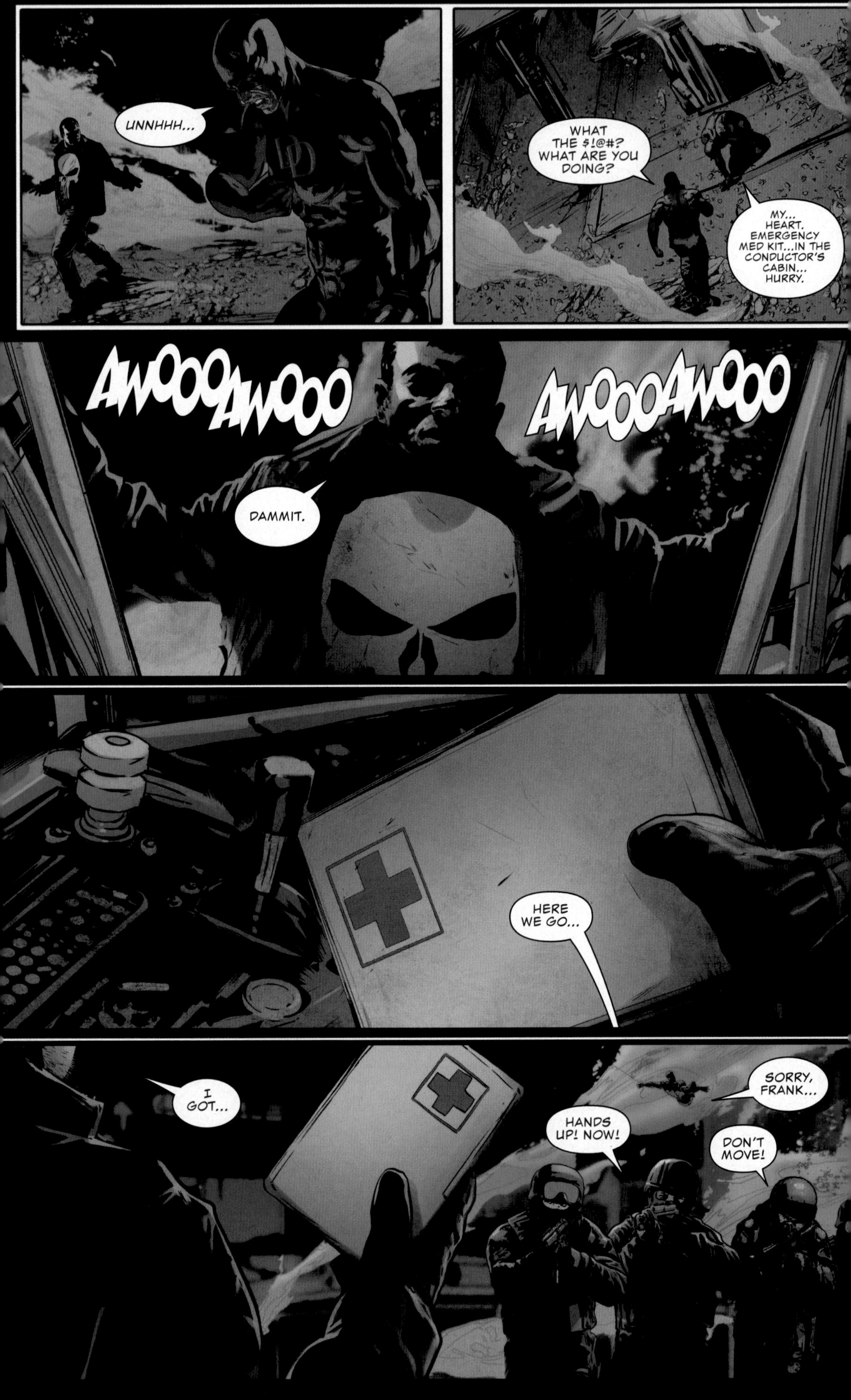
UNNHHH...
WHAT THE $!@#? WHAT ARE YOU DOING?
MY... HEART. EMERGENCY MED KIT...IN THE CONDUCTOR'S CABIN... HURRY.
AWOOOAWOOO
AWOOOAWOOO
DAMMIT.
HERE WE GO...
I GOT...
SORRY, FRANK...
HANDS UP! NOW!
DON'T MOVE!

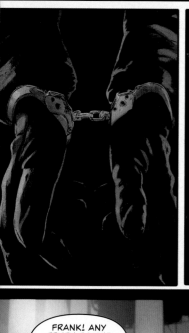

"...LOOKS LIKE IT CAUGHT UP WITH YOU TODAY AFTER ALL."

UP AND AT 'EM, KILLER, WE'RE HERE.

FRANK! ANY TRUTH TO THE RUMOR YOU WERE WORKING FOR THE RUSSIANS?

BURN IN HELL, CASTLE!

FRANK! OVER HERE!

THEY'RE GONNA THROW AWAY THE KEY FOR YOU, BOY!

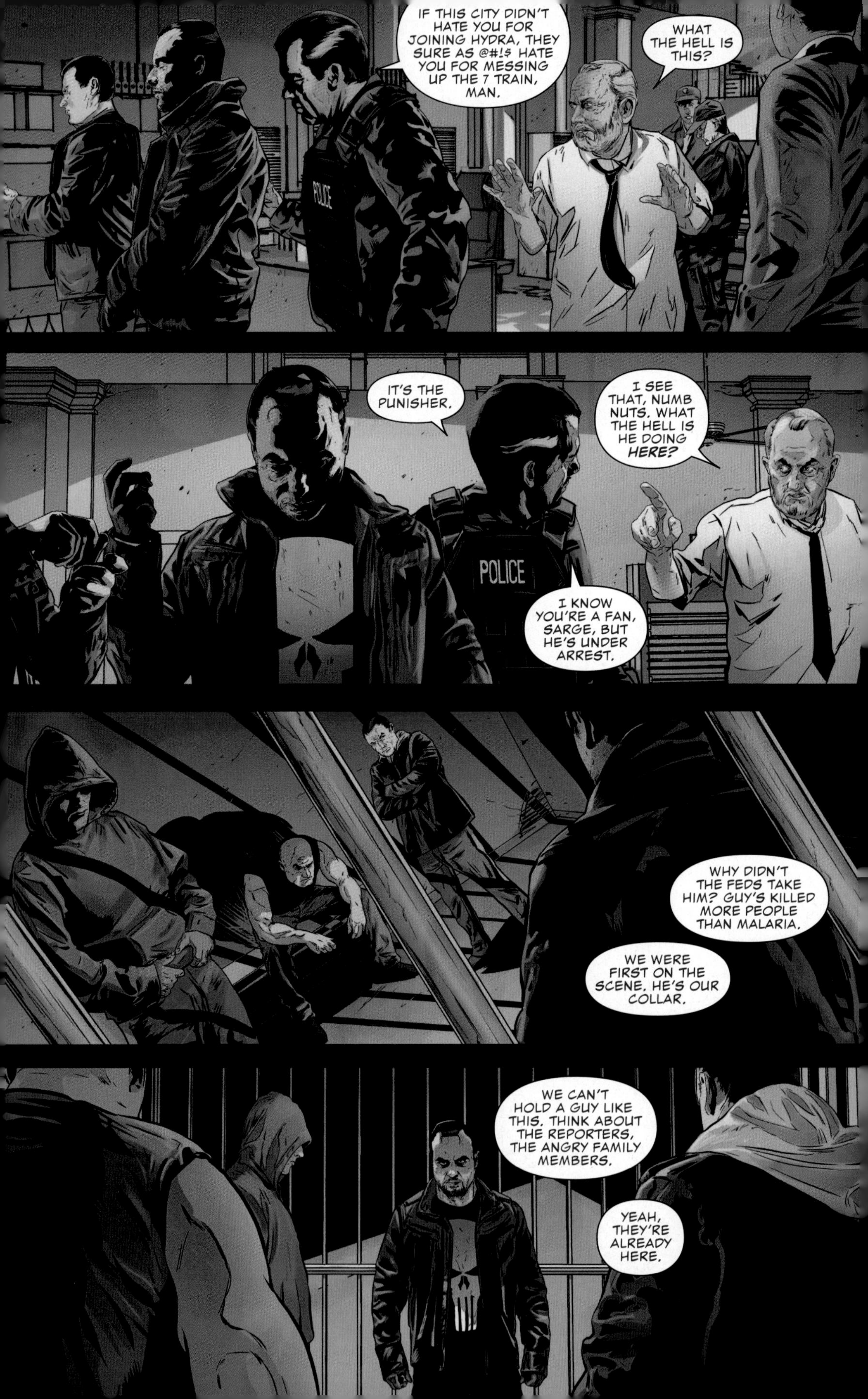
IF THIS CITY DIDN'T HATE YOU FOR JOINING HYDRA, THEY SURE AS @#!$ HATE YOU FOR MESSING UP THE 7 TRAIN, MAN.
WHAT THE HELL IS THIS?
IT'S THE PUNISHER.
I SEE THAT, NUMB NUTS. WHAT THE HELL IS HE DOING *HERE?*
I KNOW YOU'RE A FAN, SARGE, BUT HE'S UNDER ARREST.
POLICE
WHY DIDN'T THE FEDS TAKE HIM? GUY'S KILLED MORE PEOPLE THAN MALARIA.
WE WERE FIRST ON THE SCENE. HE'S OUR COLLAR.
WE CAN'T HOLD A GUY LIKE THIS. THINK ABOUT THE REPORTERS, THE ANGRY FAMILY MEMBERS.
YEAH, THEY'RE ALREADY HERE.

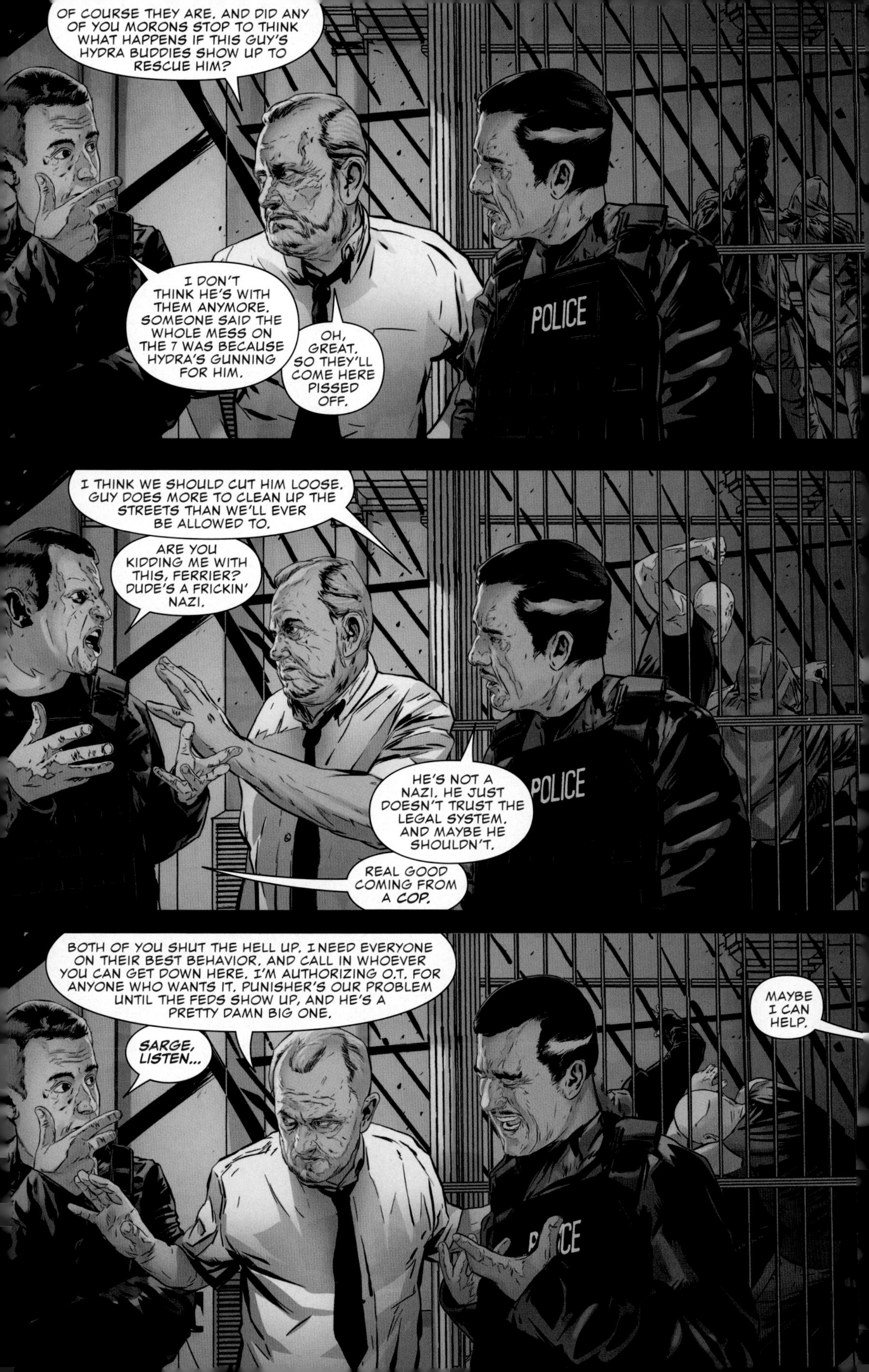

OF COURSE THEY ARE. AND DID ANY OF YOU MORONS STOP TO THINK WHAT HAPPENS IF THIS GUY'S HYDRA BUDDIES SHOW UP TO RESCUE HIM?
I DON'T THINK HE'S WITH THEM ANYMORE. SOMEONE SAID THE WHOLE MESS ON THE 7 WAS BECAUSE HYDRA'S GUNNING FOR HIM.
OH, GREAT. SO THEY'LL COME HERE PISSED OFF.
POLICE
I THINK WE SHOULD CUT HIM LOOSE. GUY DOES MORE TO CLEAN UP THE STREETS THAN WE'LL EVER BE ALLOWED TO.
ARE YOU KIDDING ME WITH THIS, FERRIER? DUDE'S A FRICKIN' NAZI.
HE'S NOT A NAZI. HE JUST DOESN'T TRUST THE LEGAL SYSTEM. AND MAYBE HE SHOULDN'T.
REAL GOOD COMING FROM A COP.
POLICE
BOTH OF YOU SHUT THE HELL UP. I NEED EVERYONE ON THEIR BEST BEHAVIOR, AND CALL IN WHOEVER YOU CAN GET DOWN HERE. I'M AUTHORIZING O.T. FOR ANYONE WHO WANTS IT. PUNISHER'S OUR PROBLEM UNTIL THE FEDS SHOW UP, AND HE'S A PRETTY DAMN BIG ONE.
SARGE, LISTEN...
MAYBE I CAN HELP.

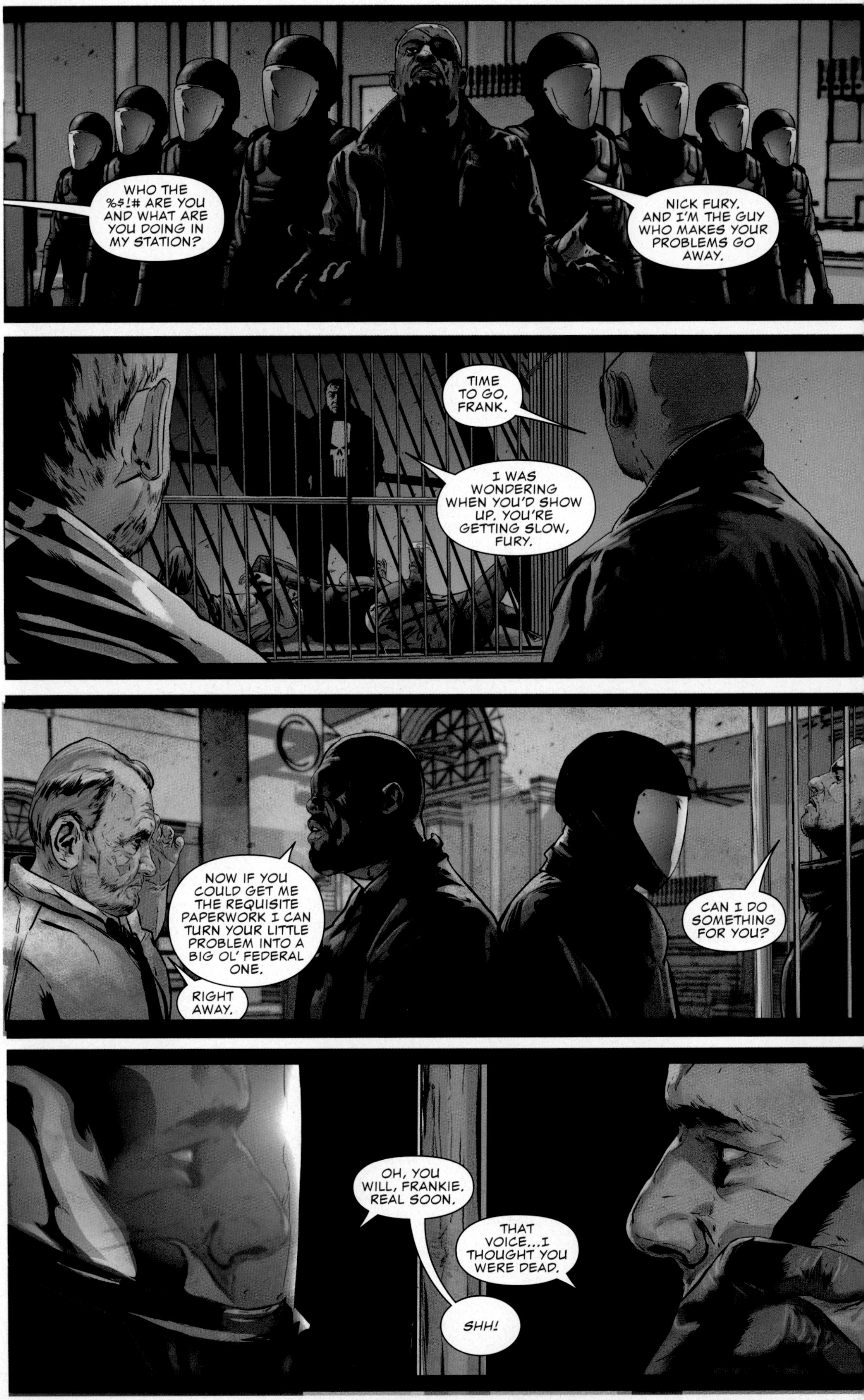
WHO THE %$!# ARE YOU AND WHAT ARE YOU DOING IN MY STATION?
NICK FURY. AND I'M THE GUY WHO MAKES YOUR PROBLEMS GO AWAY.
TIME TO GO, FRANK.
I WAS WONDERING WHEN YOU'D SHOW UP. YOU'RE GETTING SLOW, FURY.
NOW IF YOU COULD GET ME THE REQUISITE PAPERWORK I CAN TURN YOUR LITTLE PROBLEM INTO A BIG OL' FEDERAL ONE.
RIGHT AWAY.
CAN I DO SOMETHING FOR YOU?
OH, YOU WILL, FRANKIE. REAL SOON.
THAT VOICE...I THOUGHT YOU WERE DEAD.
SHH!

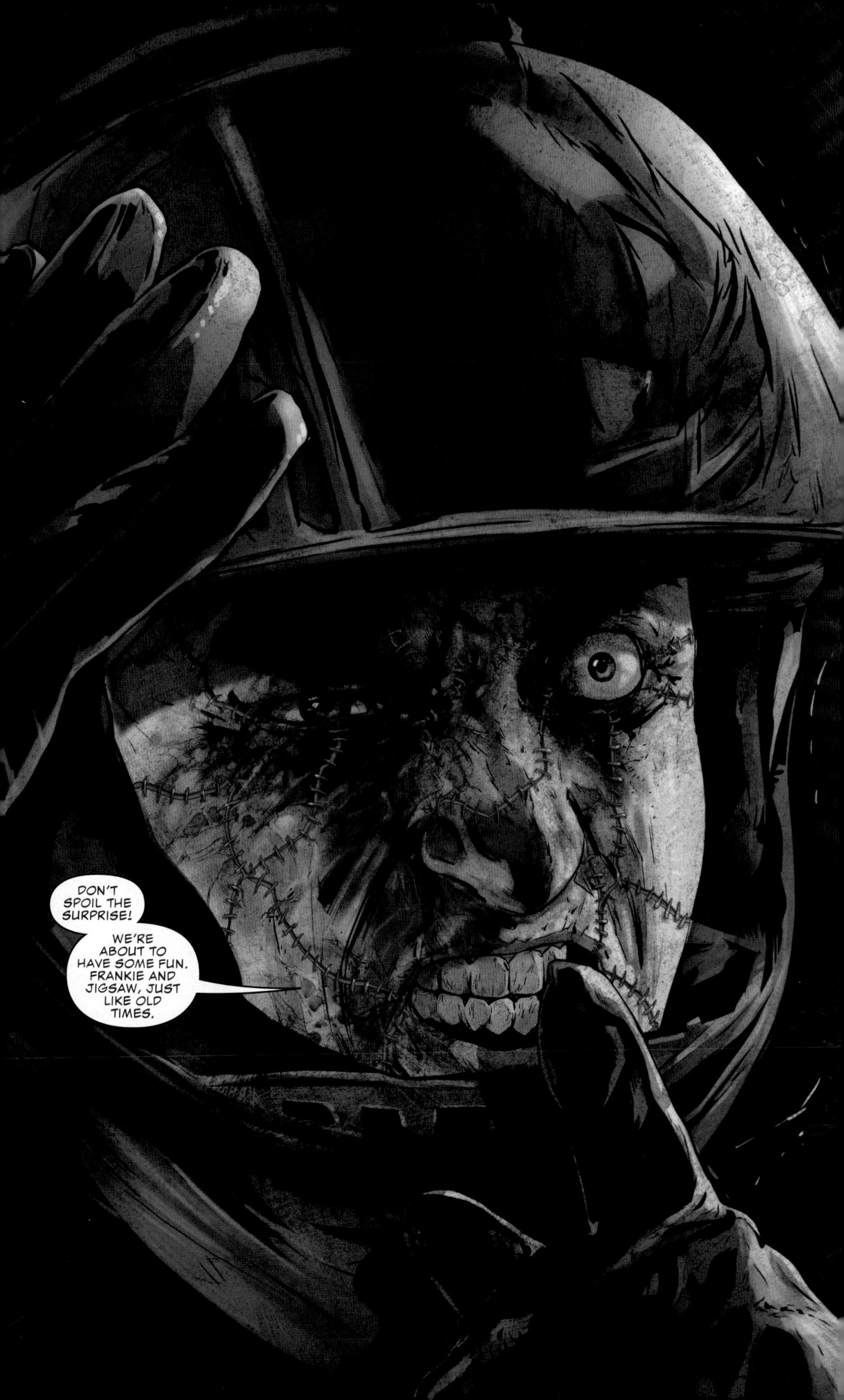
DON'T SPOIL THE SURPRISE!
WE'RE ABOUT TO HAVE SOME FUN. FRANKIE AND JIGSAW, JUST LIKE OLD TIMES.

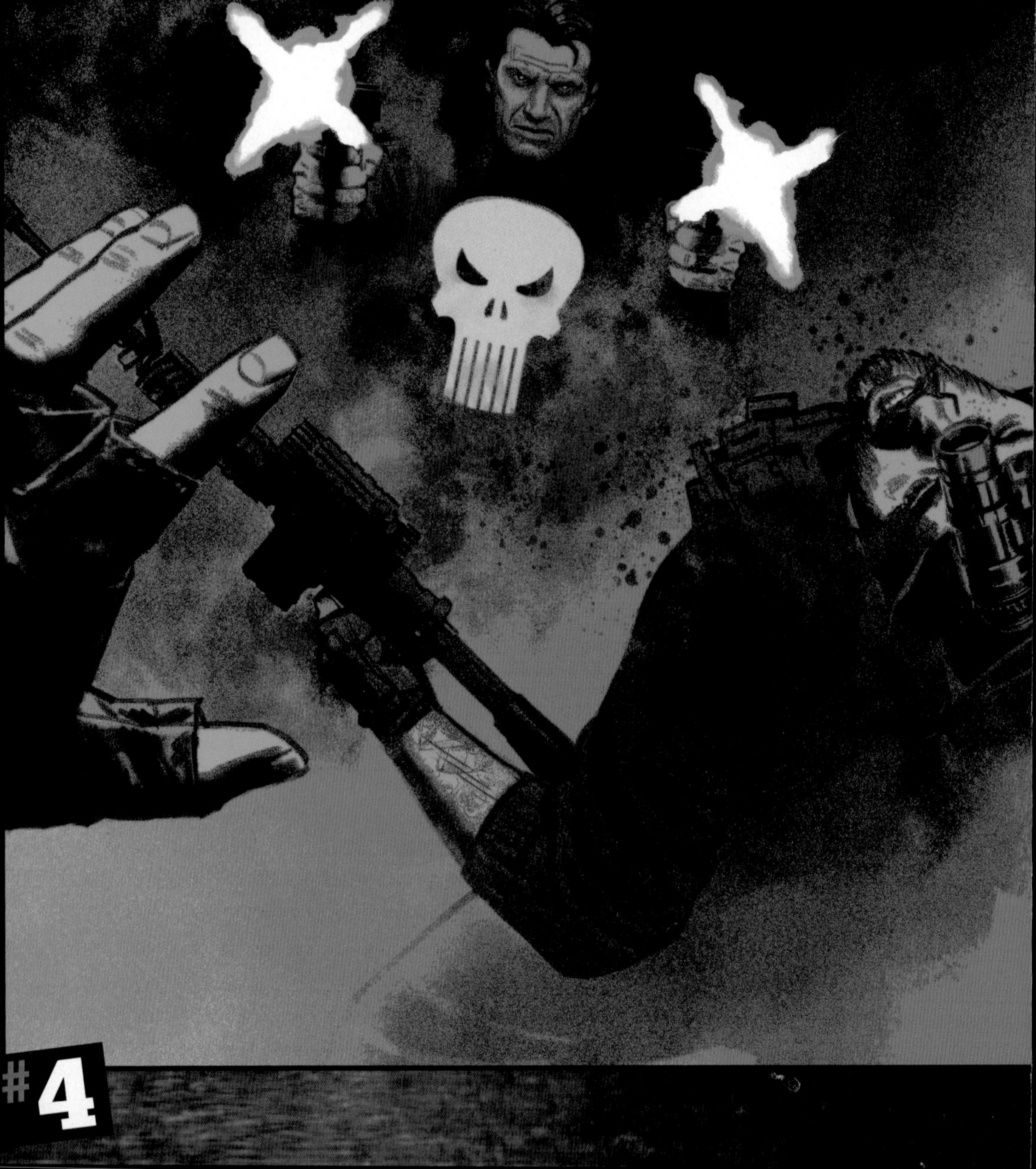
#4

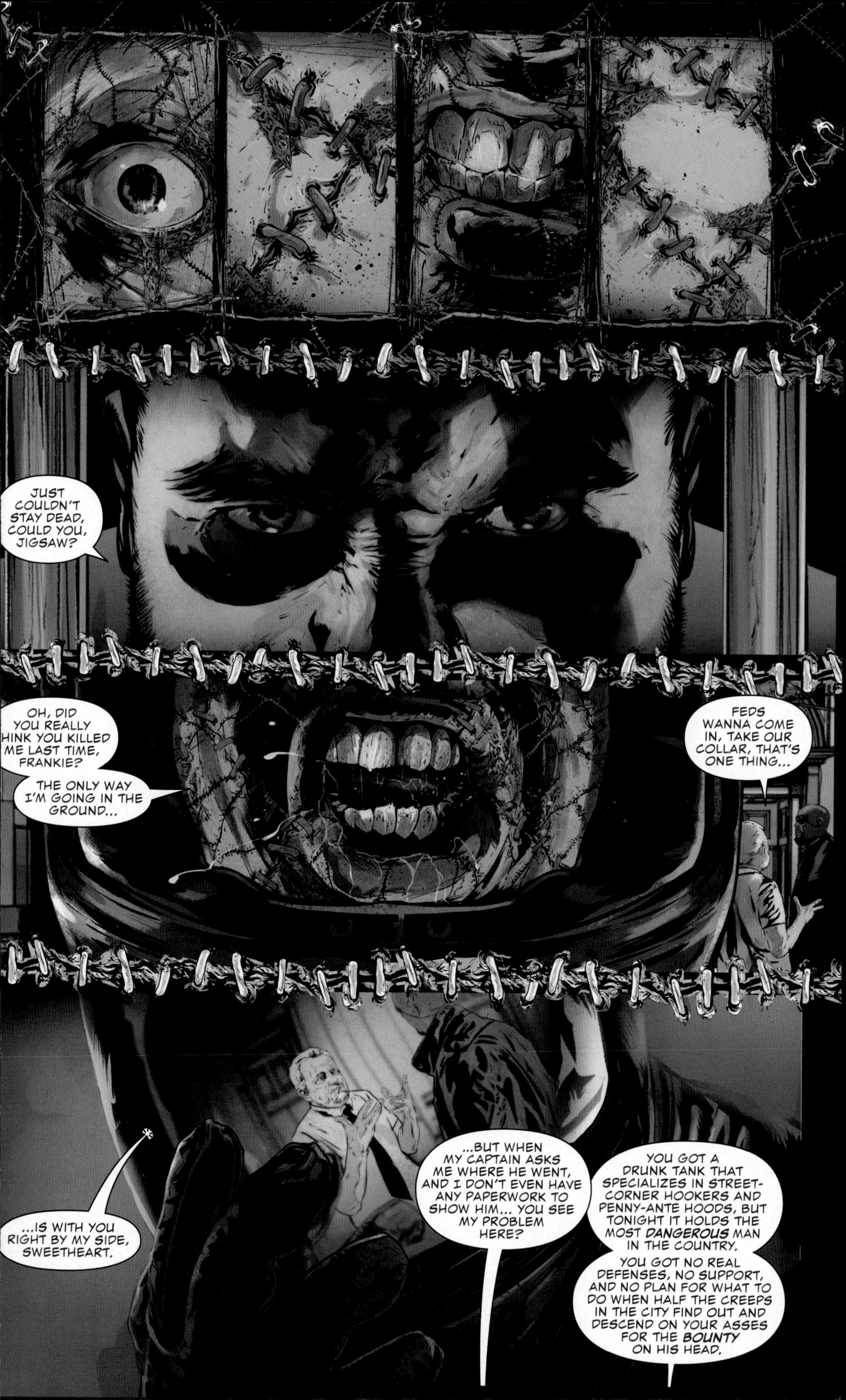

JUST COULDN'T STAY DEAD, COULD YOU, JIGSAW?
OH, DID YOU REALLY HINK YOU KILLED ME LAST TIME, FRANKIE?
THE ONLY WAY I'M GOING IN THE GROUND...
FEDS WANNA COME IN, TAKE OUR COLLAR, THAT'S ONE THING...
...IS WITH YOU RIGHT BY MY SIDE, SWEETHEART.
...BUT WHEN MY CAPTAIN ASKS ME WHERE HE WENT, AND I DON'T EVEN HAVE ANY PAPERWORK TO SHOW HIM... YOU SEE MY PROBLEM HERE?
YOU GOT A DRUNK TANK THAT SPECIALIZES IN STREET-CORNER HOOKERS AND PENNY-ANTE HOODS, BUT TONIGHT IT HOLDS THE MOST *DANGEROUS* MAN IN THE COUNTRY.
YOU GOT NO REAL DEFENSES, NO SUPPORT, AND NO PLAN FOR WHAT TO DO WHEN HALF THE CREEPS IN THE CITY FIND OUT AND DESCEND ON YOUR ASSES FOR THE *BOUNTY* ON HIS HEAD.

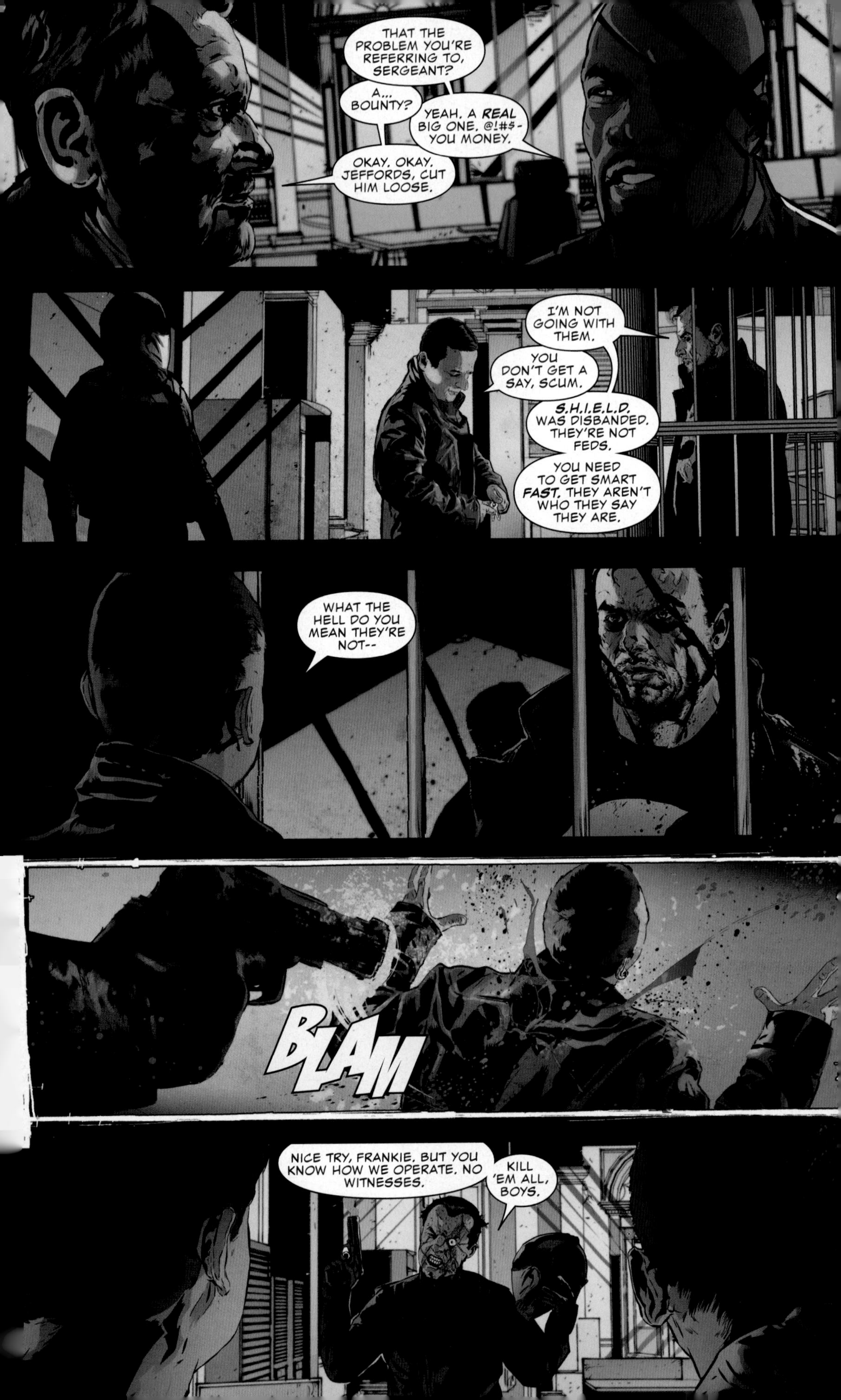
THAT THE PROBLEM YOU'RE REFERRING TO, SERGEANT?
A... BOUNTY?
YEAH. A REAL BIG ONE. @!#$-YOU MONEY.
OKAY. OKAY. JEFFORDS, CUT HIM LOOSE.
I'M NOT GOING WITH THEM.
YOU DON'T GET A SAY, SCUM.
S.H.I.E.L.D. WAS DISBANDED. THEY'RE NOT FEDS.
YOU NEED TO GET SMART FAST. THEY AREN'T WHO THEY SAY THEY ARE.
WHAT THE HELL DO YOU MEAN THEY'RE NOT--
BLAM
NICE TRY, FRANKIE. BUT YOU KNOW HOW WE OPERATE. NO WITNESSES.
KILL 'EM ALL, BOYS.

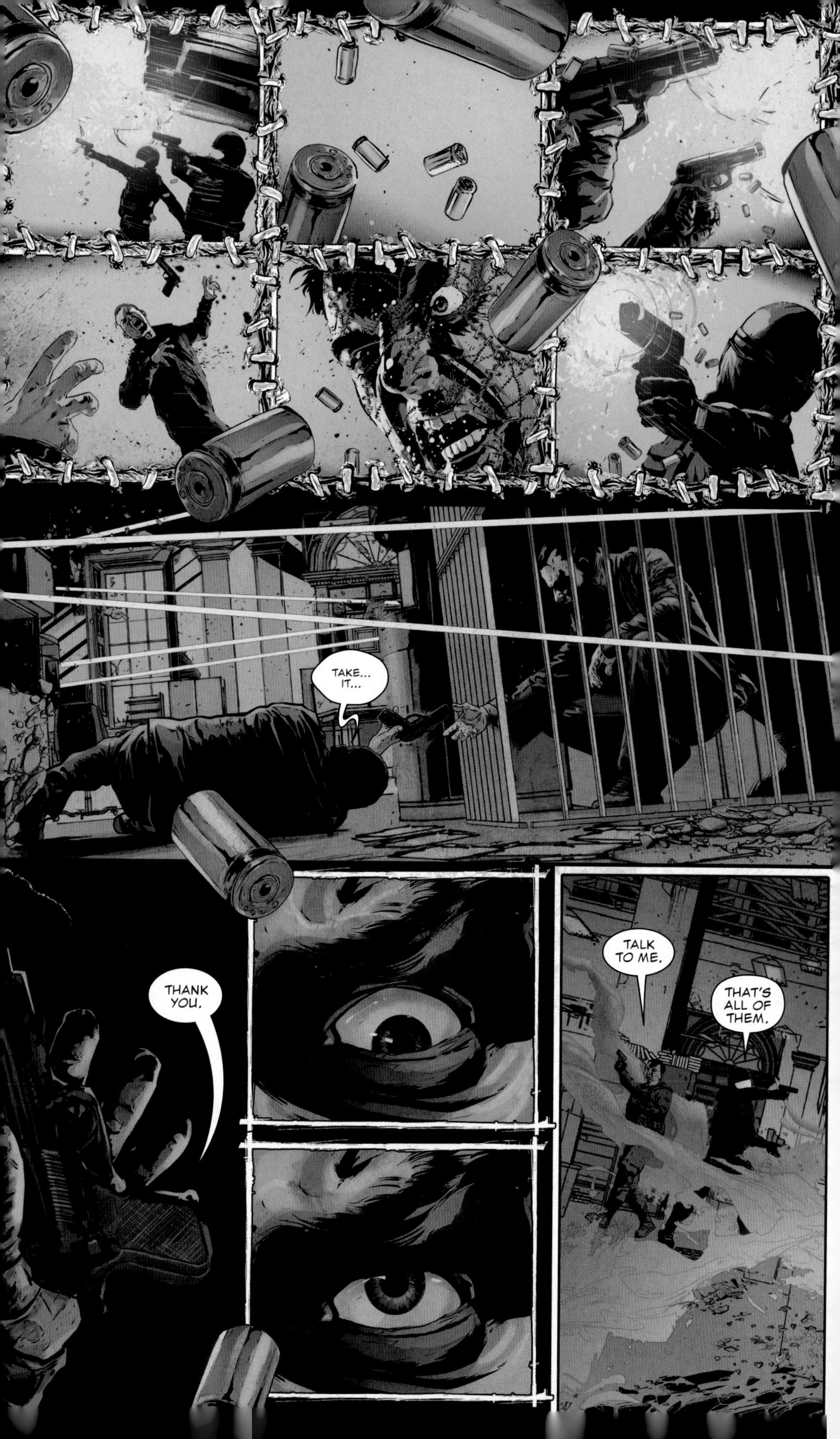
TAKE... IT...
THANK YOU.
TALK TO ME.
THAT'S ALL OF THEM.

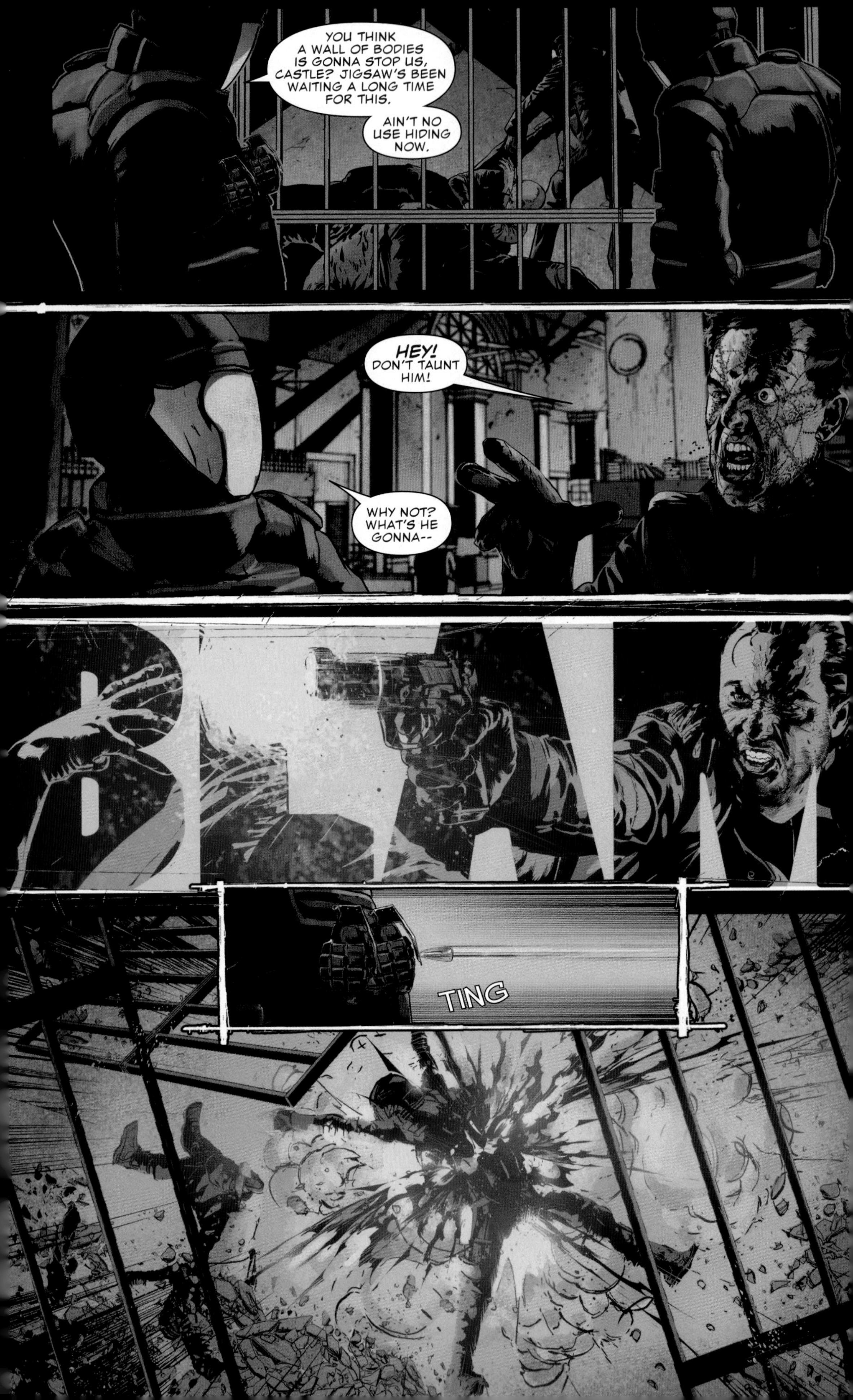

YOU THINK A WALL OF BODIES IS GONNA STOP US, CASTLE? JIGSAW'S BEEN WAITING A LONG TIME FOR THIS.
AIN'T NO USE HIDING NOW.
HEY! DON'T TAUNT HIM!
WHY NOT? WHAT'S HE GONNA--
TING

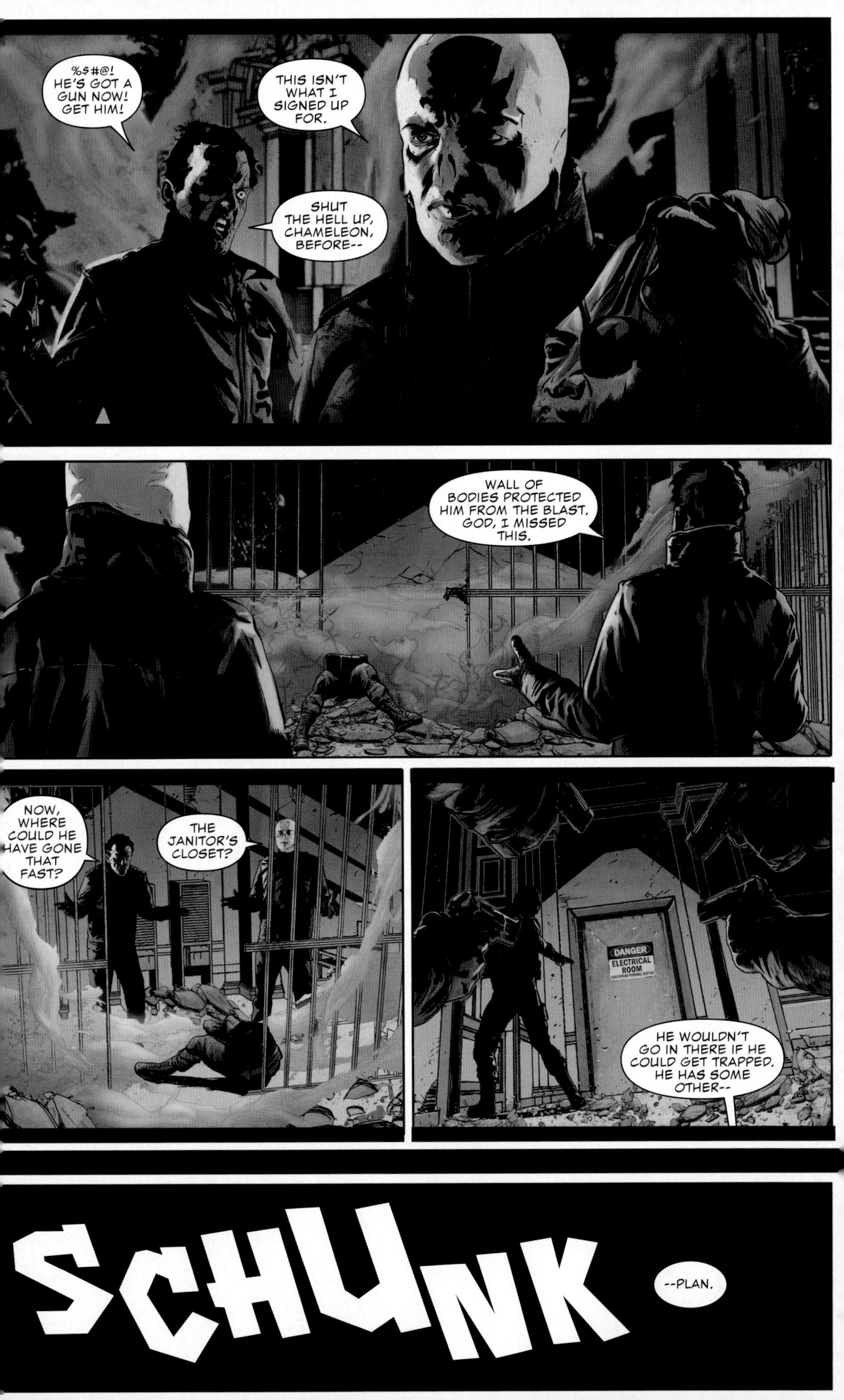
%$#@! HE'S GOT A GUN NOW! GET HIM!
THIS ISN'T WHAT I SIGNED UP FOR.
SHUT THE HELL UP, CHAMELEON, BEFORE--
WALL OF BODIES PROTECTED HIM FROM THE BLAST. GOD, I MISSED THIS.
NOW, WHERE COULD HE HAVE GONE THAT FAST?
THE JANITOR'S CLOSET?
DANGER
ELECTRICAL ROOM
HE WOULDN'T GO IN THERE IF HE COULD GET TRAPPED. HE HAS SOME OTHER--
SCHUNK
--PLAN.

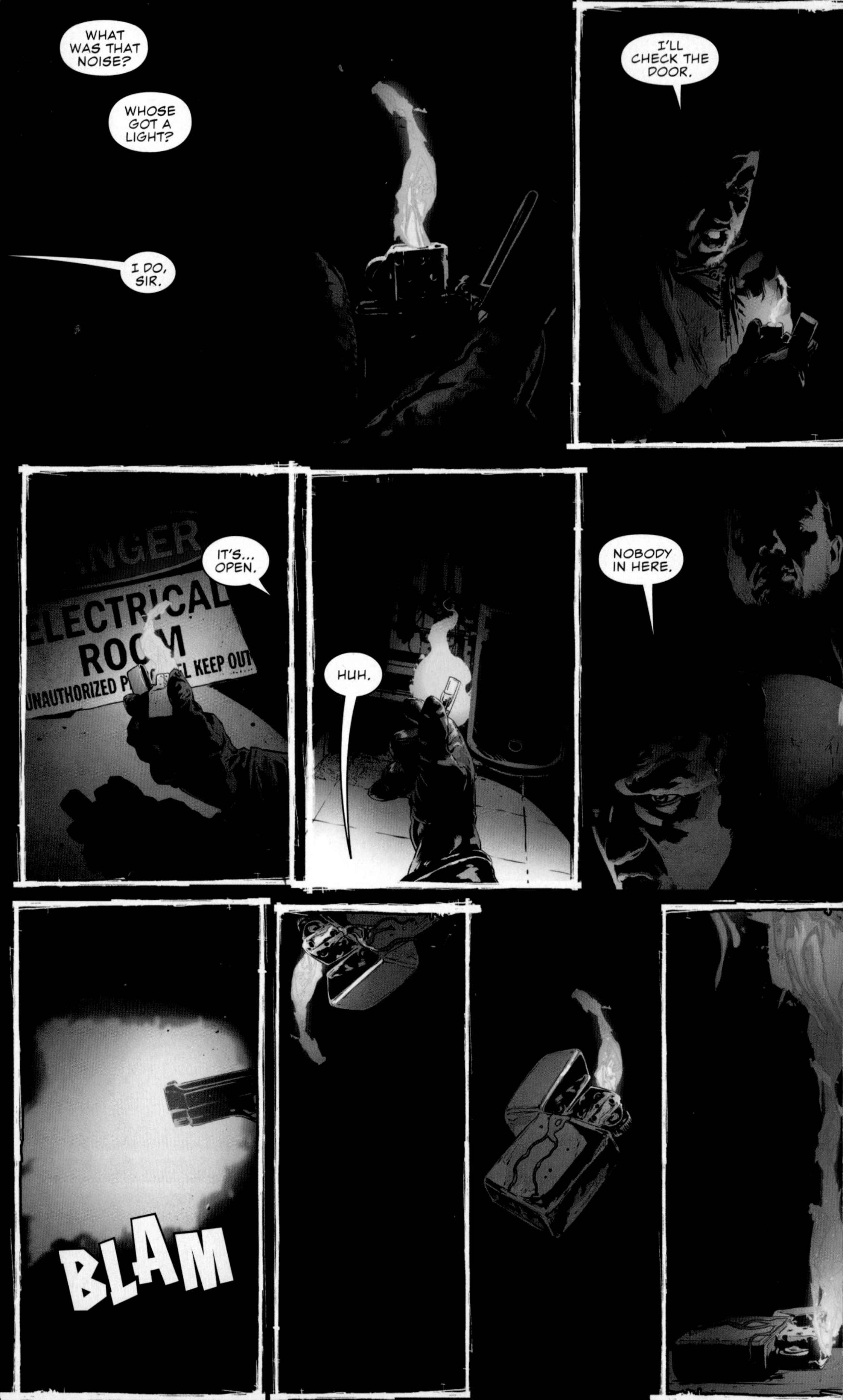
WHAT WAS THAT NOISE?
WHOSE GOT A LIGHT?
I DO, SIR.
I'LL CHECK THE DOOR.
ELECTRICAL ROOM
IT'S... OPEN.
HUH.
NOBODY IN HERE.
BLAM

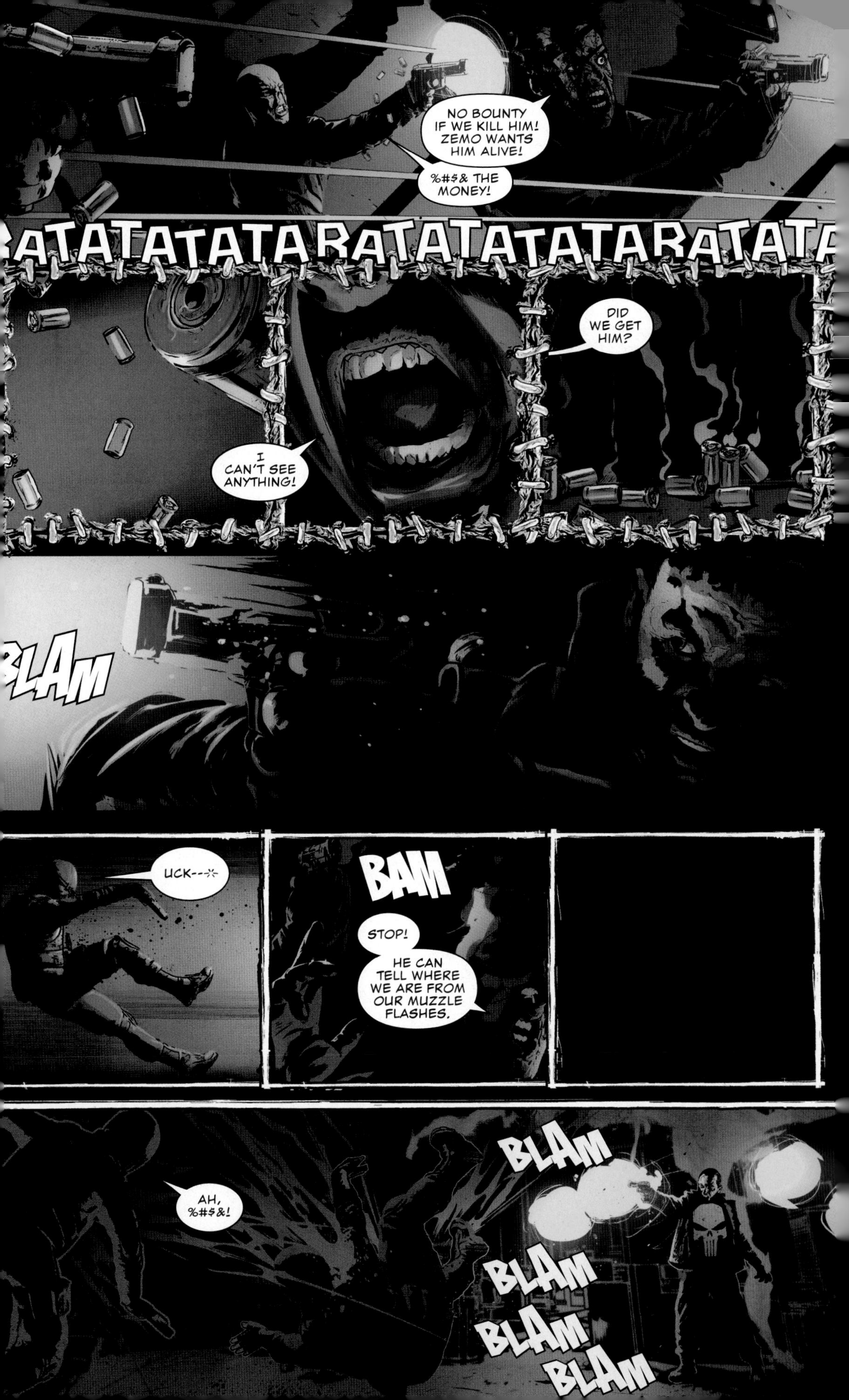
NO BOUNTY IF WE KILL HIM! ZEMO WANTS HIM ALIVE!
%#$& THE MONEY!
RATATATATA RATATATATARATATA
I CAN'T SEE ANYTHING!
DID WE GET HIM?
BLAM
UCK--
BAM
STOP!
HE CAN TELL WHERE WE ARE FROM OUR MUZZLE FLASHES.
BLAM
AH, %#$&!
BLAM
BLAM
BLAM

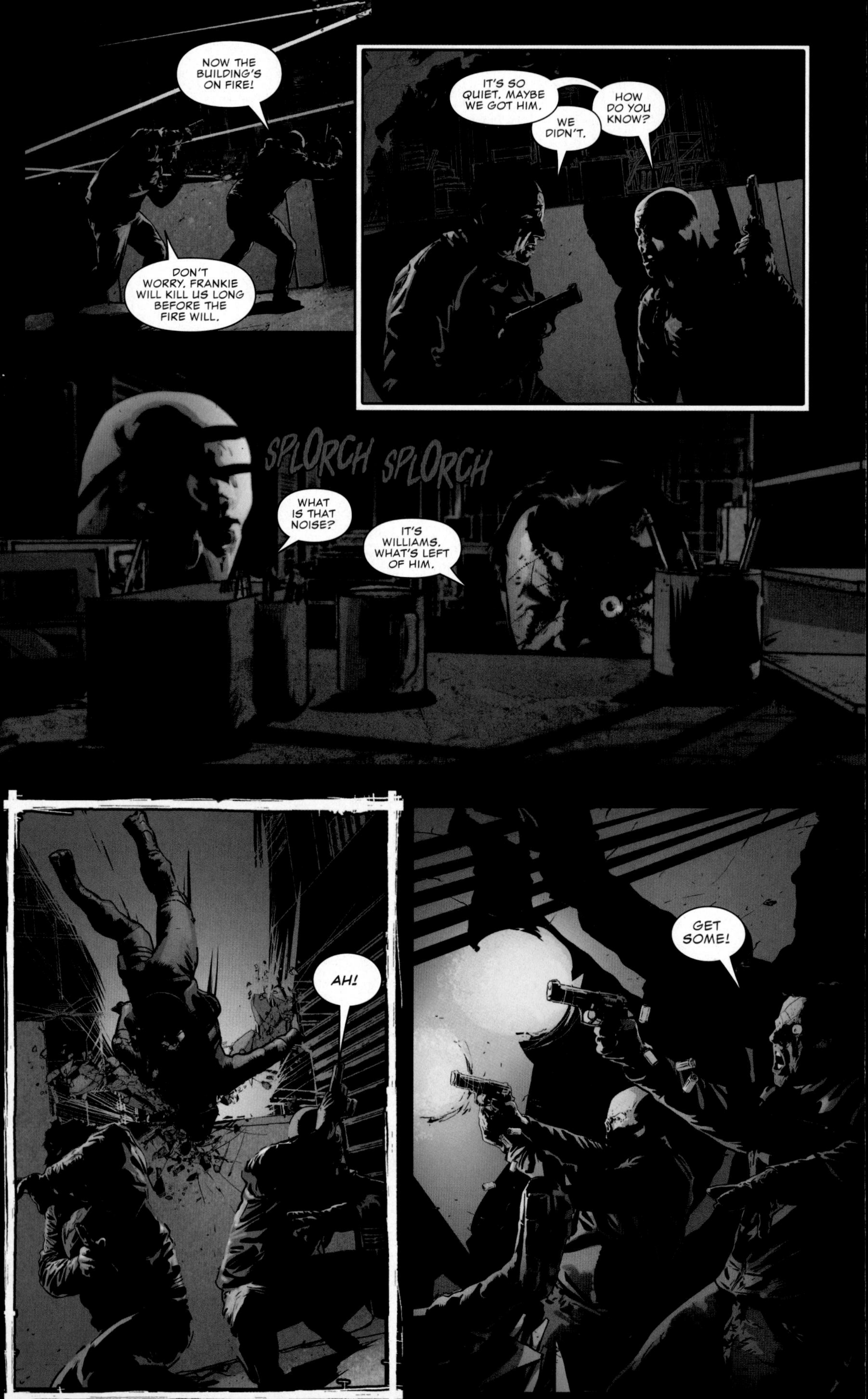
NOW THE BUILDING'S ON FIRE!
DON'T WORRY. FRANKIE WILL KILL US LONG BEFORE THE FIRE WILL.
IT'S SO QUIET. MAYBE WE GOT HIM.
HOW DO YOU KNOW?
WE DIDN'T.
SPLORCH SPLORCH
WHAT IS THAT NOISE?
IT'S WILLIAMS. WHAT'S LEFT OF HIM.
AH!
GET SOME!

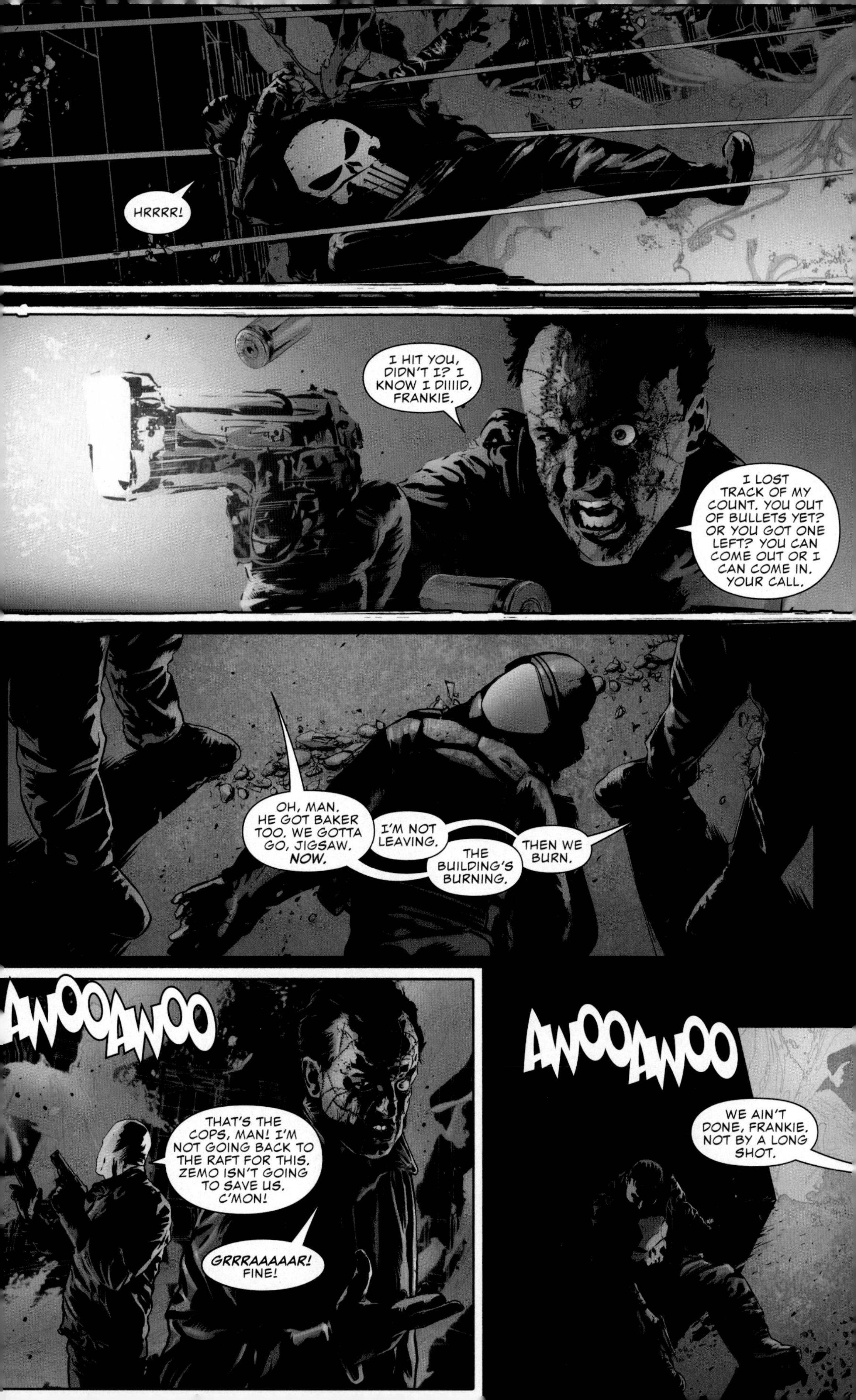
HRRRR!
I HIT YOU, DIDN'T I? I KNOW I DIIIID, FRANKIE.
I LOST TRACK OF MY COUNT. YOU OUT OF BULLETS YET? OR YOU GOT ONE LEFT? YOU CAN COME OUT OR I CAN COME IN. YOUR CALL.
OH, MAN. HE GOT BAKER TOO. WE GOTTA GO, JIGSAW. NOW.
I'M NOT LEAVING.
THE BUILDING'S BURNING.
THEN WE BURN.
AWOOAWOO
THAT'S THE COPS, MAN! I'M NOT GOING BACK TO THE RAFT FOR THIS. ZEMO ISN'T GOING TO SAVE US. C'MON!
GRRRAAAAAR! FINE!
AWOOAWOO
WE AIN'T DONE, FRANKIE. NOT BY A LONG SHOT.

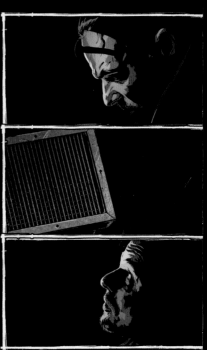

AWOOAWOO

SHOULDN'T WE WAIT FOR THE FIRE DEPARTMENT?

CIVILIANS HEARD GUNSHOTS. FOR ALL WE KNOW THE PUNISHER IS IN THERE EXECUTING EVERYONE. WE'RE GOING IN.

UNNNHH.

MOVE! MOVE! MOVE!

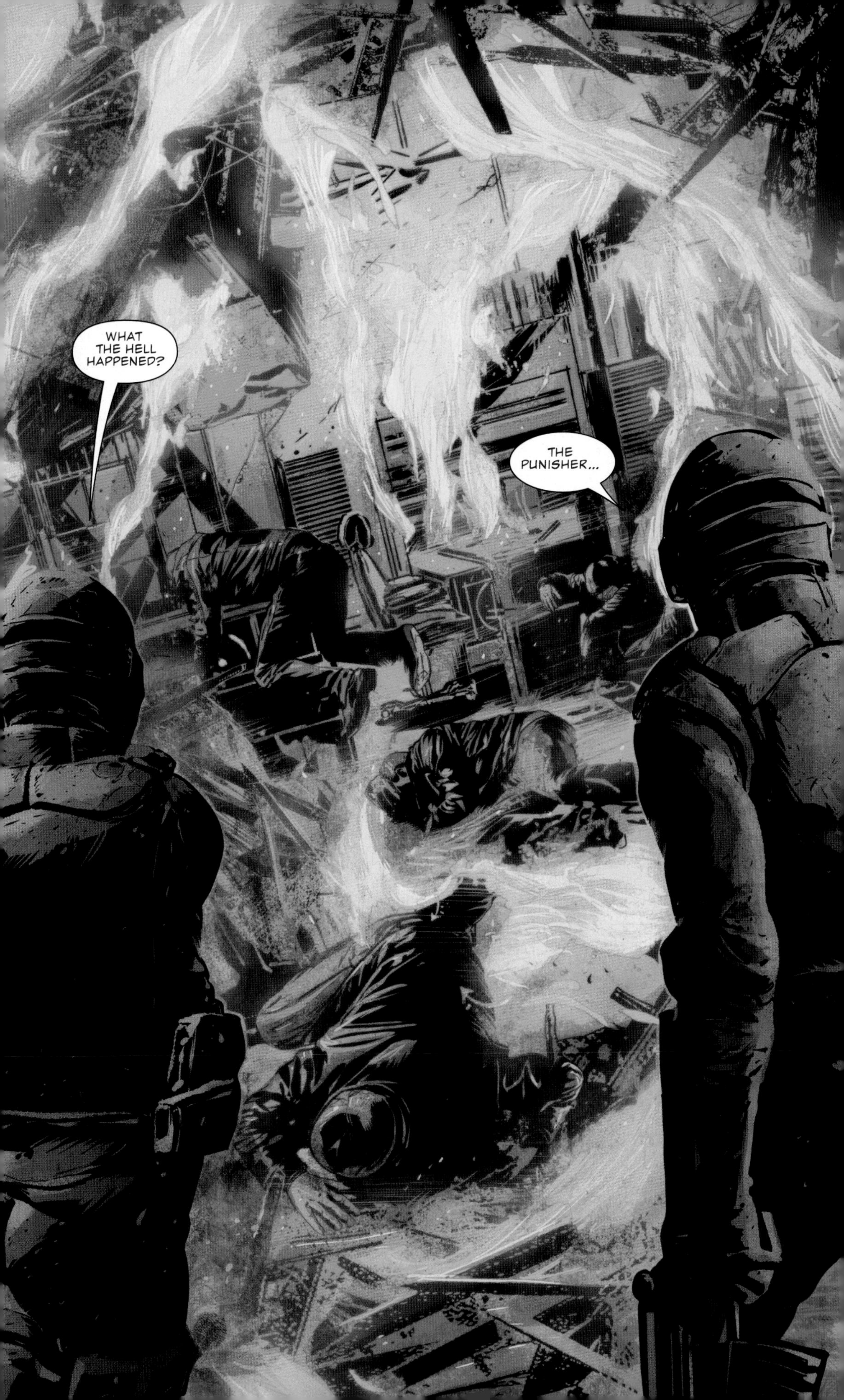
WHAT THE HELL HAPPENED?
THE PUNISHER...

"...HE KILLED EVERYONE."

SOURCES TELL US AS MANY AS FIFTEEN OFFICERS HAVE BEEN KILLED.

"IT'S SAFE TO SAY THAT THE HUNT FOR FRANK CASTLE IS THE TOP PRIORITY OF EVERY MEMBER OF THE LAW ENFORCEMENT COMMUNITY TONIGHT. OUR THOUGHTS GO OUT TO THE FAMILIES OF THE OFFICERS."

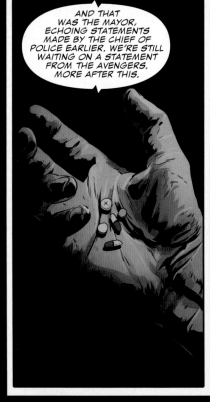

AND THAT WAS THE MAYOR, ECHOING STATEMENTS MADE BY THE CHIEF OF POLICE EARLIER. WE'RE STILL WAITING ON A STATEMENT FROM THE AVENGERS. MORE AFTER THIS.

THIS IS THE ONLY PRODUCT GUARANTEED TO MAKE BLENDING DRINKS EASIER.

NO MORE DIRTY SPOONS. NO MORE--

YOU'RE SLIPPING. OLD YOU WOULD HAVE ALREADY PUT TWO IN MY SKULL.

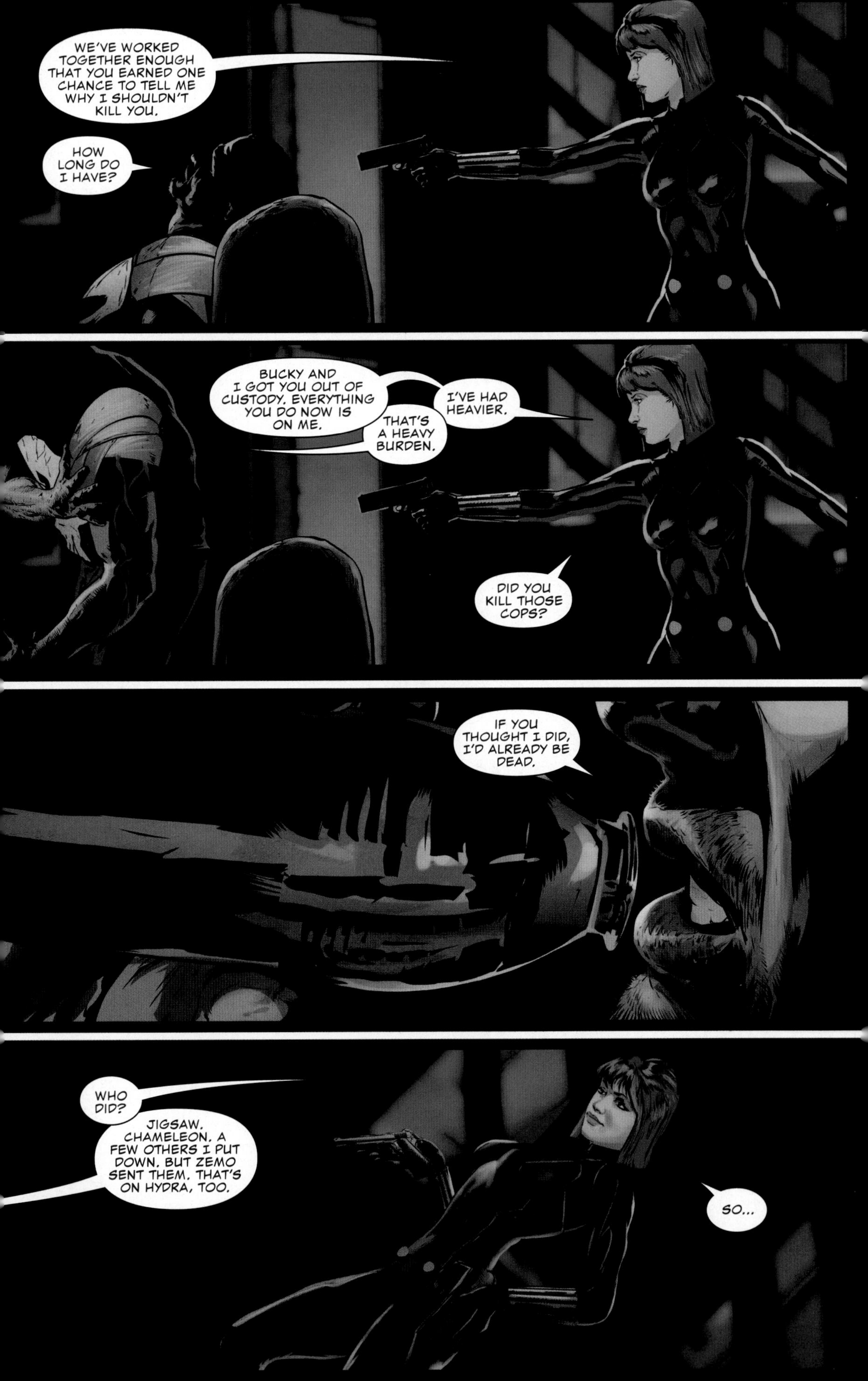
WE'VE WORKED TOGETHER ENOUGH THAT YOU EARNED ONE CHANCE TO TELL ME WHY I SHOULDN'T KILL YOU.
HOW LONG DO I HAVE?
BUCKY AND I GOT YOU OUT OF CUSTODY. EVERYTHING YOU DO NOW IS ON ME.
THAT'S A HEAVY BURDEN.
I'VE HAD HEAVIER.
DID YOU KILL THOSE COPS?
IF YOU THOUGHT I DID, I'D ALREADY BE DEAD.
WHO DID?
JIGSAW. CHAMELEON. A FEW OTHERS I PUT DOWN. BUT ZEMO SENT THEM. THAT'S ON HYDRA, TOO.
SO...

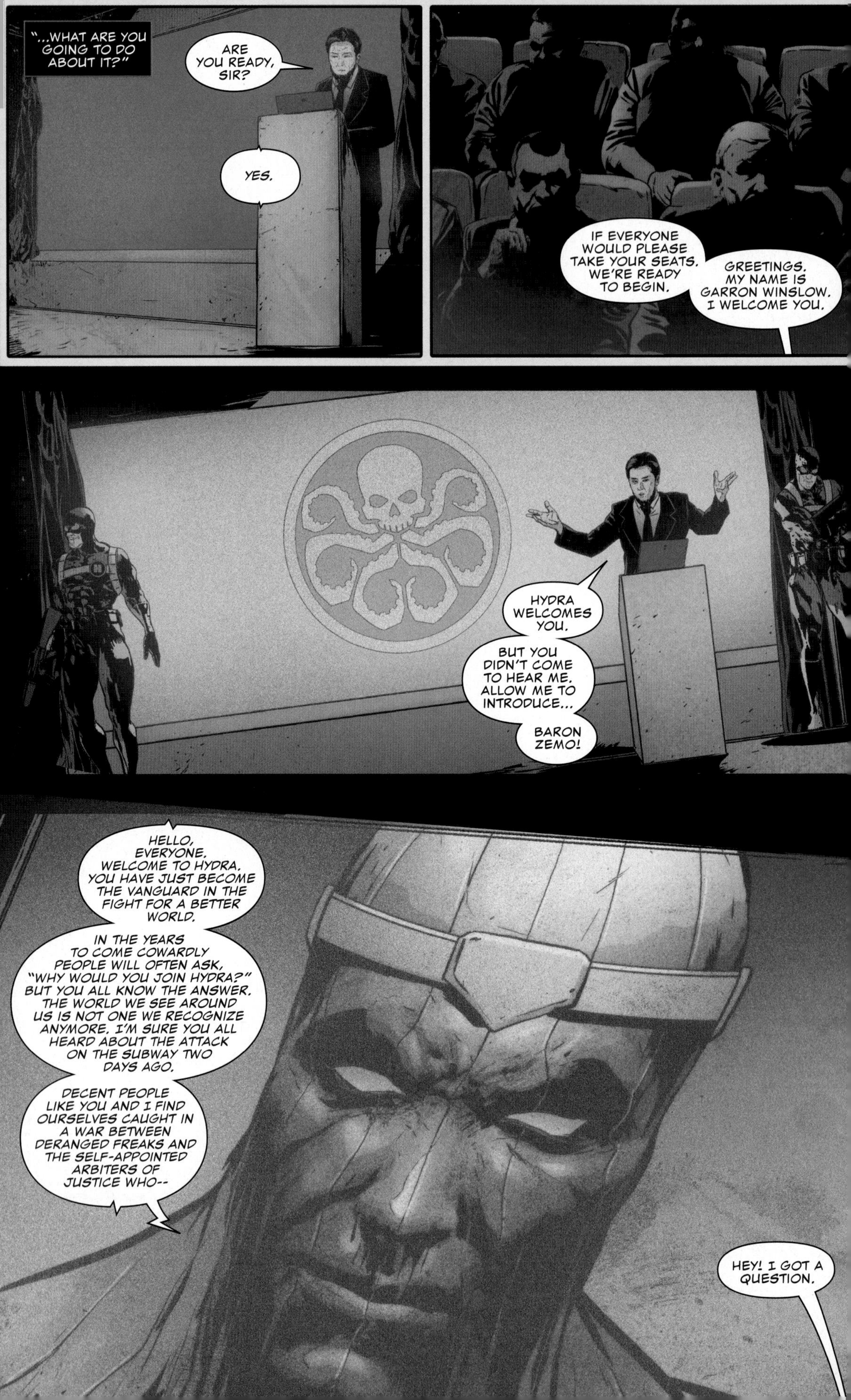
"...WHAT ARE YOU GOING TO DO ABOUT IT?"
ARE YOU READY, SIR?
YES.
IF EVERYONE WOULD PLEASE TAKE YOUR SEATS. WE'RE READY TO BEGIN.
GREETINGS. MY NAME IS GARRON WINSLOW. I WELCOME YOU.
HYDRA WELCOMES YOU.
BUT YOU DIDN'T COME TO HEAR ME. ALLOW ME TO INTRODUCE...
BARON ZEMO!
HELLO, EVERYONE. WELCOME TO HYDRA. YOU HAVE JUST BECOME THE VANGUARD IN THE FIGHT FOR A BETTER WORLD.
IN THE YEARS TO COME COWARDLY PEOPLE WILL OFTEN ASK, "WHY WOULD YOU JOIN HYDRA?" BUT YOU ALL KNOW THE ANSWER. THE WORLD WE SEE AROUND US IS NOT ONE WE RECOGNIZE ANYMORE. I'M SURE YOU ALL HEARD ABOUT THE ATTACK ON THE SUBWAY TWO DAYS AGO.
DECENT PEOPLE LIKE YOU AND I FIND OURSELVES CAUGHT IN A WAR BETWEEN DERANGED FREAKS AND THE SELF-APPOINTED ARBITERS OF JUSTICE WHO--
HEY! I GOT A QUESTION.

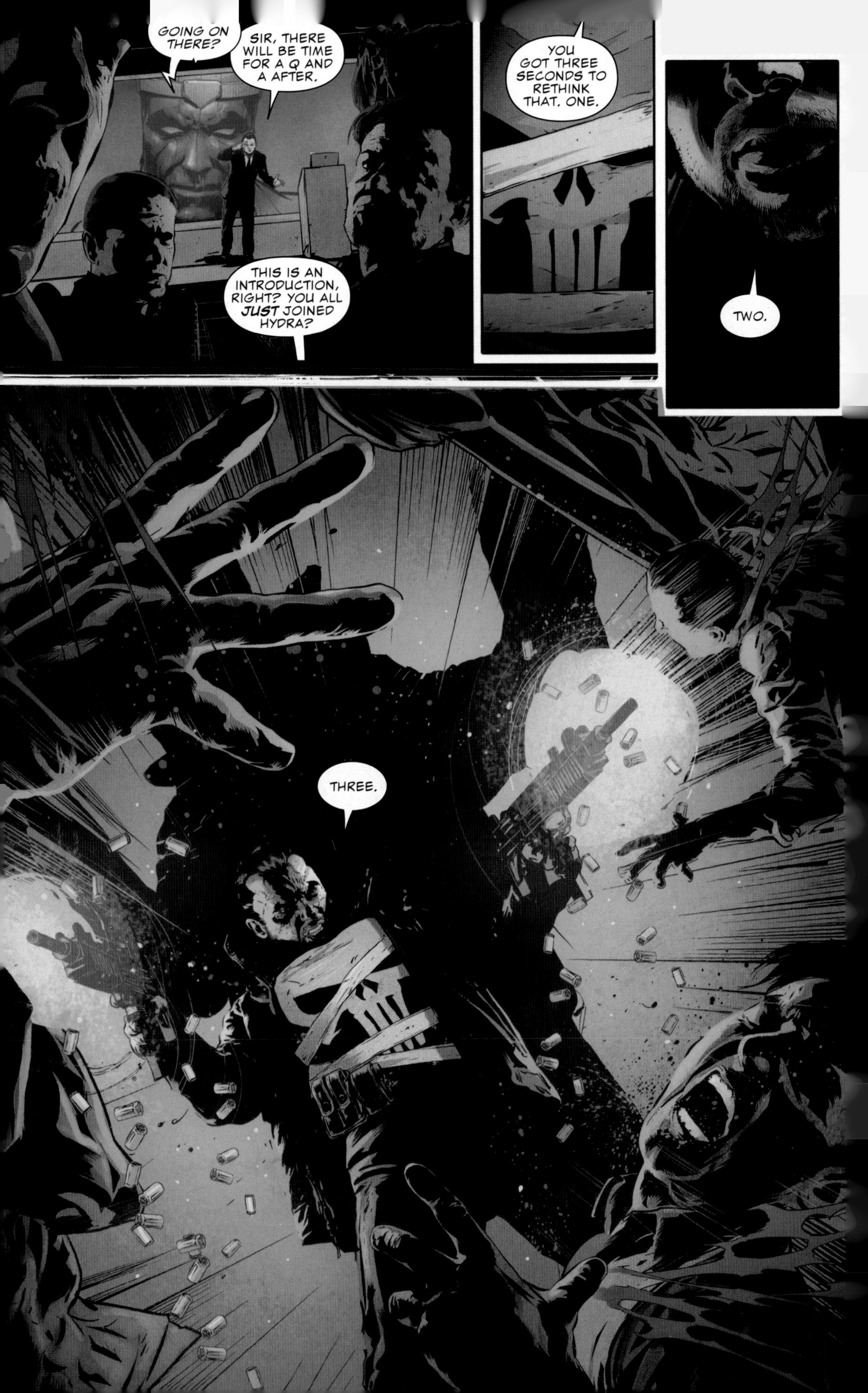
GOING ON THERE?
SIR, THERE WILL BE TIME FOR A Q AND A AFTER.
THIS IS AN INTRODUCTION, RIGHT? YOU ALL JUST JOINED HYDRA?
YOU GOT THREE SECONDS TO RETHINK THAT. ONE.
TWO.
THREE.

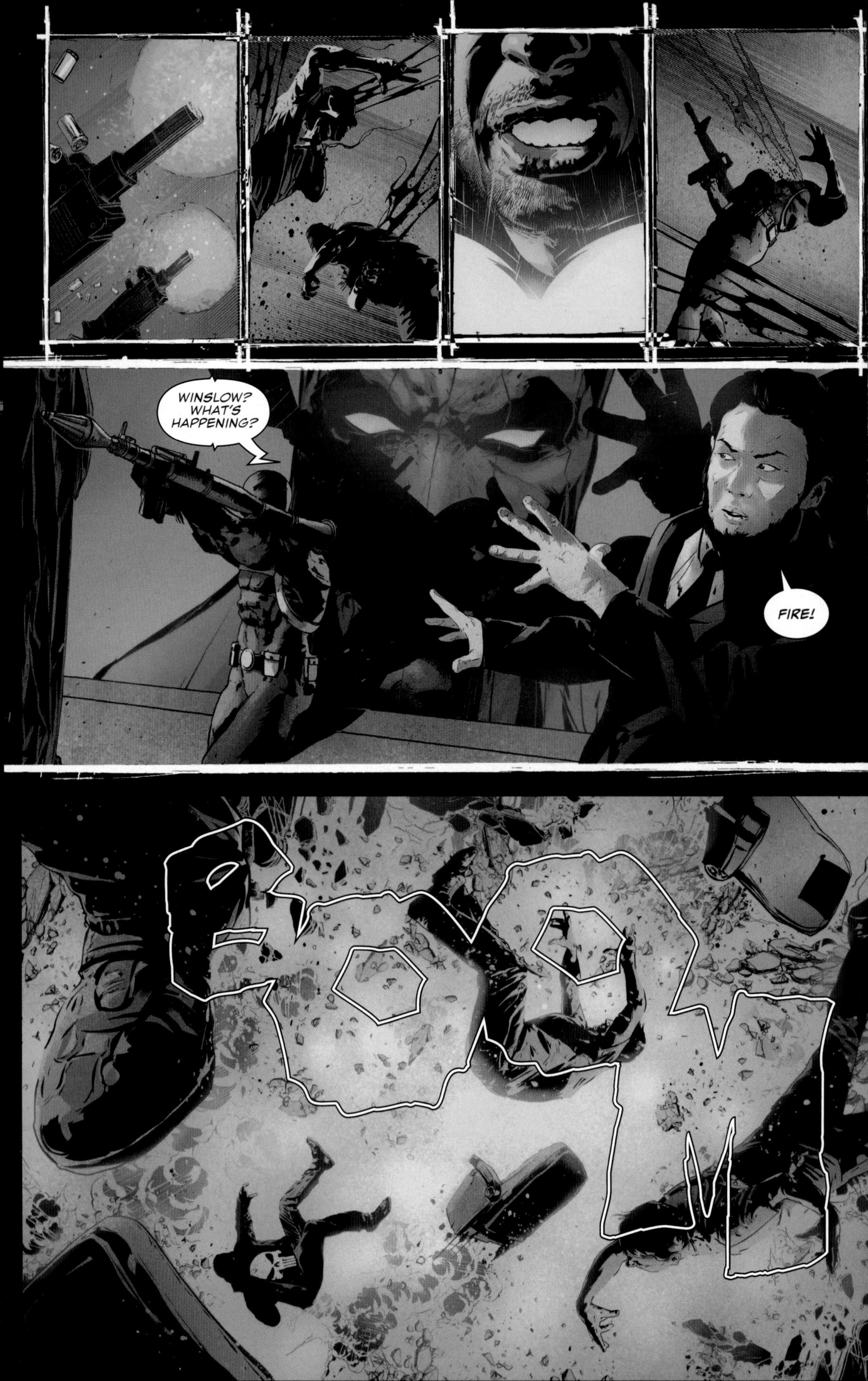
WINSLOW? WHAT'S HAPPENING?
FIRE!
BOOOM

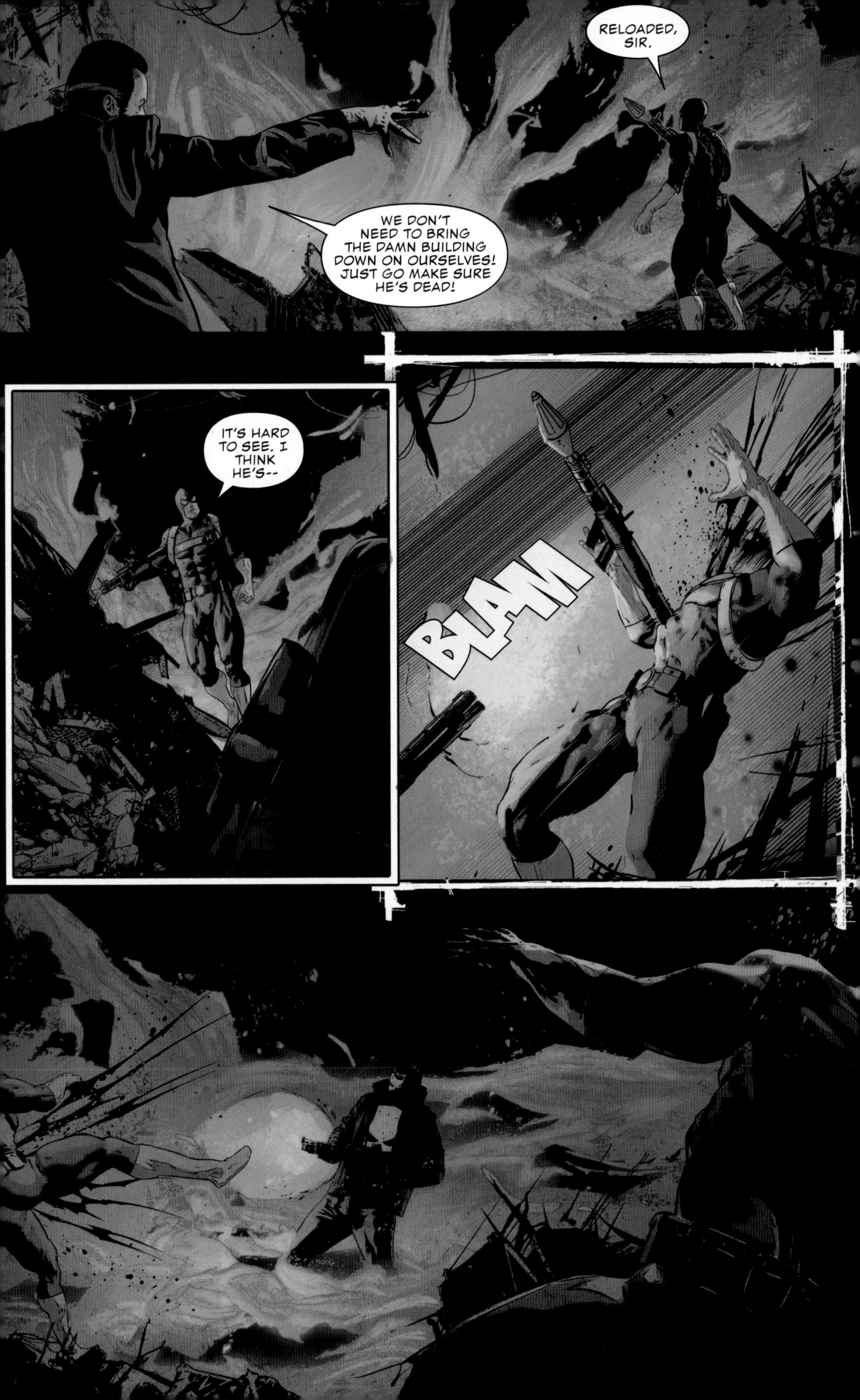
RELOADED, SIR.
WE DON'T NEED TO BRING THE DAMN BUILDING DOWN ON OURSELVES! JUST GO MAKE SURE HE'S DEAD!
IT'S HARD TO SEE. I THINK HE'S--
BLAM

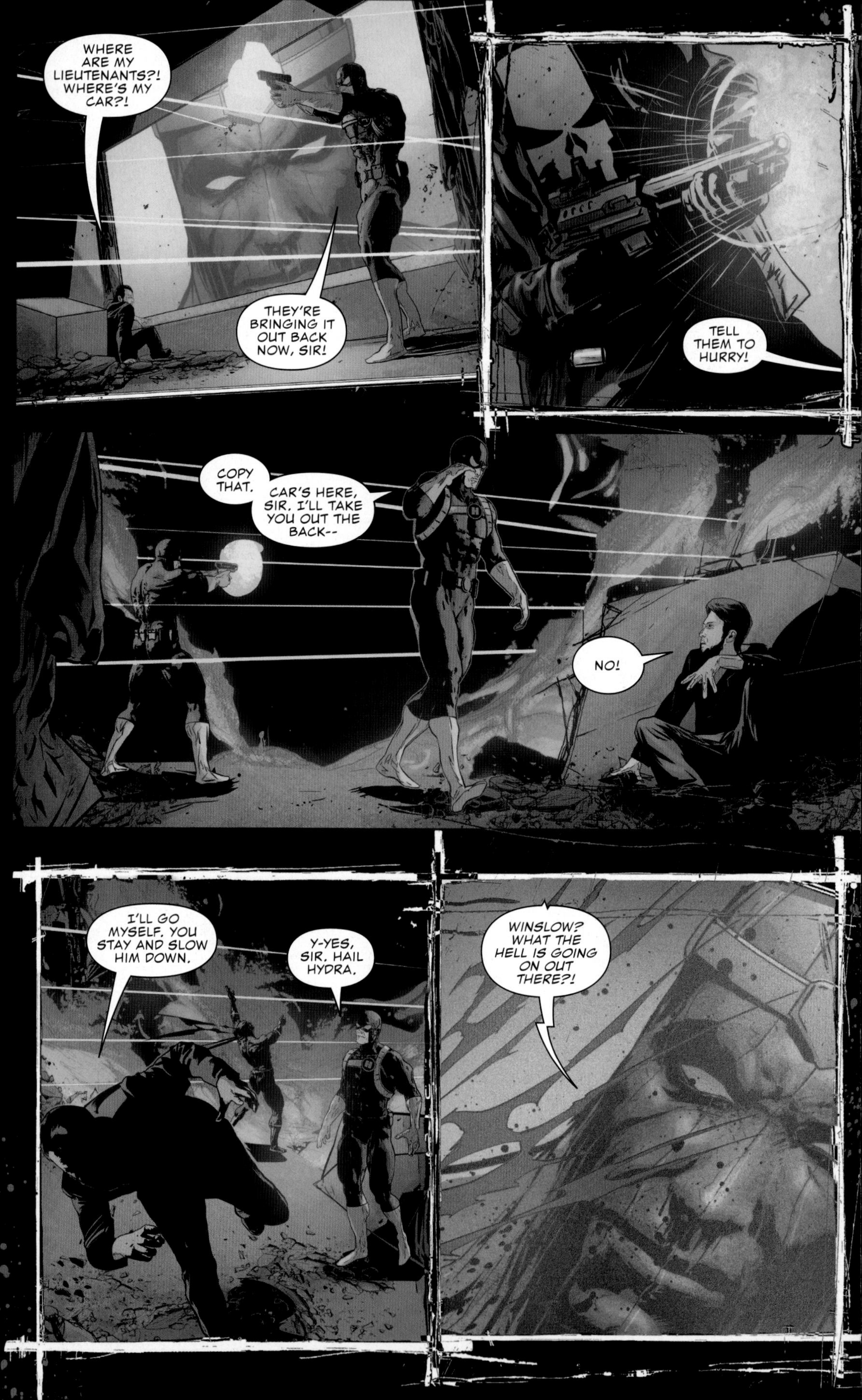

WHERE ARE MY LIEUTENANTS?! WHERE'S MY CAR?!
THEY'RE BRINGING IT OUT BACK NOW, SIR!
TELL THEM TO HURRY!
COPY THAT.
CAR'S HERE, SIR. I'LL TAKE YOU OUT THE BACK--
NO!
I'LL GO MYSELF. YOU STAY AND SLOW HIM DOWN.
Y-YES, SIR. HAIL HYDRA.
WINSLOW? WHAT THE HELL IS GOING ON OUT THERE?!

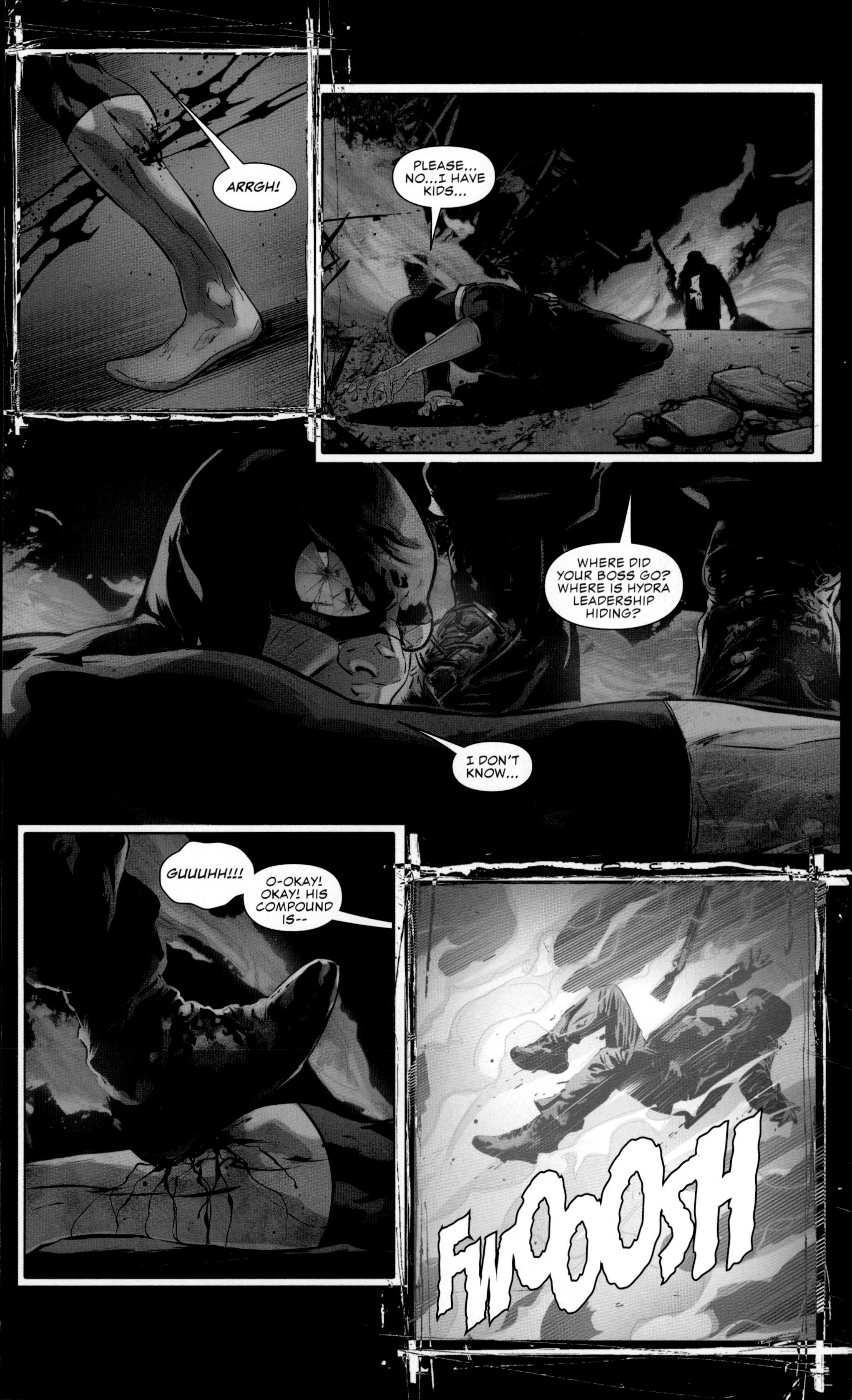
ARRGH!
PLEASE... NO...I HAVE KIDS...
WHERE DID YOUR BOSS GO? WHERE IS HYDRA LEADERSHIP HIDING?
I DON'T KNOW...
GUUUHH!!!
O-OKAY! OKAY! HIS COMPOUND IS--
FWOOOSH

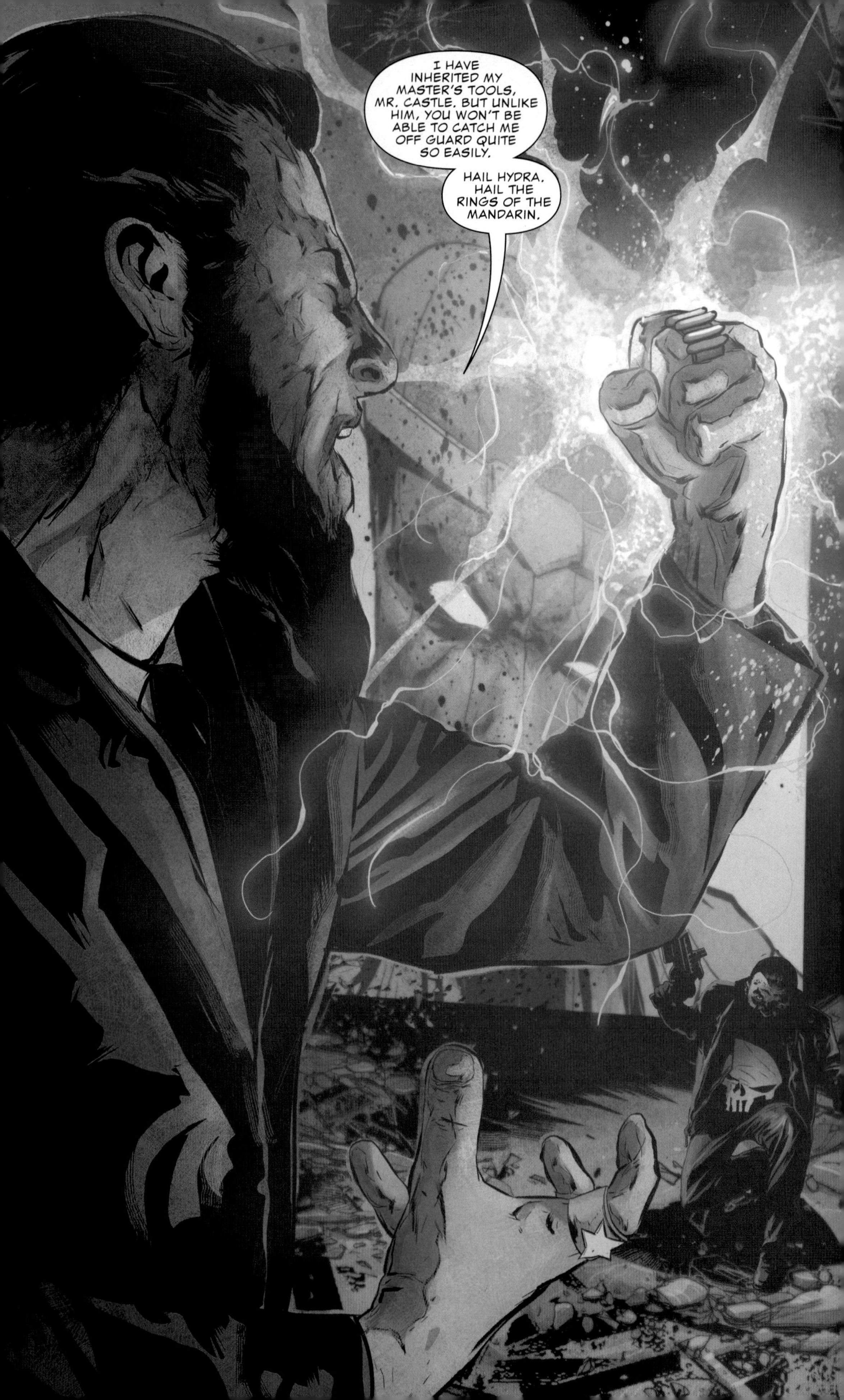
I HAVE INHERITED MY MASTER'S TOOLS, MR. CASTLE. BUT UNLIKE HIM, YOU WON'T BE ABLE TO CATCH ME OFF GUARD QUITE SO EASILY.
HAIL HYDRA. HAIL THE RINGS OF THE MANDARIN.

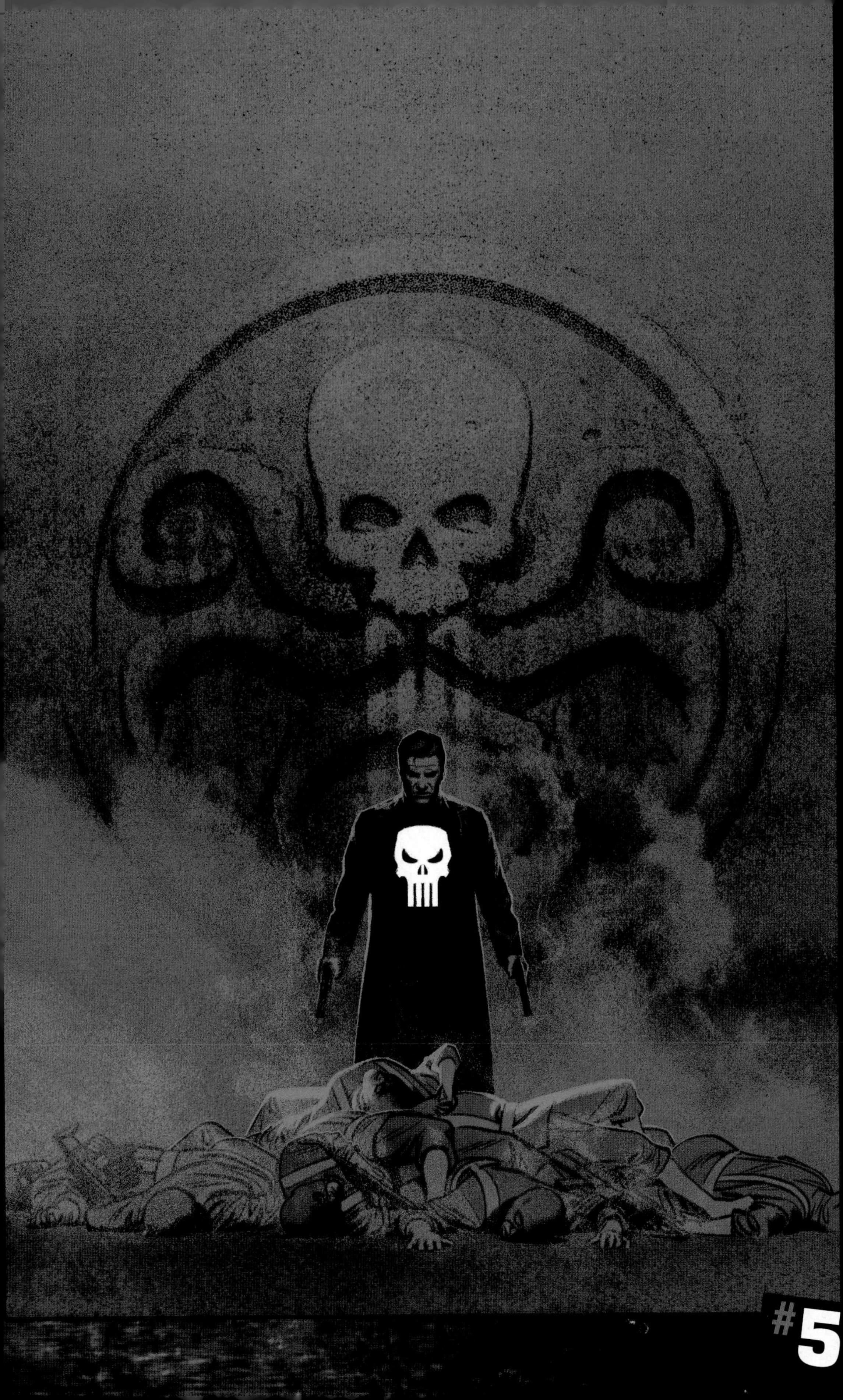
#5

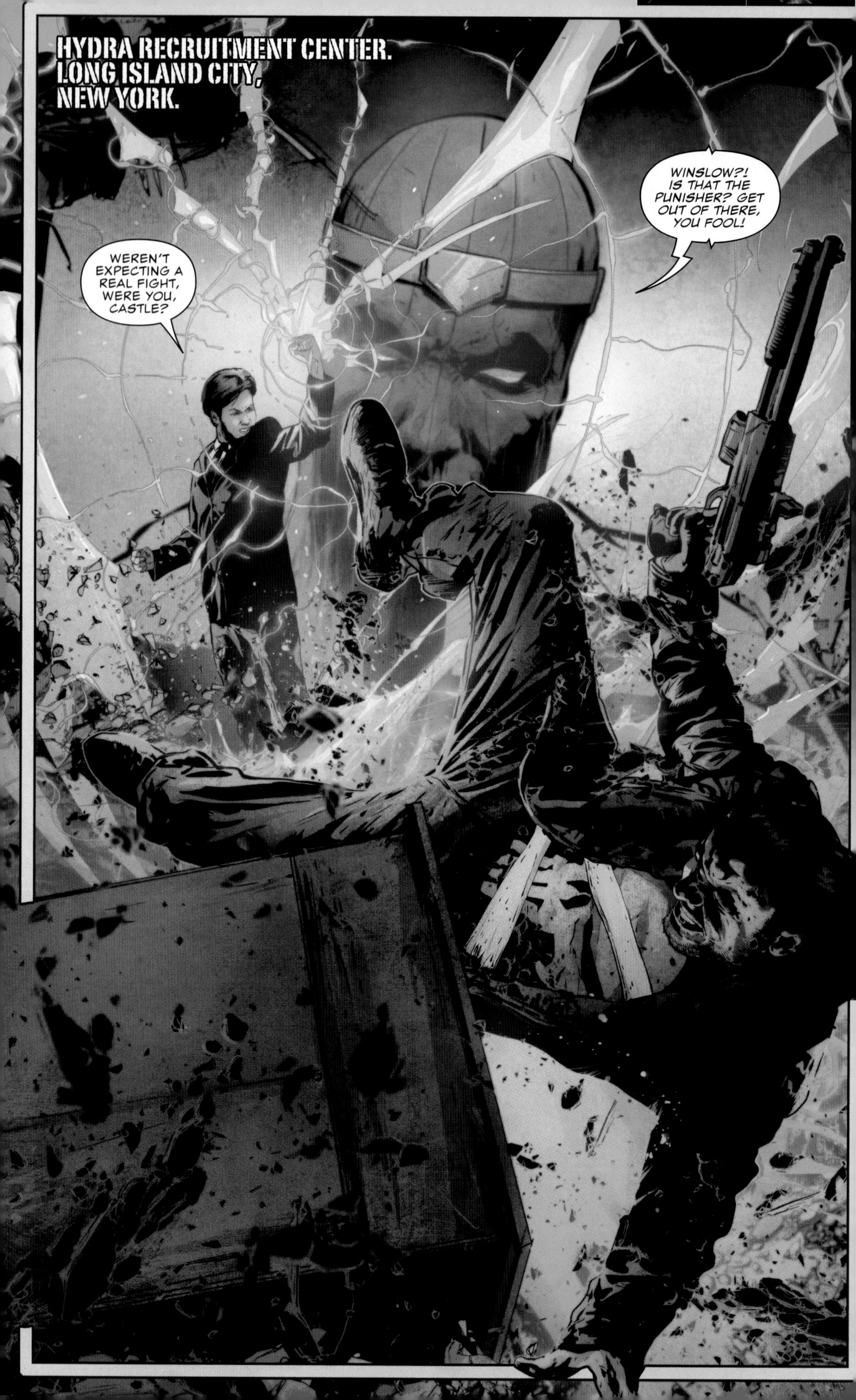
HYDRA RECRUITMENT CENTER. LONG ISLAND CITY, NEW YORK.
WEREN'T EXPECTING A REAL FIGHT, WERE YOU, CASTLE?
WINSLOW?! IS THAT THE PUNISHER? GET OUT OF THERE, YOU FOOL!

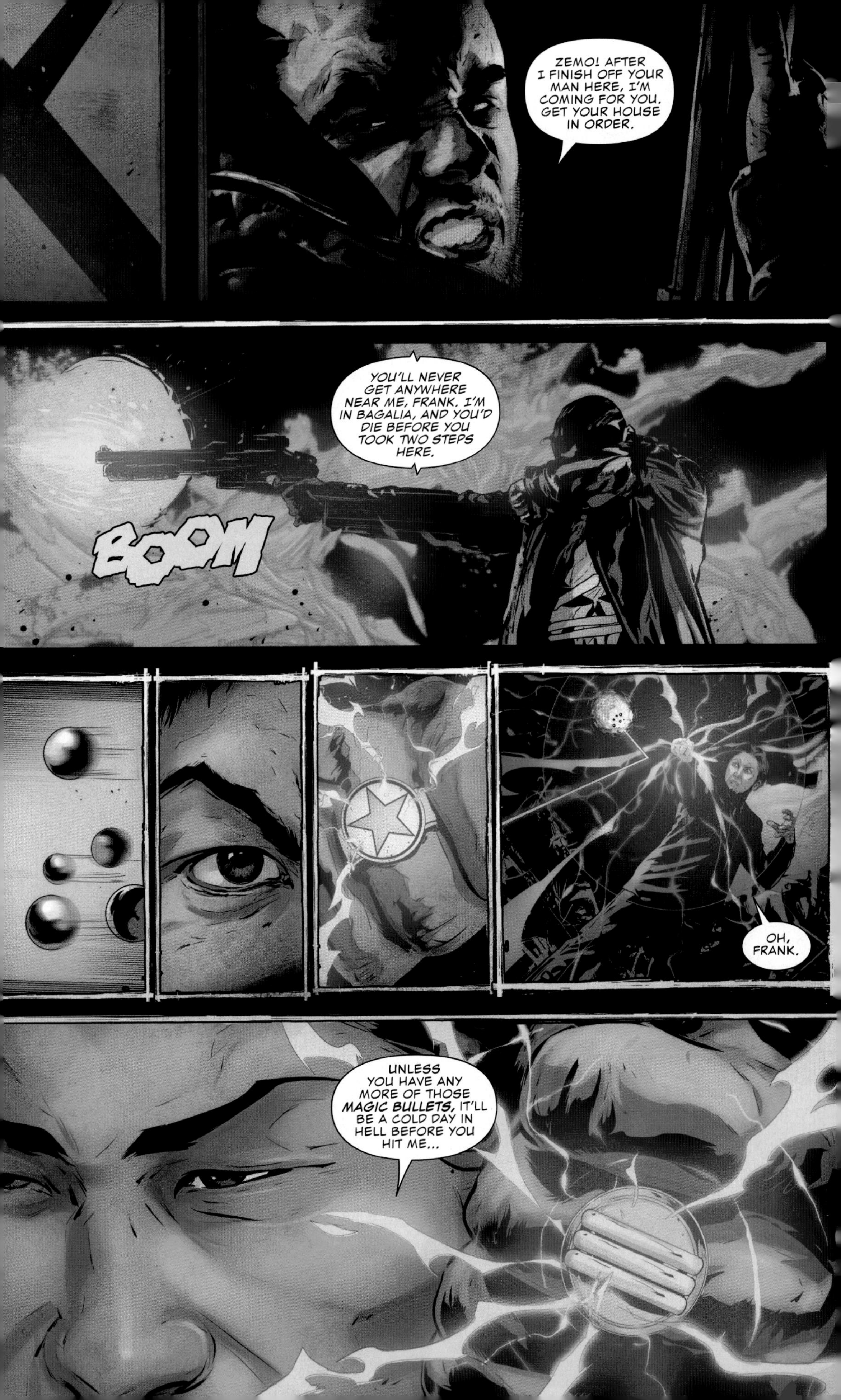
ZEMO! AFTER I FINISH OFF YOUR MAN HERE, I'M COMING FOR YOU. GET YOUR HOUSE IN ORDER.
YOU'LL NEVER GET ANYWHERE NEAR ME, FRANK. I'M IN BAGALIA, AND YOU'D DIE BEFORE YOU TOOK TWO STEPS HERE.
BOOM
OH, FRANK.
UNLESS YOU HAVE ANY MORE OF THOSE **MAGIC BULLETS,** IT'LL BE A COLD DAY IN HELL BEFORE YOU HIT ME...

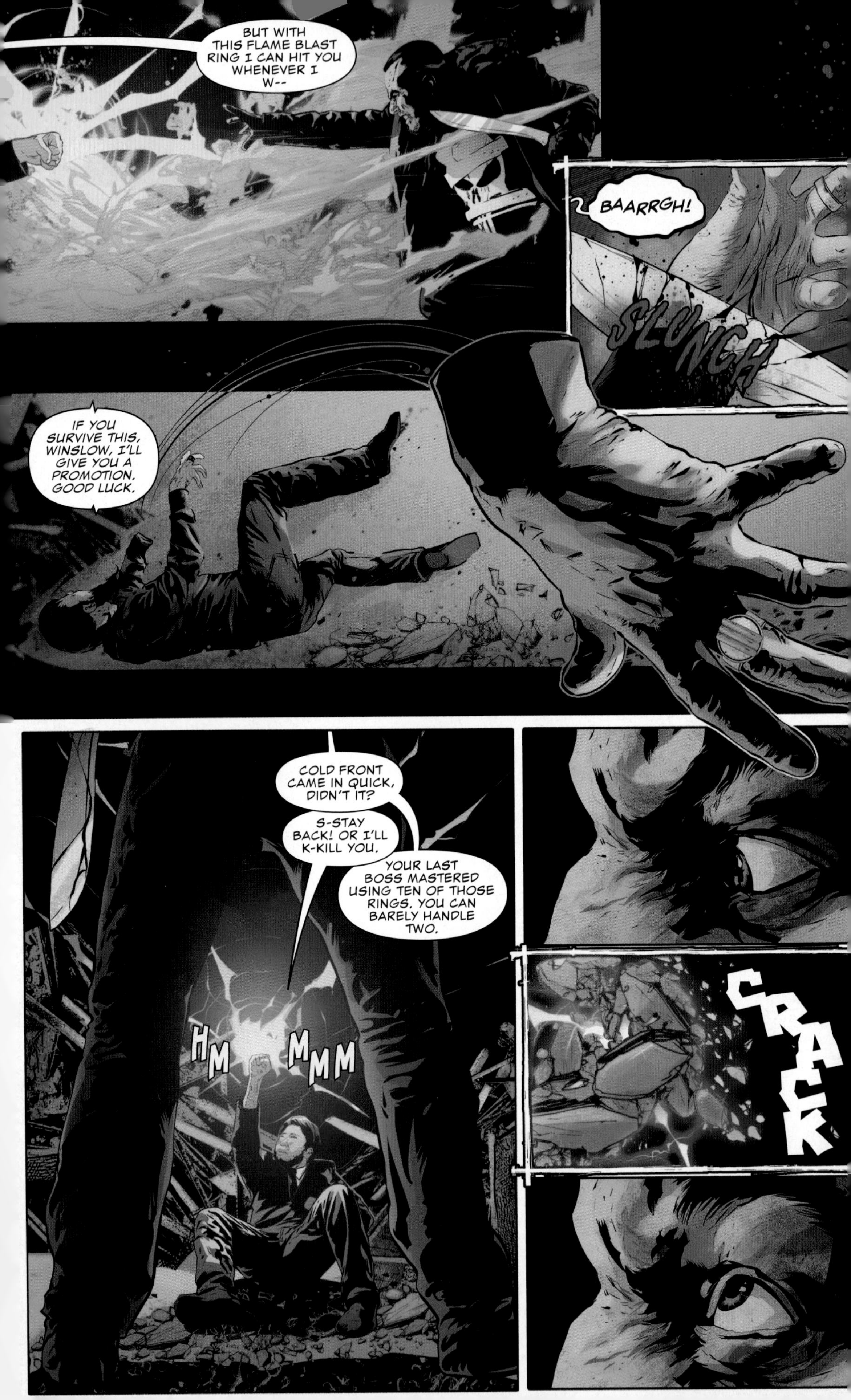
BUT WITH THIS FLAME BLAST RING I CAN HIT YOU WHENEVER I W--
BAARRGH!
SLUNCH
IF YOU SURVIVE THIS, WINSLOW, I'LL GIVE YOU A PROMOTION. GOOD LUCK.
COLD FRONT CAME IN QUICK, DIDN'T IT?
S-STAY BACK! OR I'LL K-KILL YOU.
YOUR LAST BOSS MASTERED USING TEN OF THOSE RINGS. YOU CAN BARELY HANDLE TWO.
HMMMM
CRACK

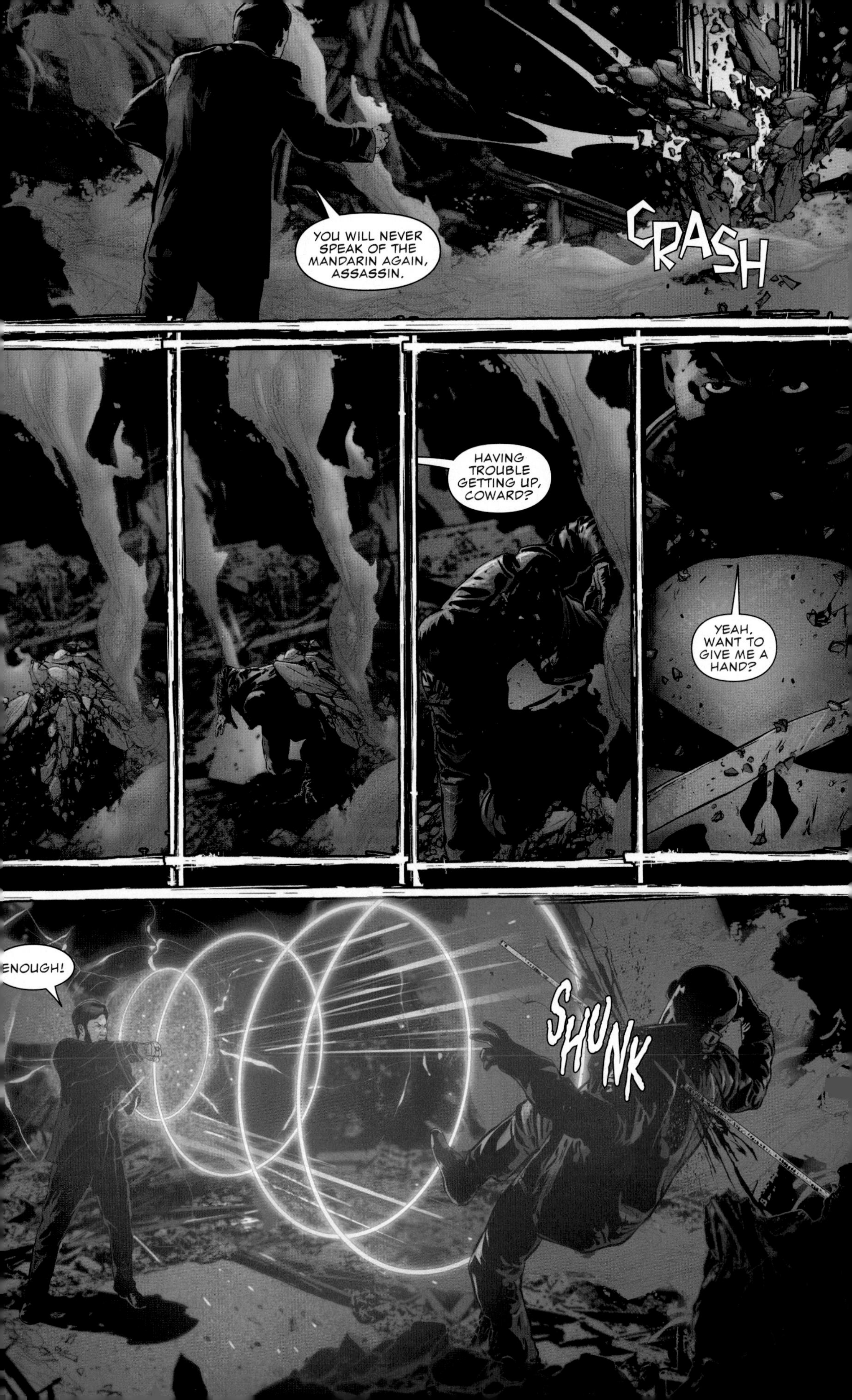
YOU WILL NEVER SPEAK OF THE MANDARIN AGAIN, ASSASSIN.
CRASH
HAVING TROUBLE GETTING UP, COWARD?
YEAH. WANT TO GIVE ME A HAND?
ENOUGH!
SHUNK

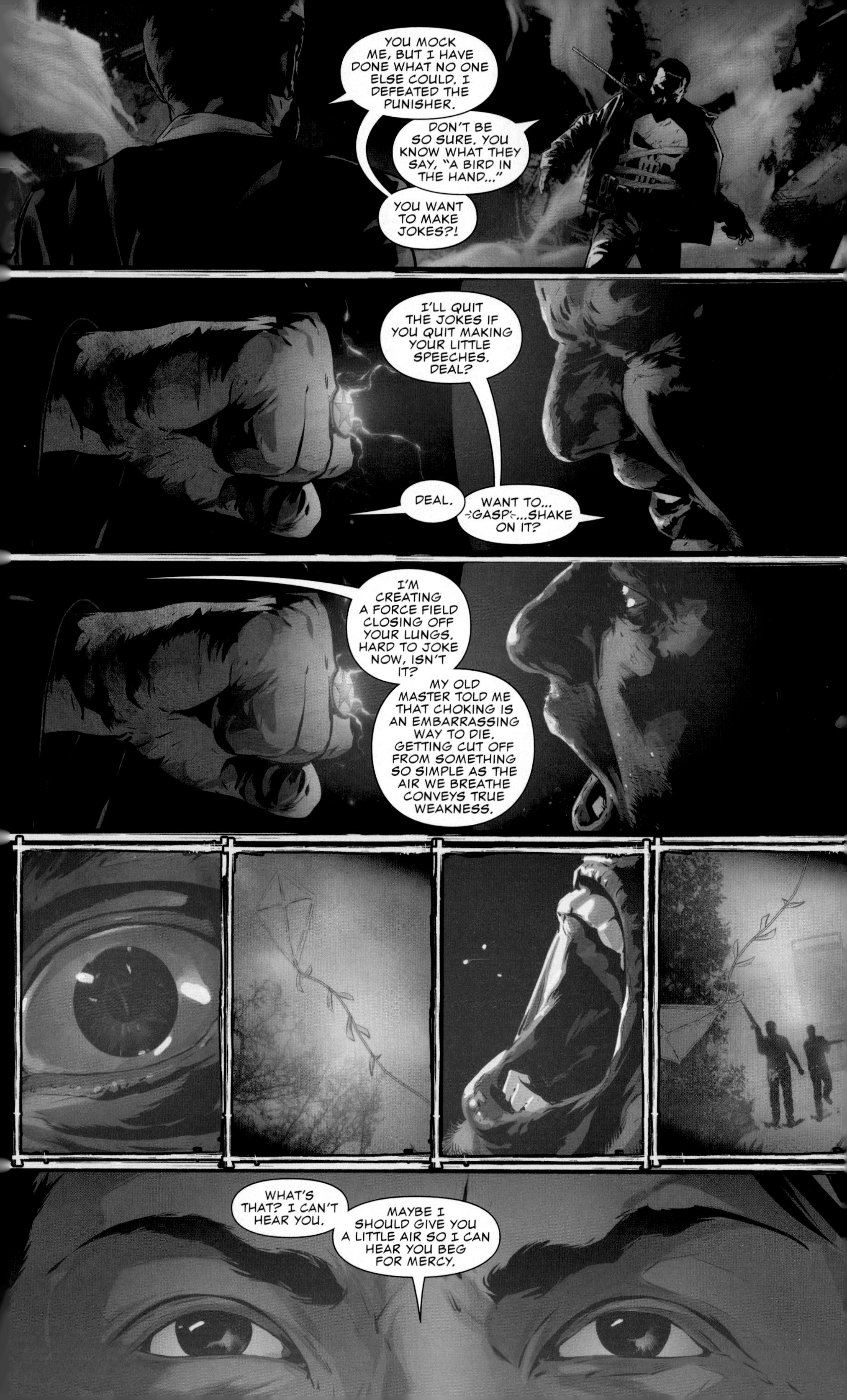

YOU MOCK ME, BUT I HAVE DONE WHAT NO ONE ELSE COULD. I DEFEATED THE PUNISHER.
DON'T BE SO SURE. YOU KNOW WHAT THEY SAY, "A BIRD IN THE HAND..."
YOU WANT TO MAKE JOKES?!
I'LL QUIT THE JOKES IF YOU QUIT MAKING YOUR LITTLE SPEECHES. DEAL?
DEAL.
WANT TO... -GASP-...SHAKE ON IT?
I'M CREATING A FORCE FIELD CLOSING OFF YOUR LUNGS. HARD TO JOKE NOW, ISN'T IT?
MY OLD MASTER TOLD ME THAT CHOKING IS AN EMBARRASSING WAY TO DIE. GETTING CUT OFF FROM SOMETHING SO SIMPLE AS THE AIR WE BREATHE CONVEYS TRUE WEAKNESS.
WHAT'S THAT? I CAN'T HEAR YOU.
MAYBE I SHOULD GIVE YOU A LITTLE AIR SO I CAN HEAR YOU BEG FOR MERCY.

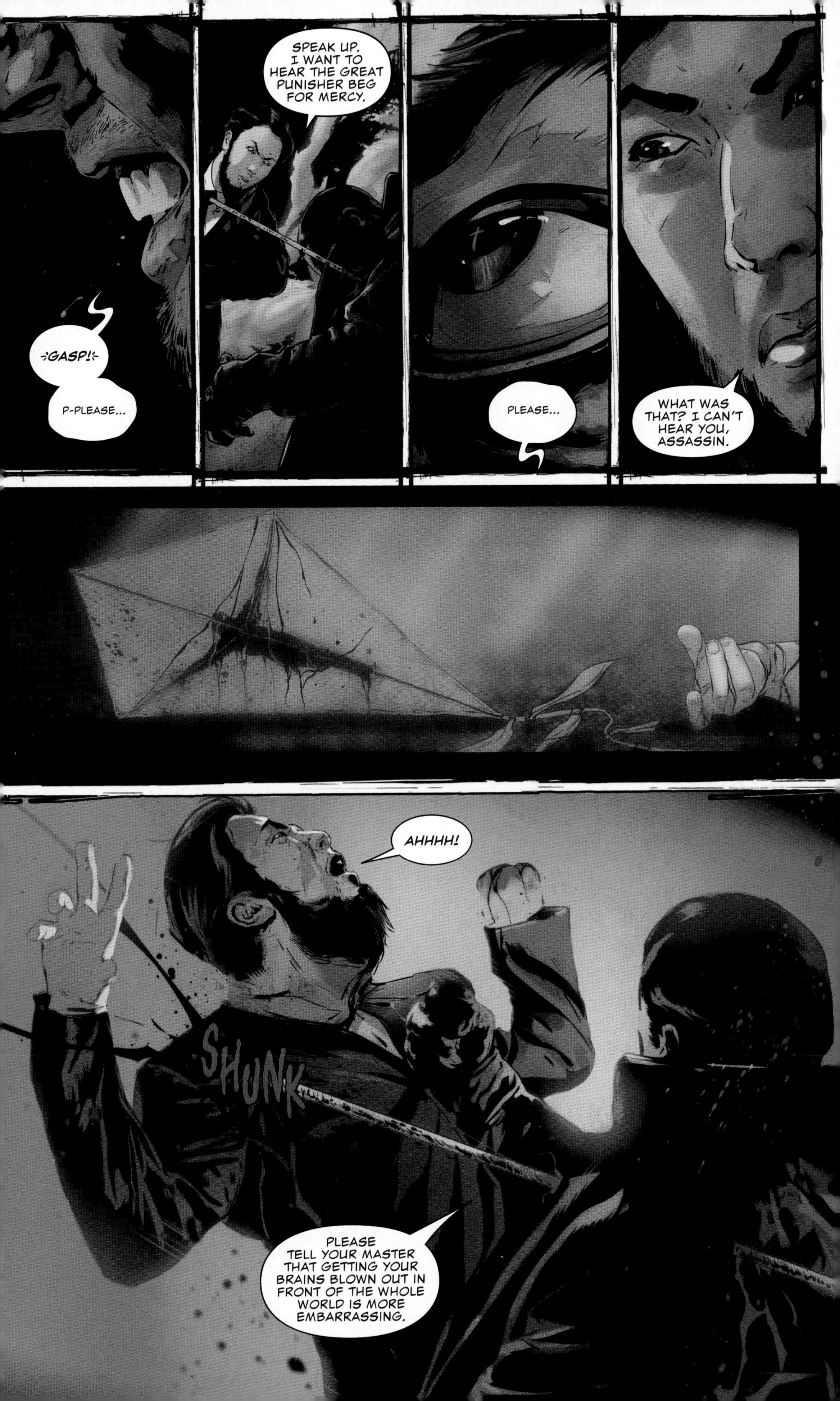

-GASP!-
P-PLEASE...
SPEAK UP. I WANT TO HEAR THE GREAT PUNISHER BEG FOR MERCY.
PLEASE...
WHAT WAS THAT? I CAN'T HEAR YOU, ASSASSIN.
AHHHH!
SHUNK
PLEASE TELL YOUR MASTER THAT GETTING YOUR BRAINS BLOWN OUT IN FRONT OF THE WHOLE WORLD IS MORE EMBARRASSING.

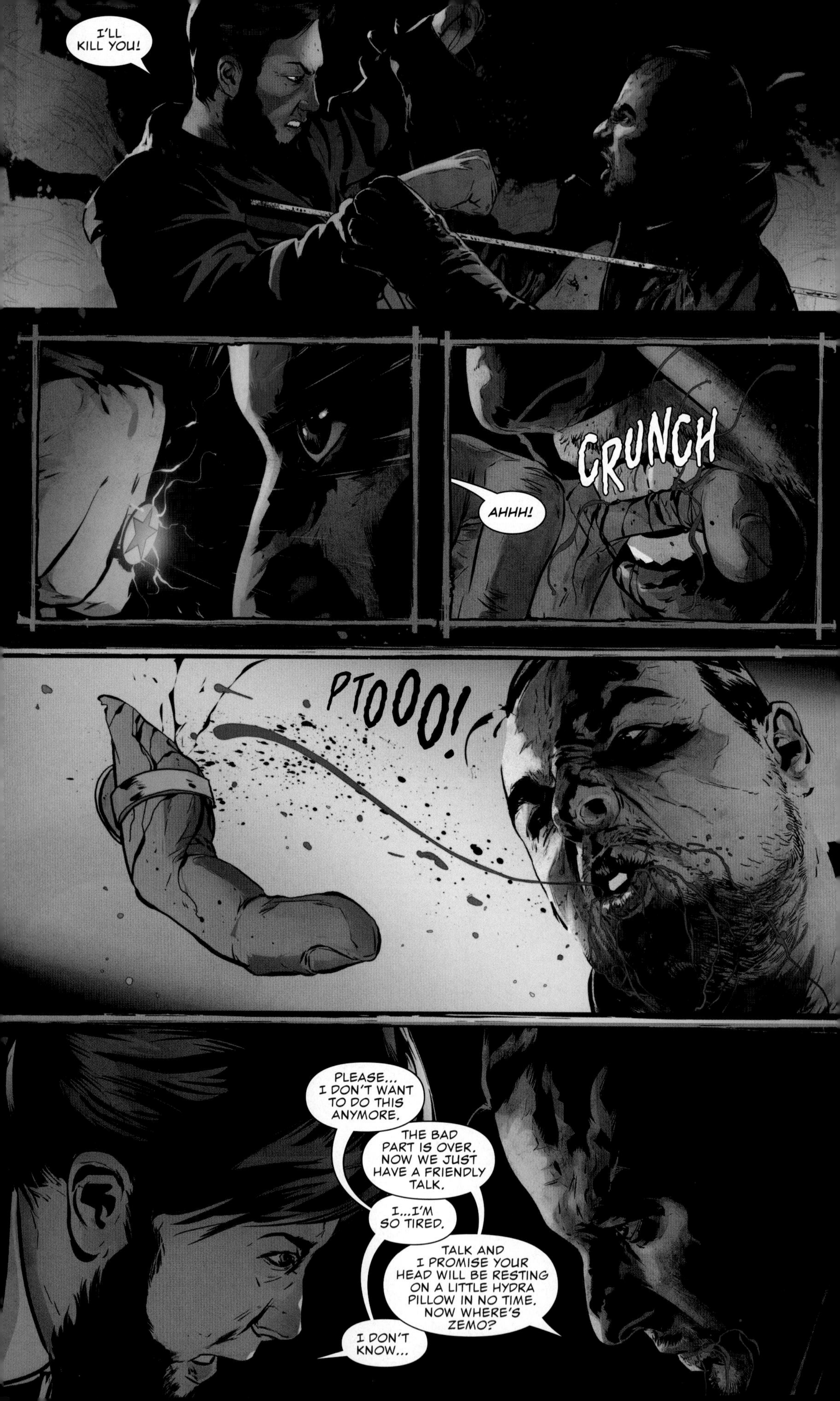
I'LL KILL YOU!
AHHH!
CRUNCH
PTOOOI!
PLEASE... I DON'T WANT TO DO THIS ANYMORE.
THE BAD PART IS OVER. NOW WE JUST HAVE A FRIENDLY TALK.
I...I'M SO TIRED.
TALK AND I PROMISE YOUR HEAD WILL BE RESTING ON A LITTLE HYDRA PILLOW IN NO TIME. NOW WHERE'S ZEMO?
I DON'T KNOW...

AND I TOLD HIM--

DAVID!

"I THOUGHT YOU WERE GONNA HELP ME NOW, WINSLOW?"

HELLO, MR. CAVERLY. A MUTUAL FRIEND SAID YOU COULD HELP ME. I'M LOOKING FOR BARON ZEMO.

"CAVERLY, YOU'RE LOOKING FOR A MAN NAMED DAVID CAVERLY."

WHAT?! WHY WOULD I HELP YOU?

BECAUSE THE LONGER IT TAKES ME TO GET ANSWERS THE LESS OF YOU YOUR WIFE WILL HAVE TO BURY.

WELCOME TO DIMMU BURGER. HOW CAN I HELP YOU?

"HE KNOWS WHERE ZEMO IS?"

WHAT THE HELL?!

HEY!

"NO, ZEMO IS EXTREMELY PARANOID. MOST OF HYDRA HAS GONE UNDERGROUND. CAVERLY'S THE ONLY CONTACT I HAVE."

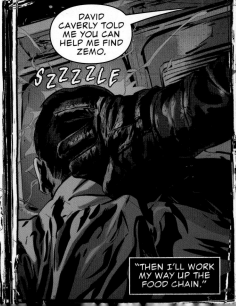

DAVID CAVERLY TOLD ME YOU CAN HELP ME FIND ZEMO.

SZZZZLE

"THEN I'LL WORK MY WAY UP THE FOOD CHAIN."

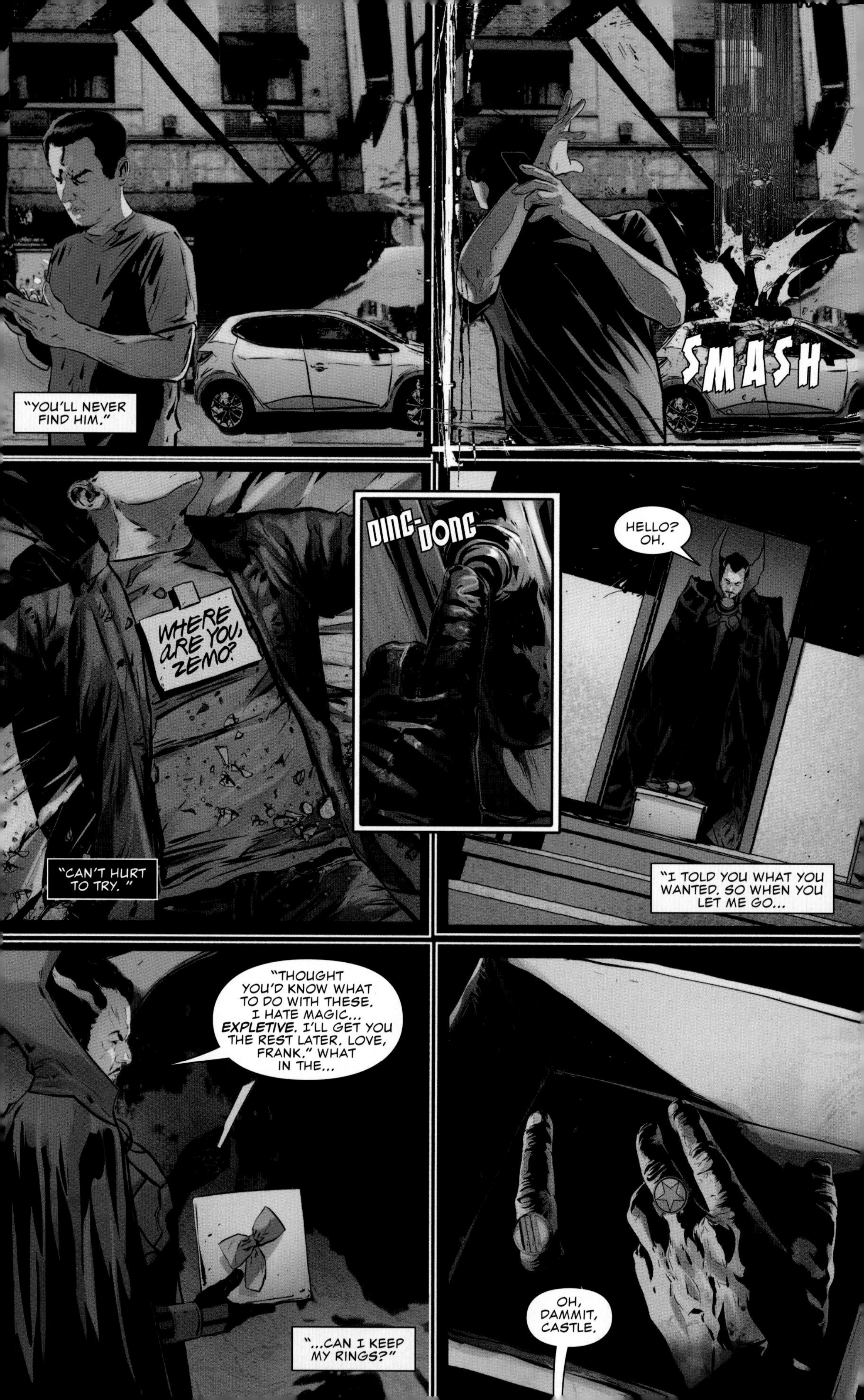
"YOU'LL NEVER FIND HIM."
SMASH
WHERE ARE YOU, ZEMO?
"CAN'T HURT TO TRY."
DING-DONG
HELLO? OH.
"I TOLD YOU WHAT YOU WANTED. SO WHEN YOU LET ME GO...
"THOUGHT YOU'D KNOW WHAT TO DO WITH THESE. I HATE MAGIC... **EXPLETIVE**. I'LL GET YOU THE REST LATER. LOVE, FRANK." WHAT IN THE...
"...CAN I KEEP MY RINGS?"
OH, DAMMIT, CASTLE.

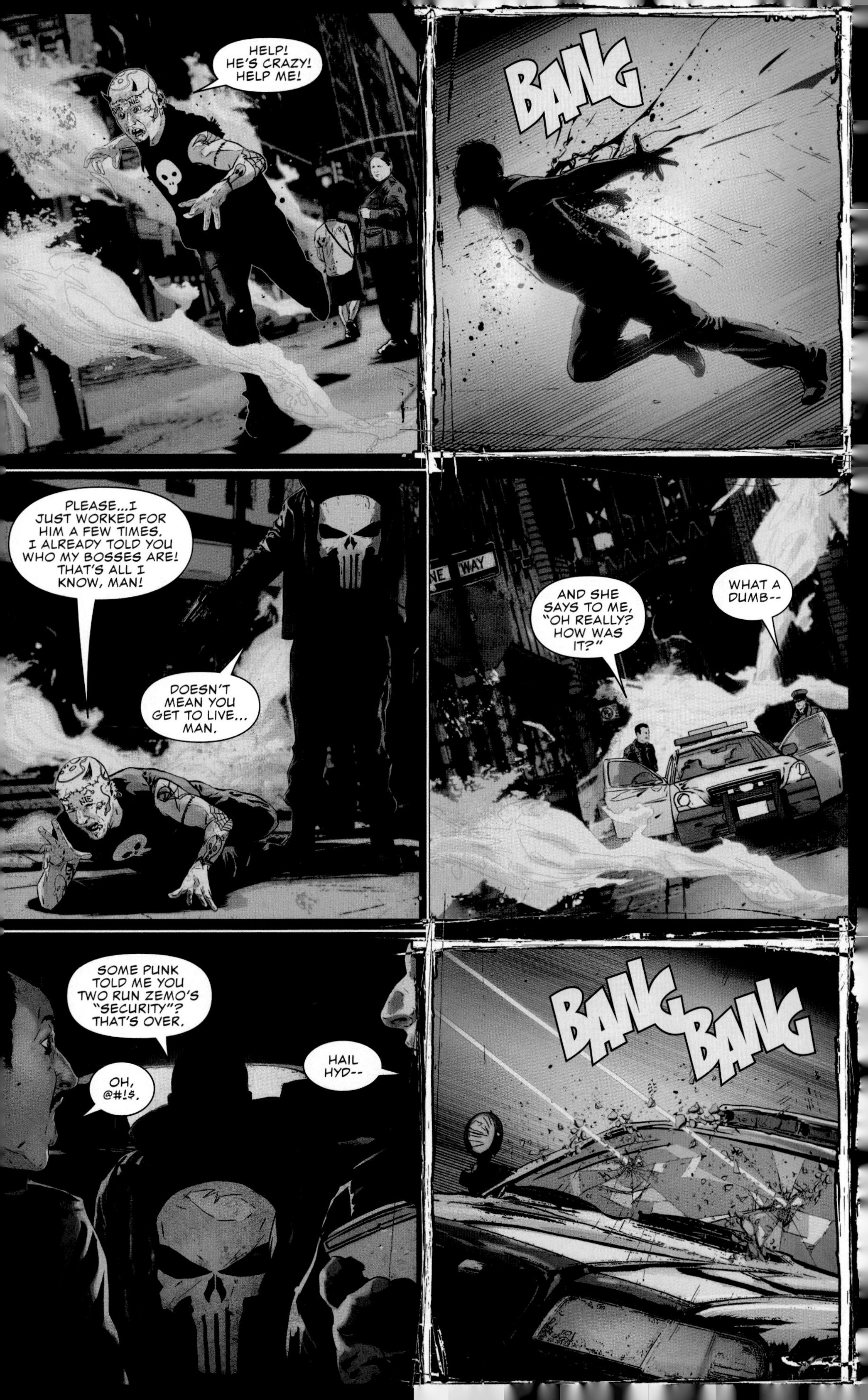
HELP! HE'S CRAZY! HELP ME!
BANG
PLEASE...I JUST WORKED FOR HIM A FEW TIMES. I ALREADY TOLD YOU WHO MY BOSSES ARE! THAT'S ALL I KNOW, MAN!
DOESN'T MEAN YOU GET TO LIVE... MAN.
ONE WAY
AND SHE SAYS TO ME, "OH REALLY? HOW WAS IT?"
WHAT A DUMB--
SOME PUNK TOLD ME YOU TWO RUN ZEMO'S "SECURITY"? THAT'S OVER.
OH, @#!$.
HAIL HYD--
BANG BANG

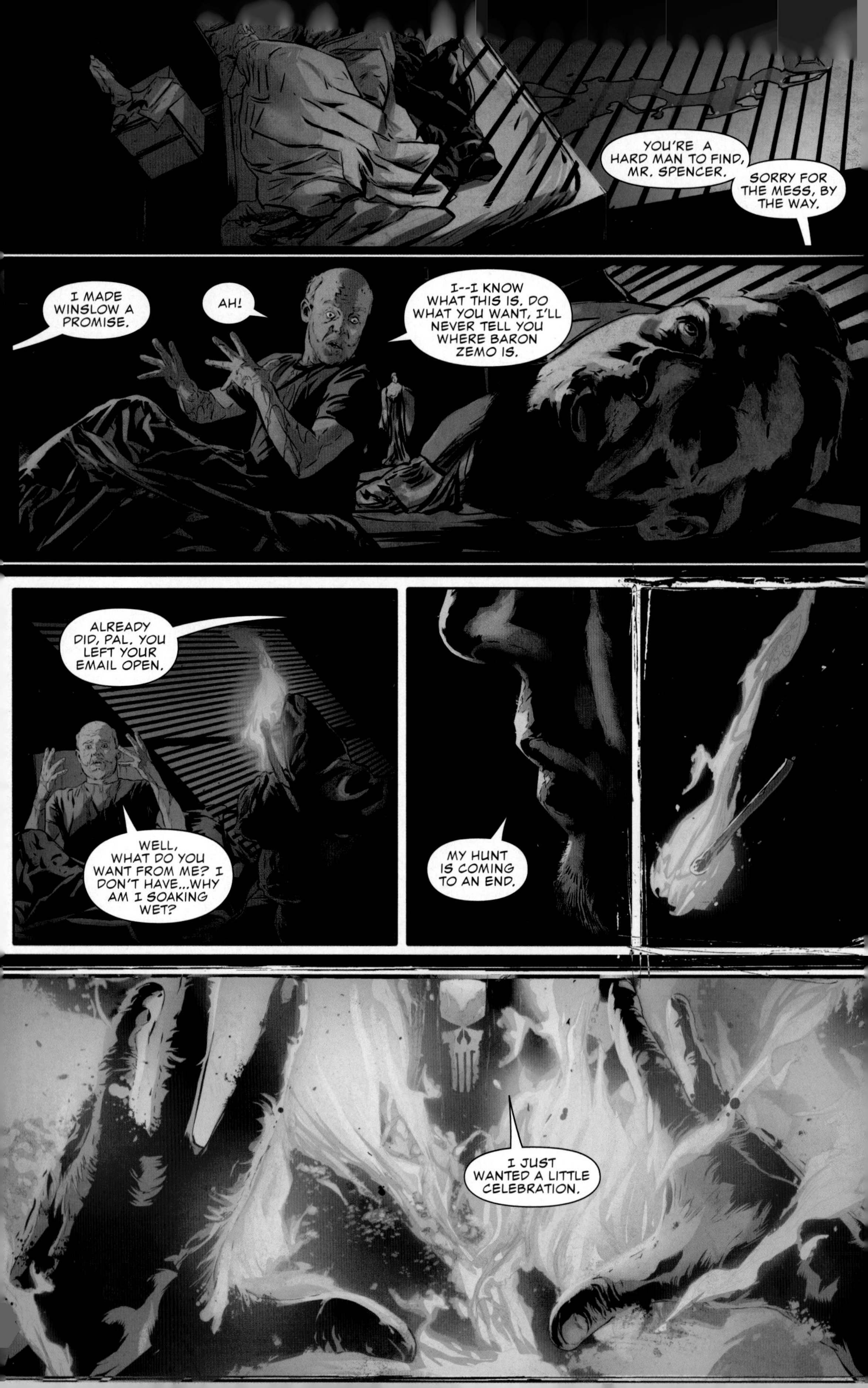
YOU'RE A HARD MAN TO FIND, MR. SPENCER.
SORRY FOR THE MESS, BY THE WAY.
I MADE WINSLOW A PROMISE.
AH!
I--I KNOW WHAT THIS IS. DO WHAT YOU WANT, I'LL NEVER TELL YOU WHERE BARON ZEMO IS.
ALREADY DID, PAL. YOU LEFT YOUR EMAIL OPEN.
WELL, WHAT DO YOU WANT FROM ME? I DON'T HAVE...WHY AM I SOAKING WET?
MY HUNT IS COMING TO AN END.
I JUST WANTED A LITTLE CELEBRATION.

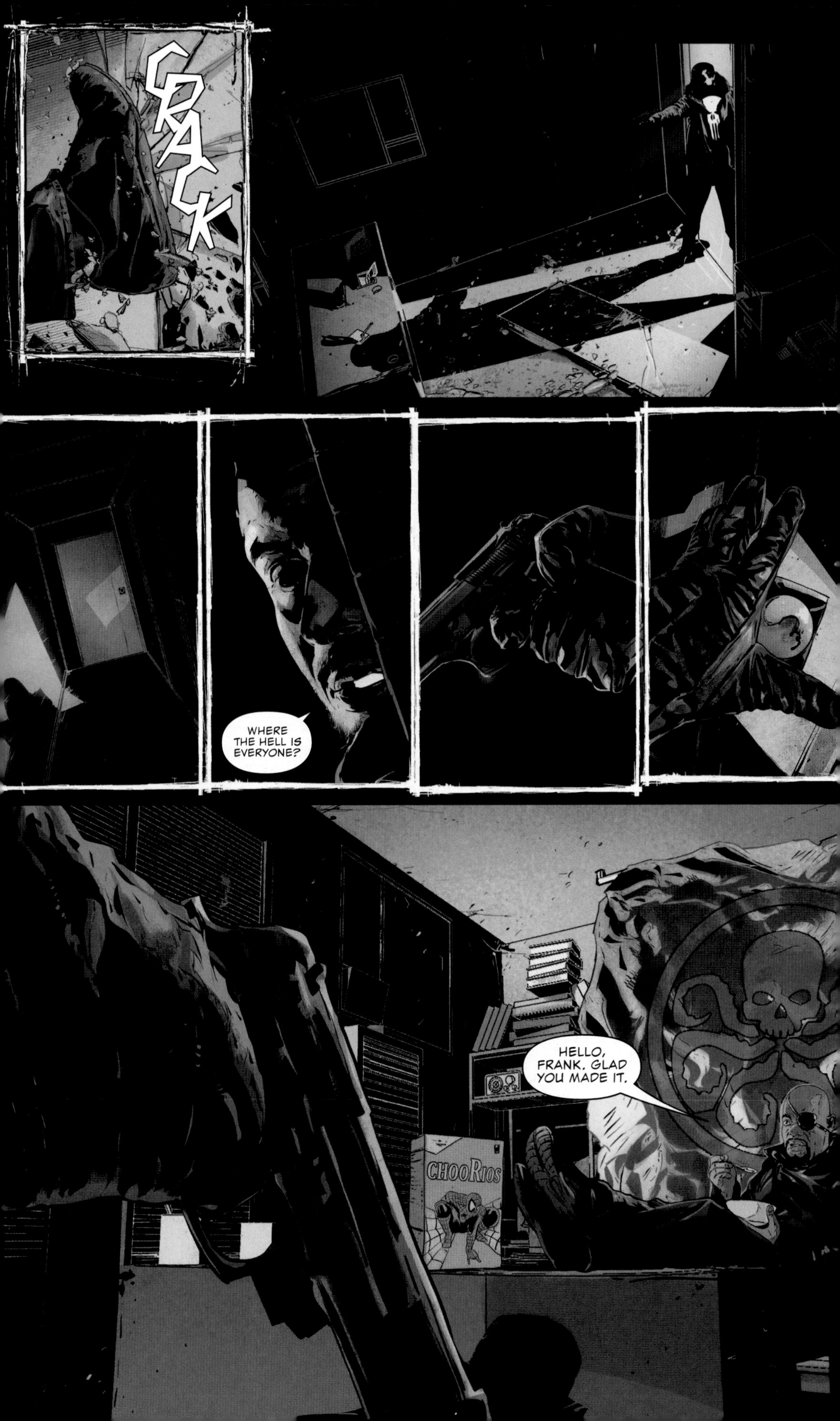

CRACK
WHERE THE HELL IS EVERYONE?
HELLO, FRANK. GLAD YOU MADE IT.
CHOORIOS

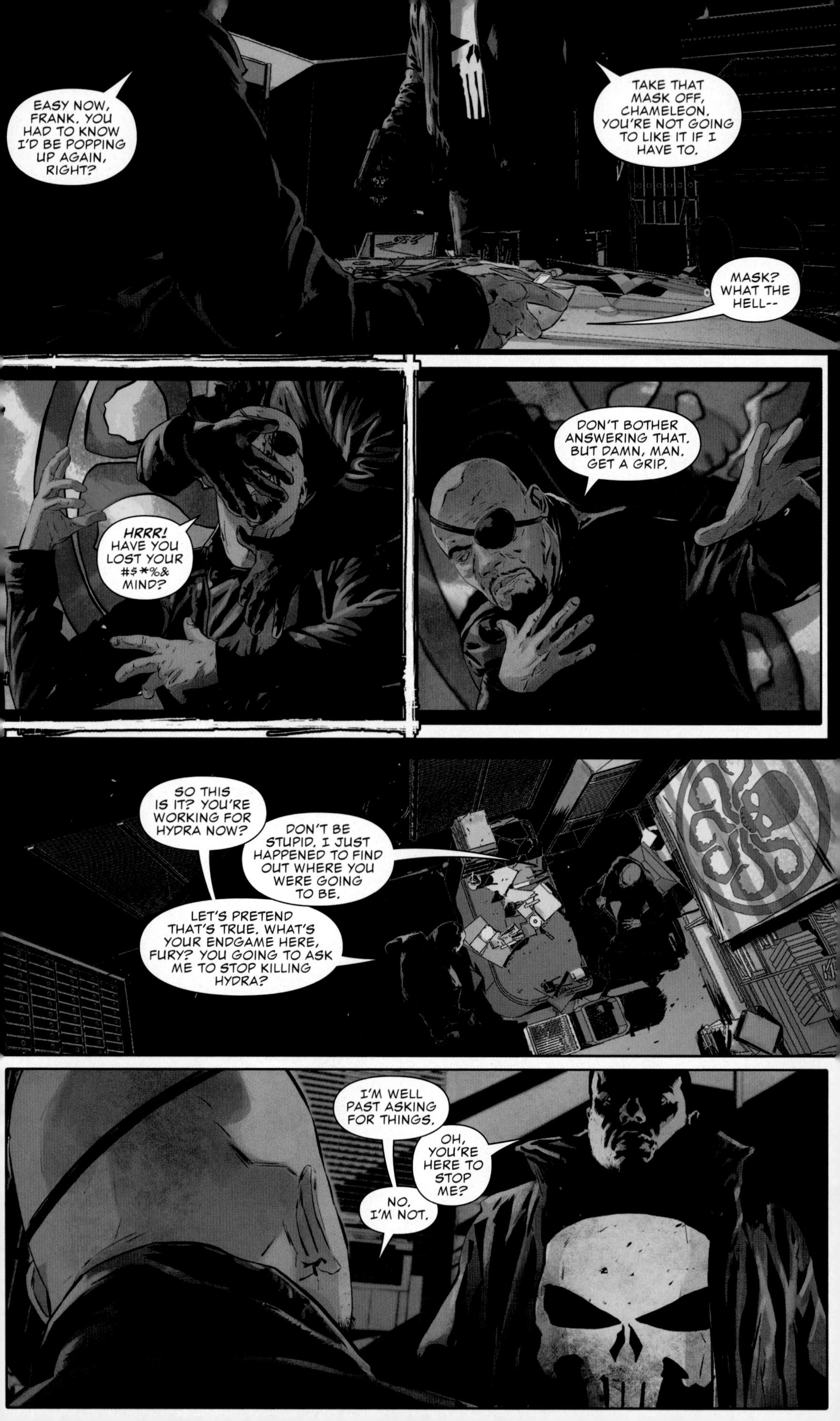

EASY NOW, FRANK. YOU HAD TO KNOW I'D BE POPPING UP AGAIN, RIGHT?
TAKE THAT MASK OFF, CHAMELEON. YOU'RE NOT GOING TO LIKE IT IF I HAVE TO.
MASK? WHAT THE HELL--
HRRR! HAVE YOU LOST YOUR #$*%& MIND?
DON'T BOTHER ANSWERING THAT. BUT DAMN, MAN. GET A GRIP.
SO THIS IS IT? YOU'RE WORKING FOR HYDRA NOW?
DON'T BE STUPID. I JUST HAPPENED TO FIND OUT WHERE YOU WERE GOING TO BE.
LET'S PRETEND THAT'S TRUE. WHAT'S YOUR ENDGAME HERE, FURY? YOU GOING TO ASK ME TO STOP KILLING HYDRA?
I'M WELL PAST ASKING FOR THINGS.
OH, YOU'RE HERE TO STOP ME?
NO. I'M NOT.

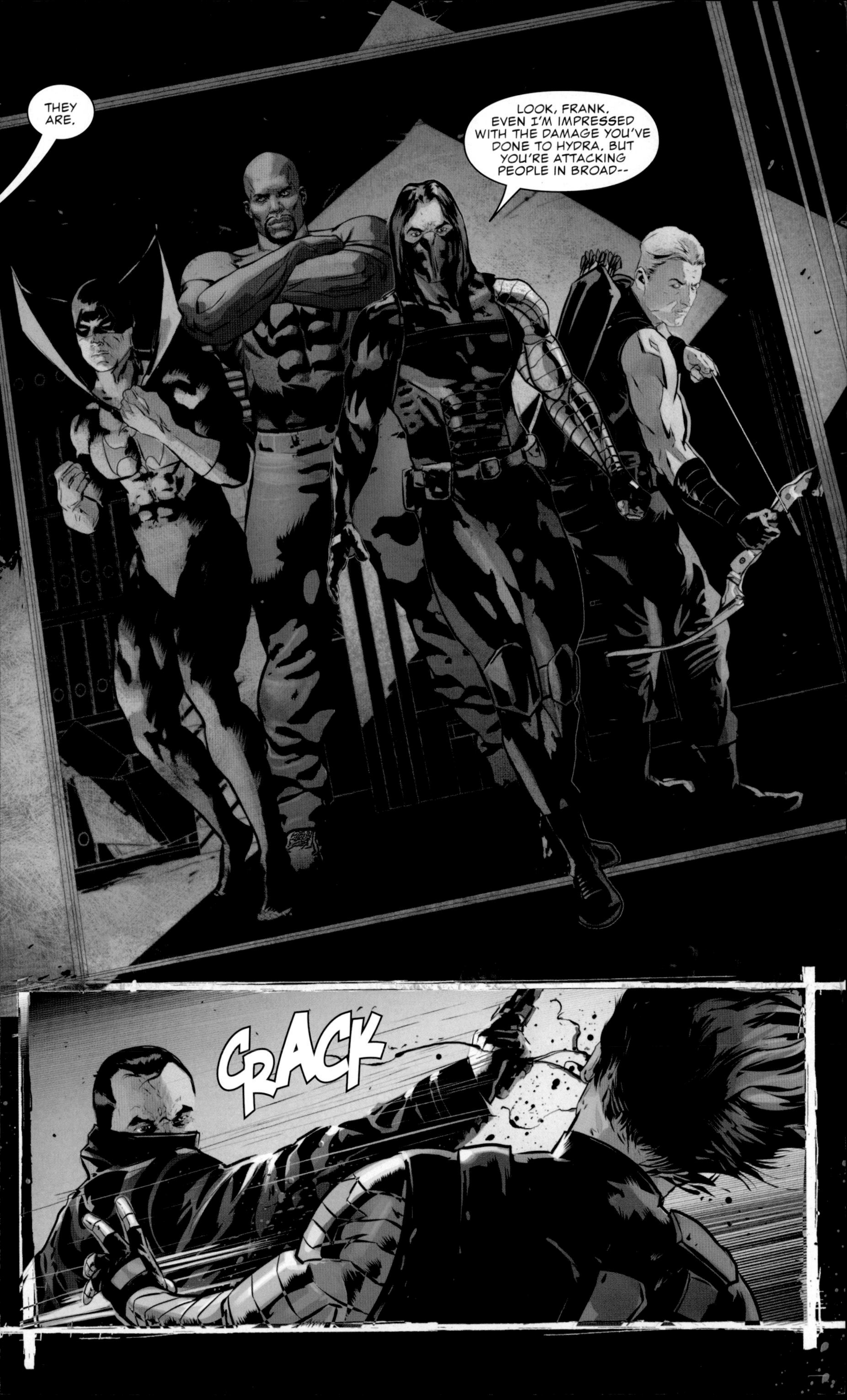
THEY ARE.
LOOK, FRANK, EVEN I'M IMPRESSED WITH THE DAMAGE YOU'VE DONE TO HYDRA, BUT YOU'RE ATTACKING PEOPLE IN BROAD--
CRACK

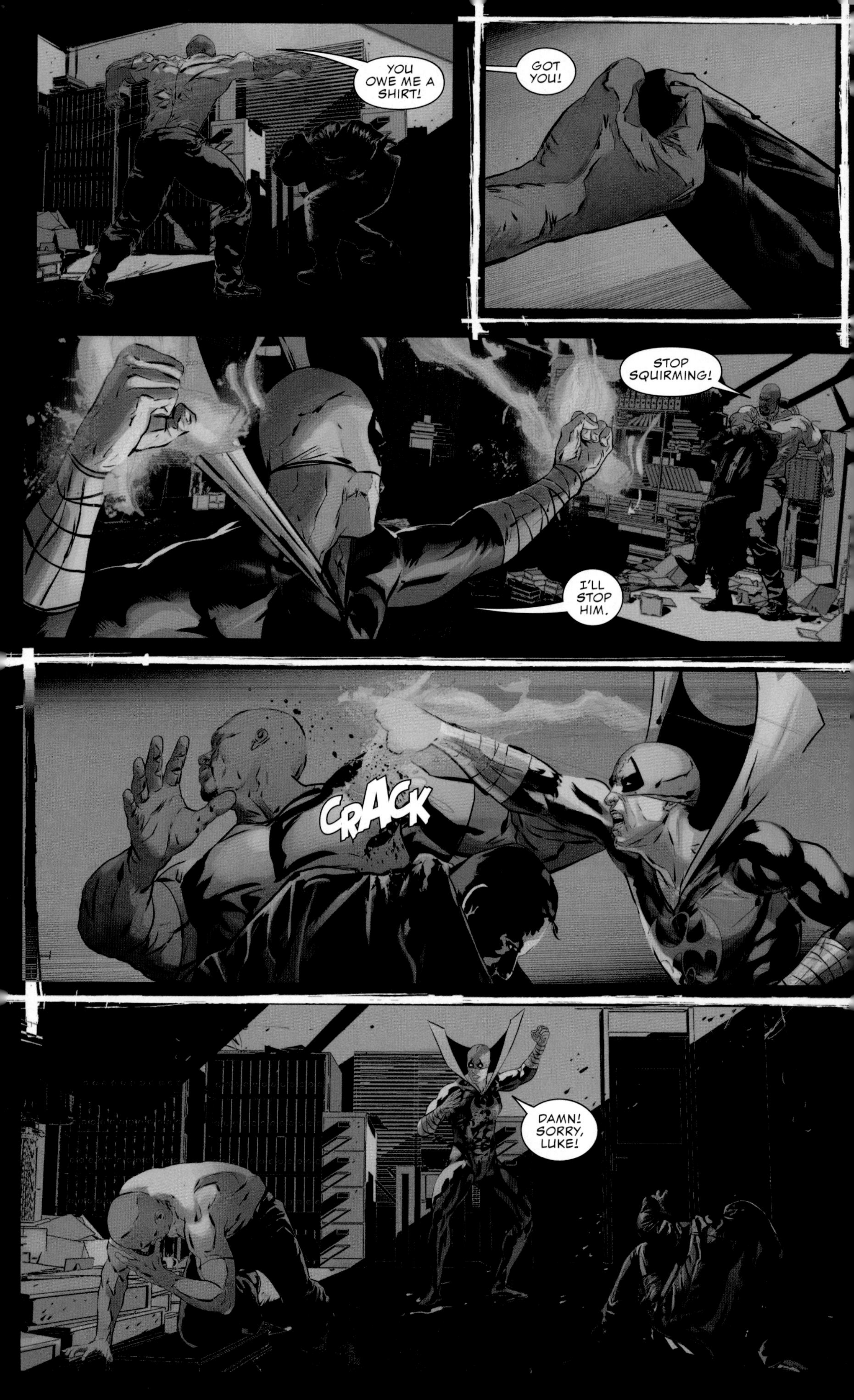
YOU OWE ME A SHIRT!
GOT YOU!
STOP SQUIRMING!
I'LL STOP HIM.
CRACK
DAMN! SORRY, LUKE!

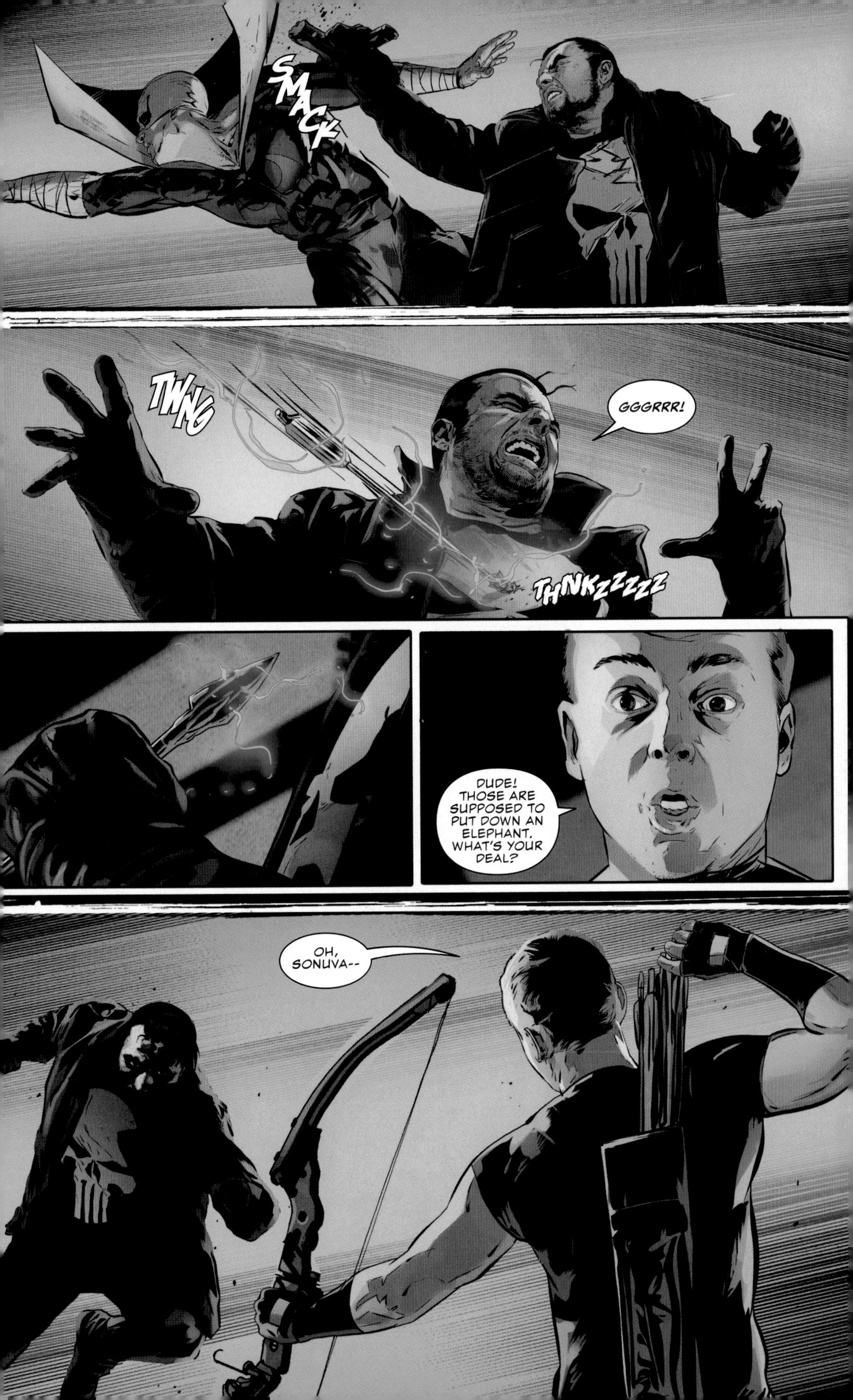
SMACK
TWNG
GGGRRR!
THNKZZZZZ
DUDE! THOSE ARE SUPPOSED TO PUT DOWN AN ELEPHANT. WHAT'S YOUR DEAL?
OH, SONUVA--

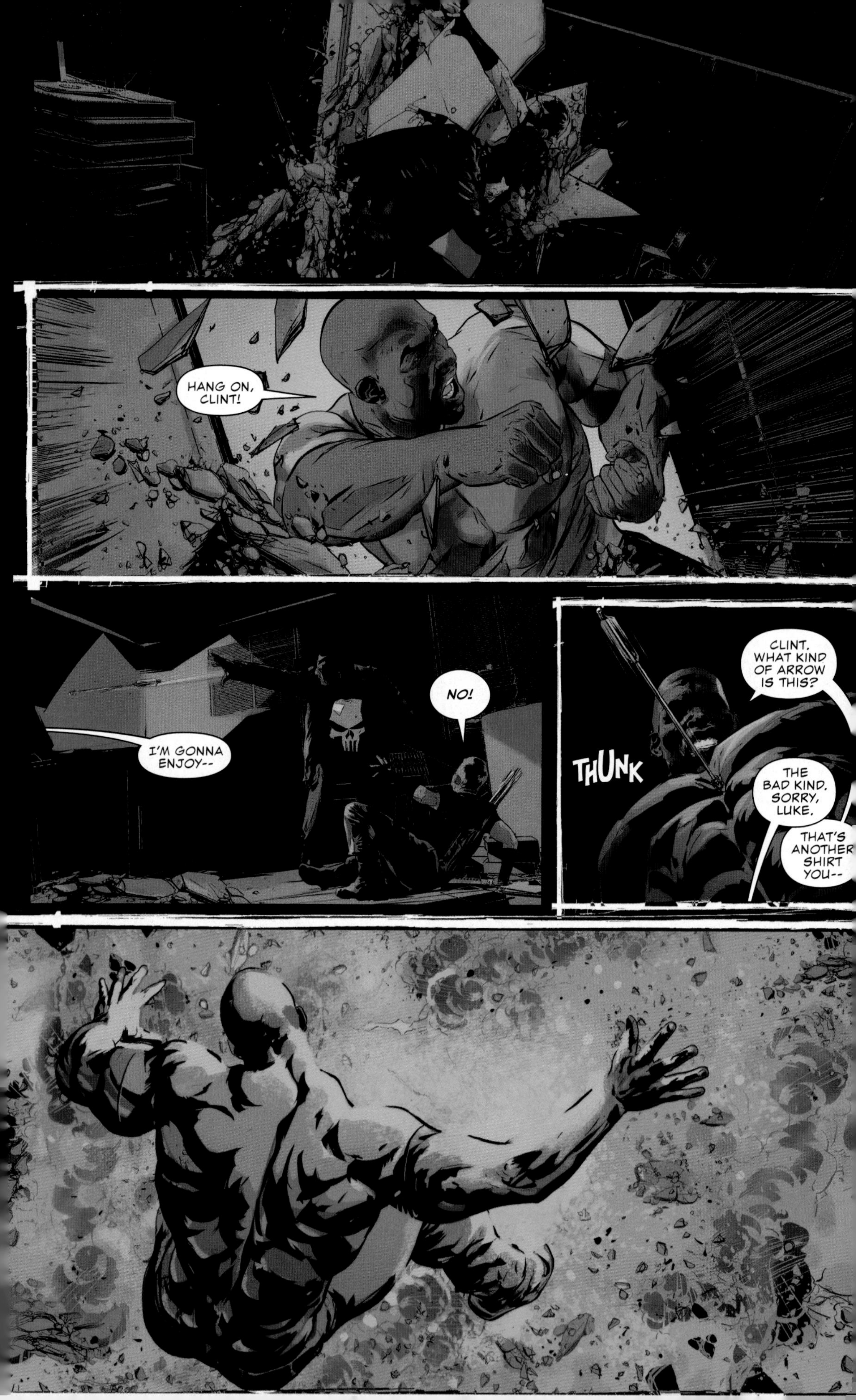
HANG ON, CLINT!
I'M GONNA ENJOY--
NO!
CLINT. WHAT KIND OF ARROW IS THIS?
THUNK
THE BAD KIND. SORRY, LUKE.
THAT'S ANOTHER SHIRT YOU--

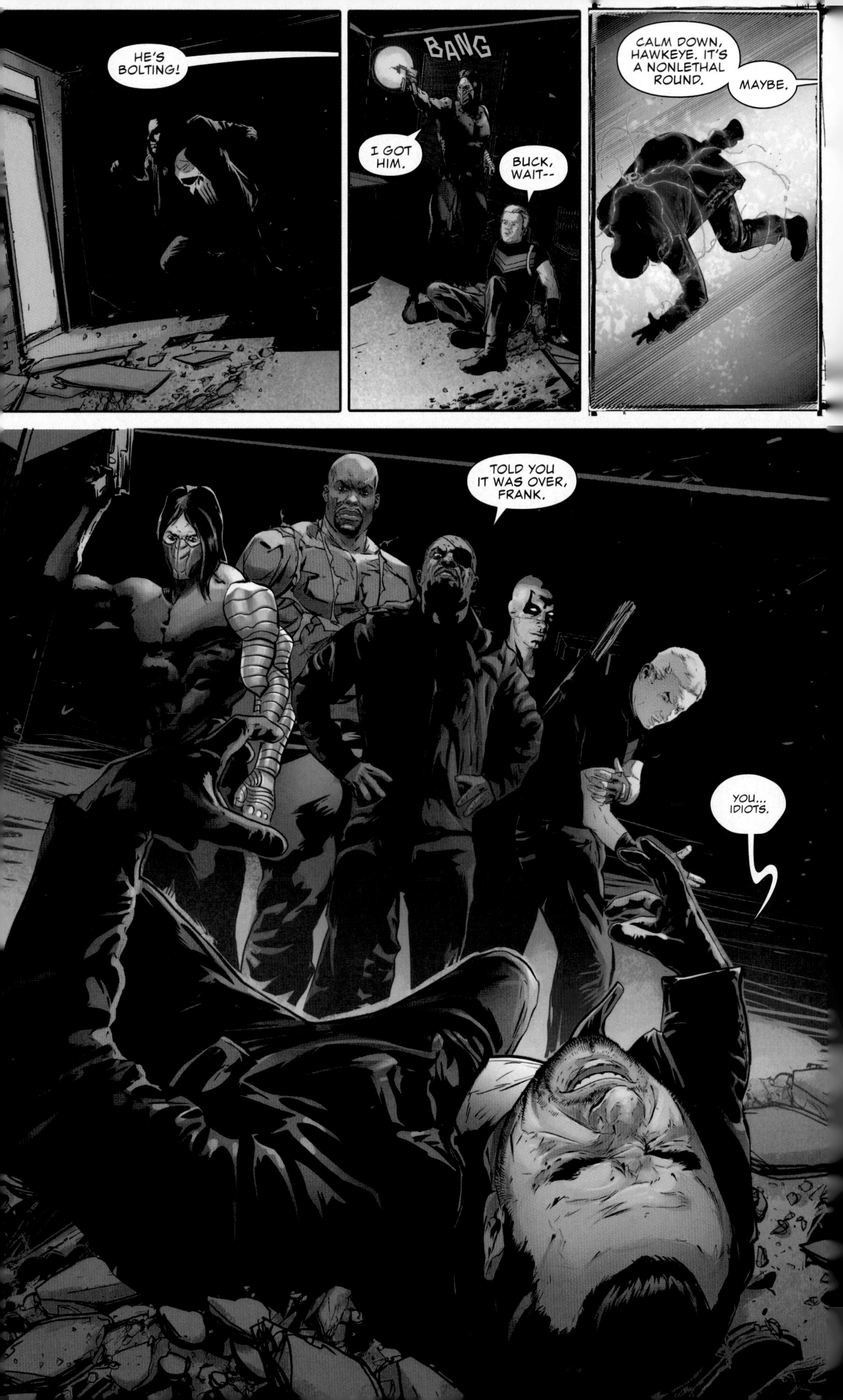
HE'S BOLTING!
BANG
I GOT HIM.
BUCK, WAIT--
CALM DOWN, HAWKEYE. IT'S A NONLETHAL ROUND.
MAYBE.
TOLD YOU IT WAS OVER, FRANK.
YOU... IDIOTS.

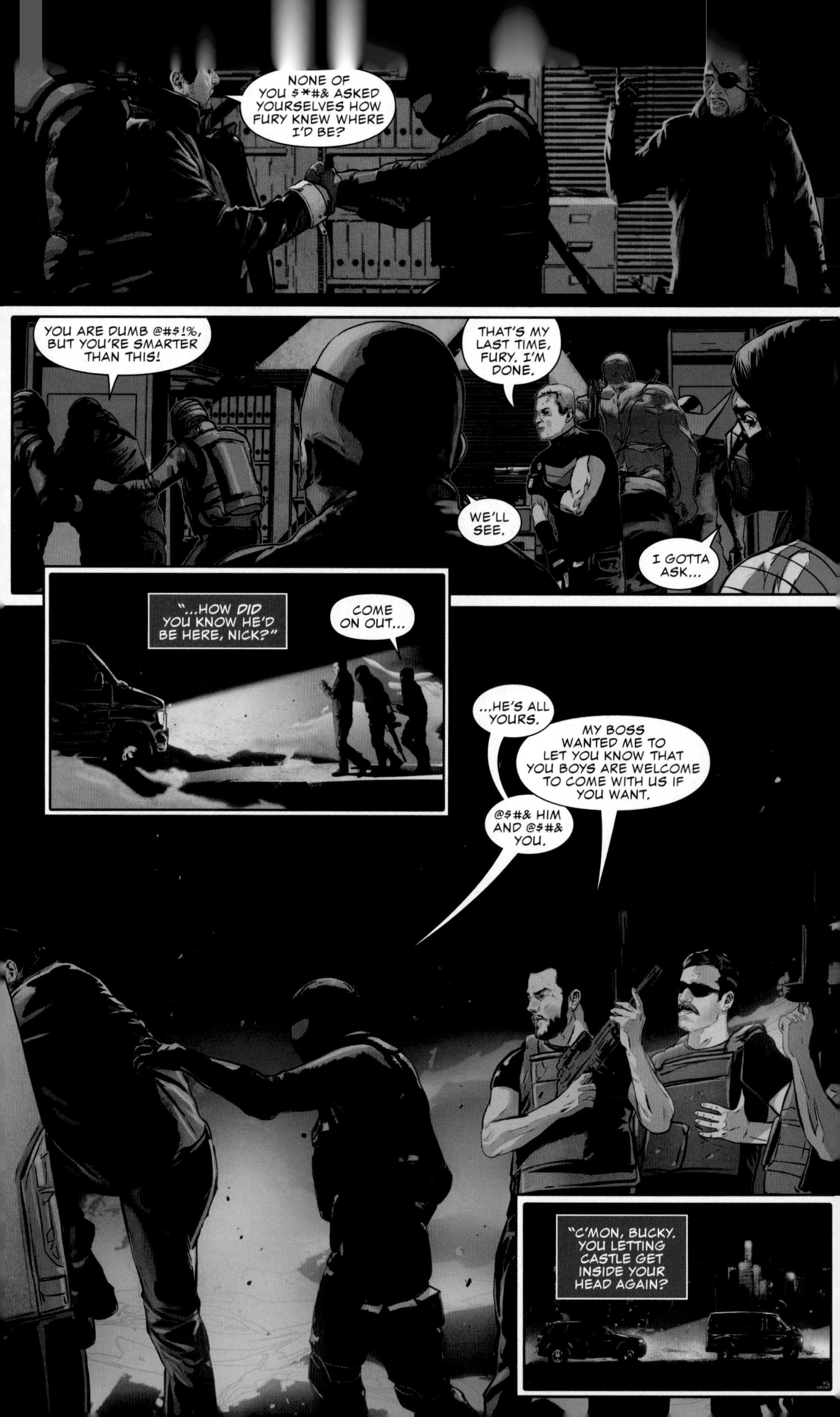
NONE OF YOU $*#& ASKED YOURSELVES HOW FURY KNEW WHERE I'D BE?
YOU ARE DUMB @#$!%, BUT YOU'RE SMARTER THAN THIS!
THAT'S MY LAST TIME, FURY. I'M DONE.
WE'LL SEE.
I GOTTA ASK...
"...HOW DID YOU KNOW HE'D BE HERE, NICK?"
COME ON OUT...
...HE'S ALL YOURS.
MY BOSS WANTED ME TO LET YOU KNOW THAT YOU BOYS ARE WELCOME TO COME WITH US IF YOU WANT.
@$#& HIM AND @$#& YOU.
"C'MON, BUCKY. YOU LETTING CASTLE GET INSIDE YOUR HEAD AGAIN?

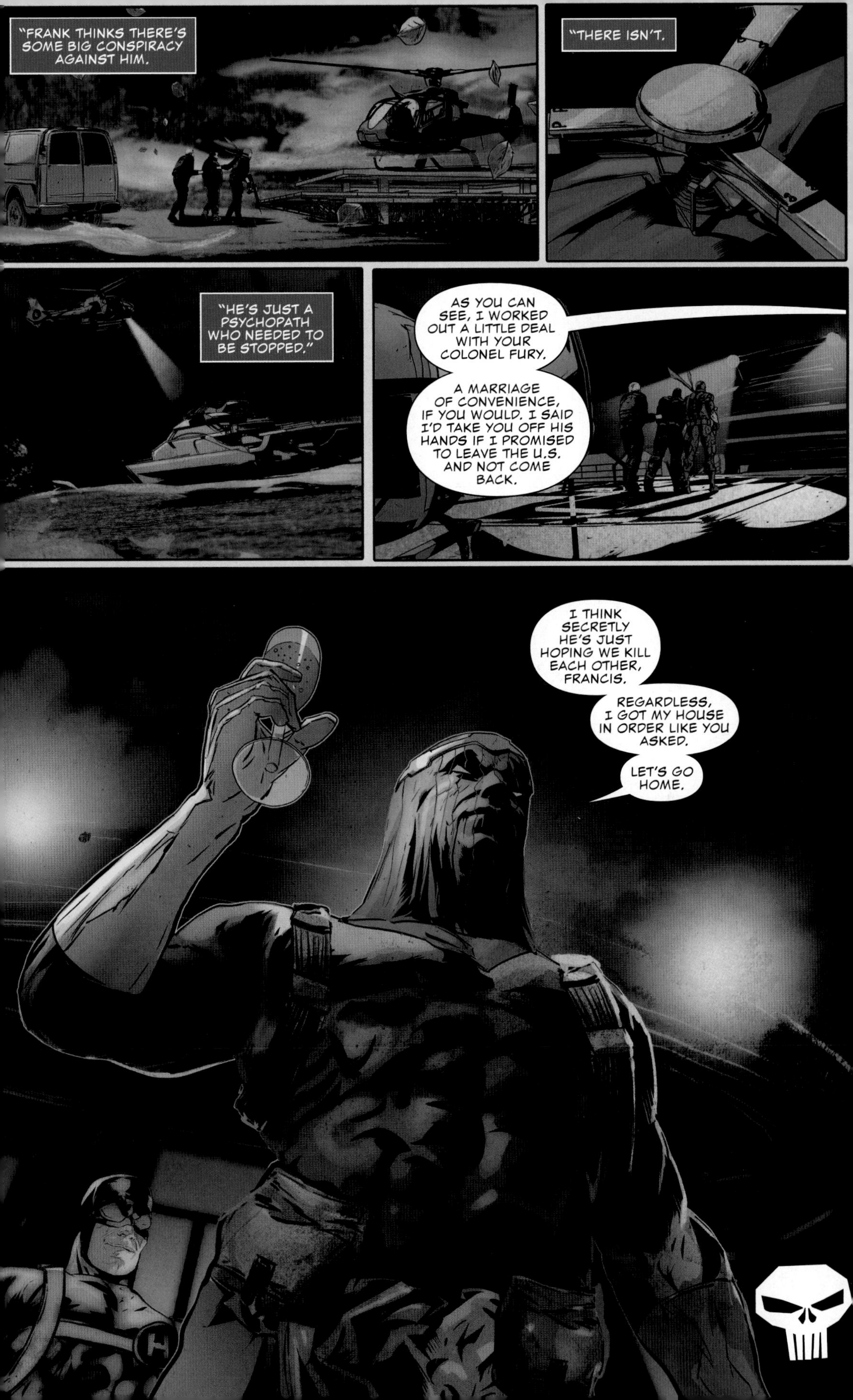
"FRANK THINKS THERE'S SOME BIG CONSPIRACY AGAINST HIM.
"THERE ISN'T.
"HE'S JUST A PSYCHOPATH WHO NEEDED TO BE STOPPED."
AS YOU CAN SEE, I WORKED OUT A LITTLE DEAL WITH YOUR COLONEL FURY.
A MARRIAGE OF CONVENIENCE, IF YOU WOULD. I SAID I'D TAKE YOU OFF HIS HANDS IF I PROMISED TO LEAVE THE U.S. AND NOT COME BACK.
I THINK SECRETLY HE'S JUST HOPING WE KILL EACH OTHER, FRANCIS.
REGARDLESS, I GOT MY HOUSE IN ORDER LIKE YOU ASKED.
LET'S GO HOME.

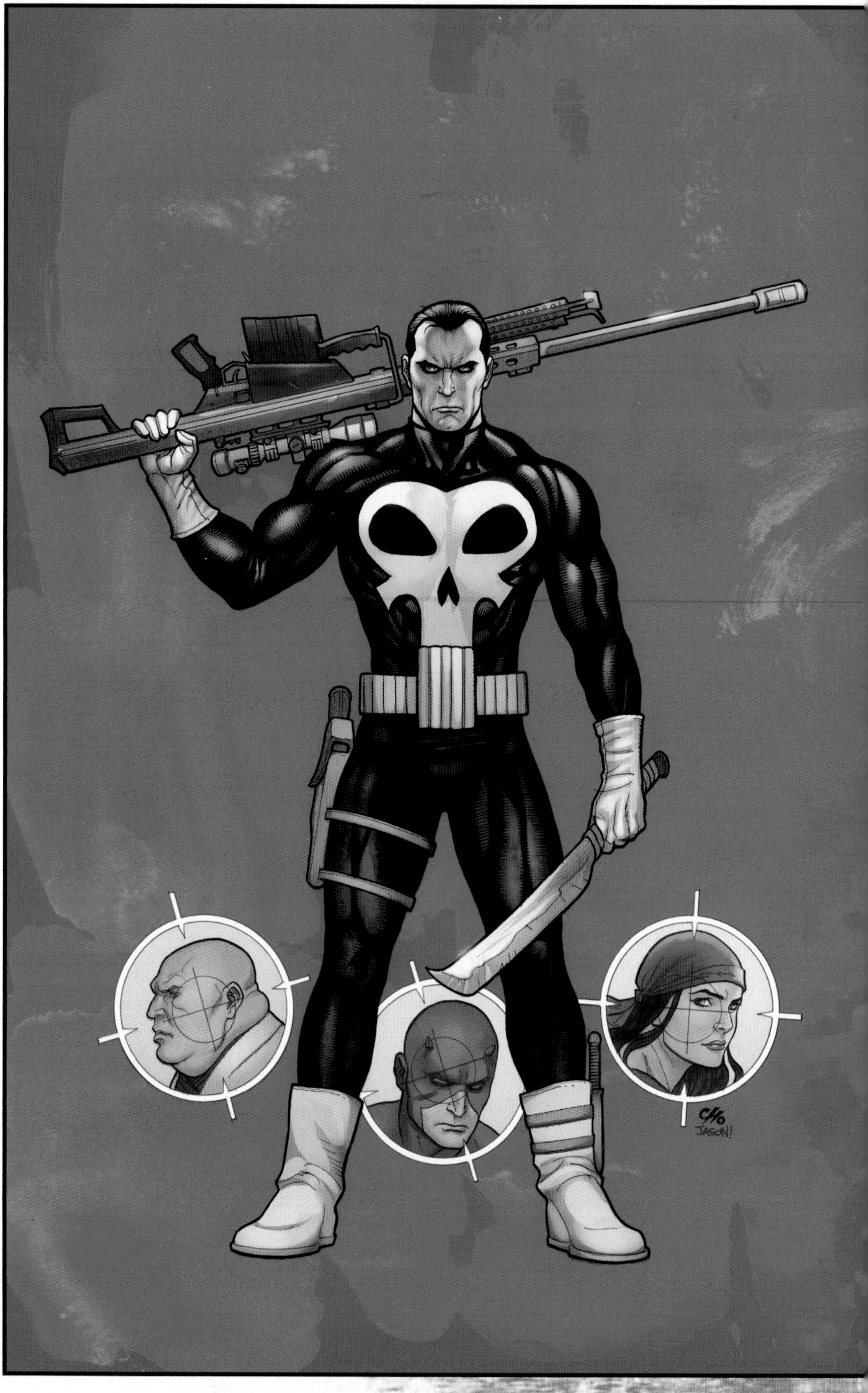
CHO
JASON!

#1 VARIANT BY FRANK CHO & JASON KEITH

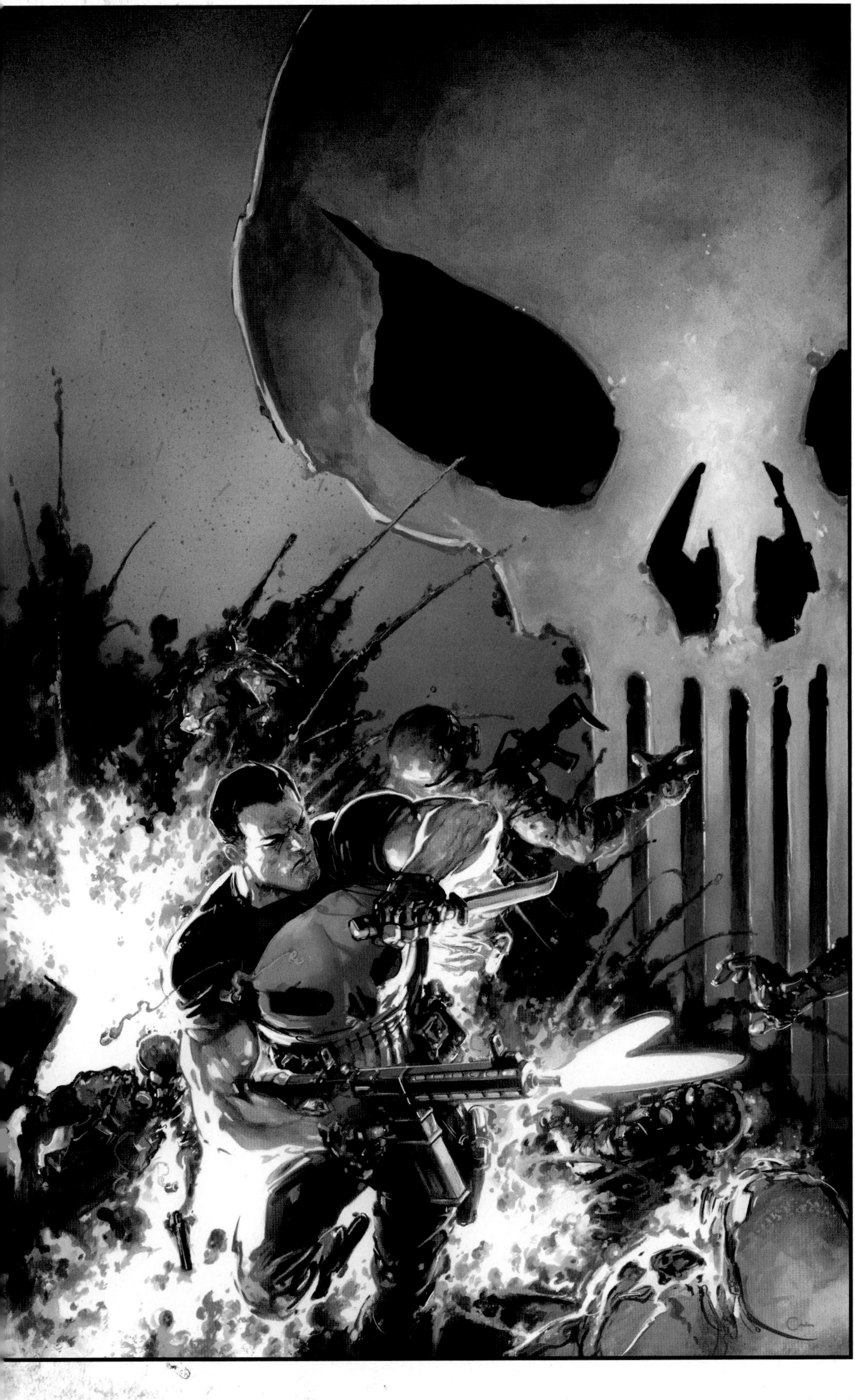

#1 **VARIANT** BY CLAYTON CRAIN

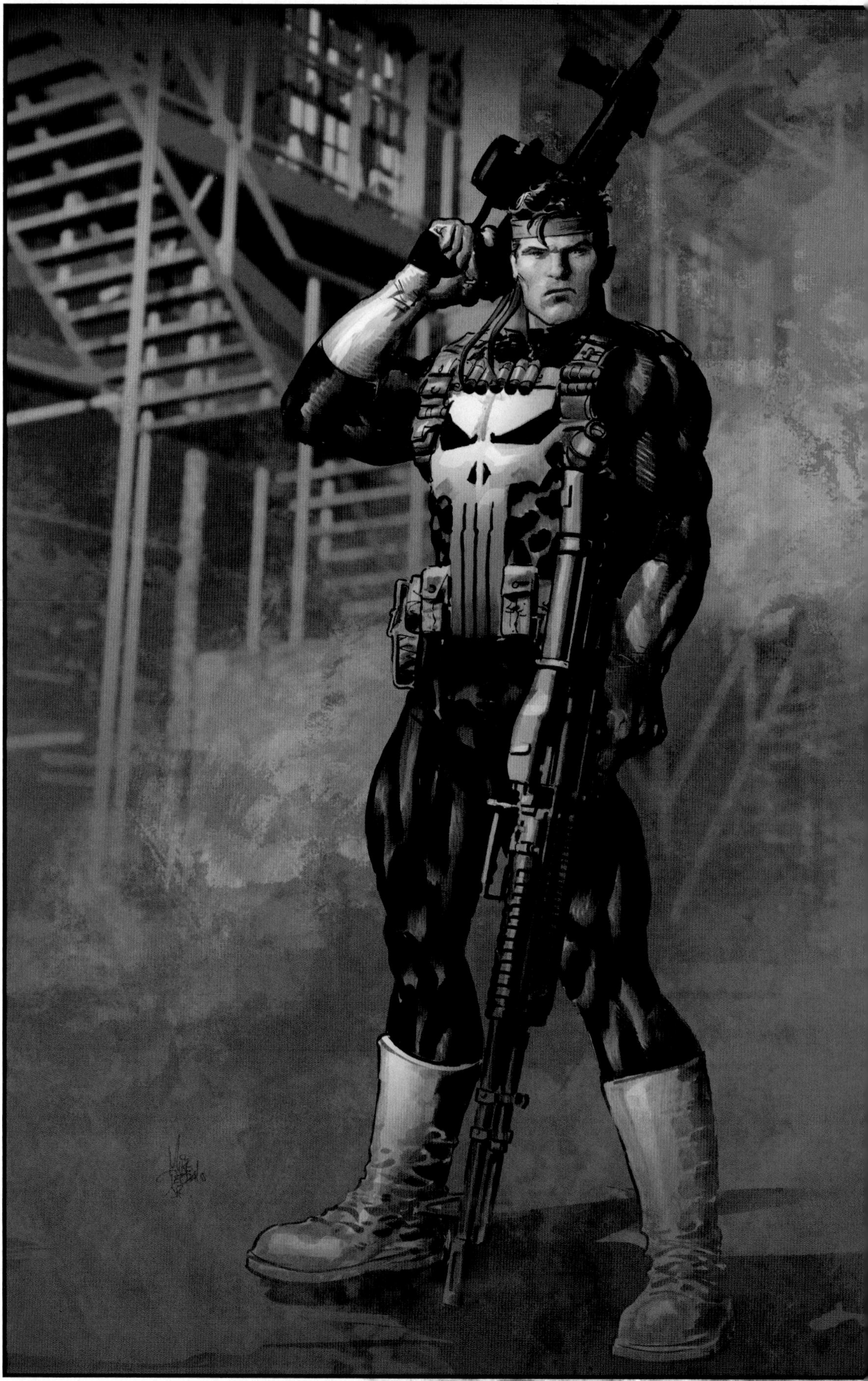

#2 VARIANT BY MIKE DEODATO JR. & RAIN BEREDO

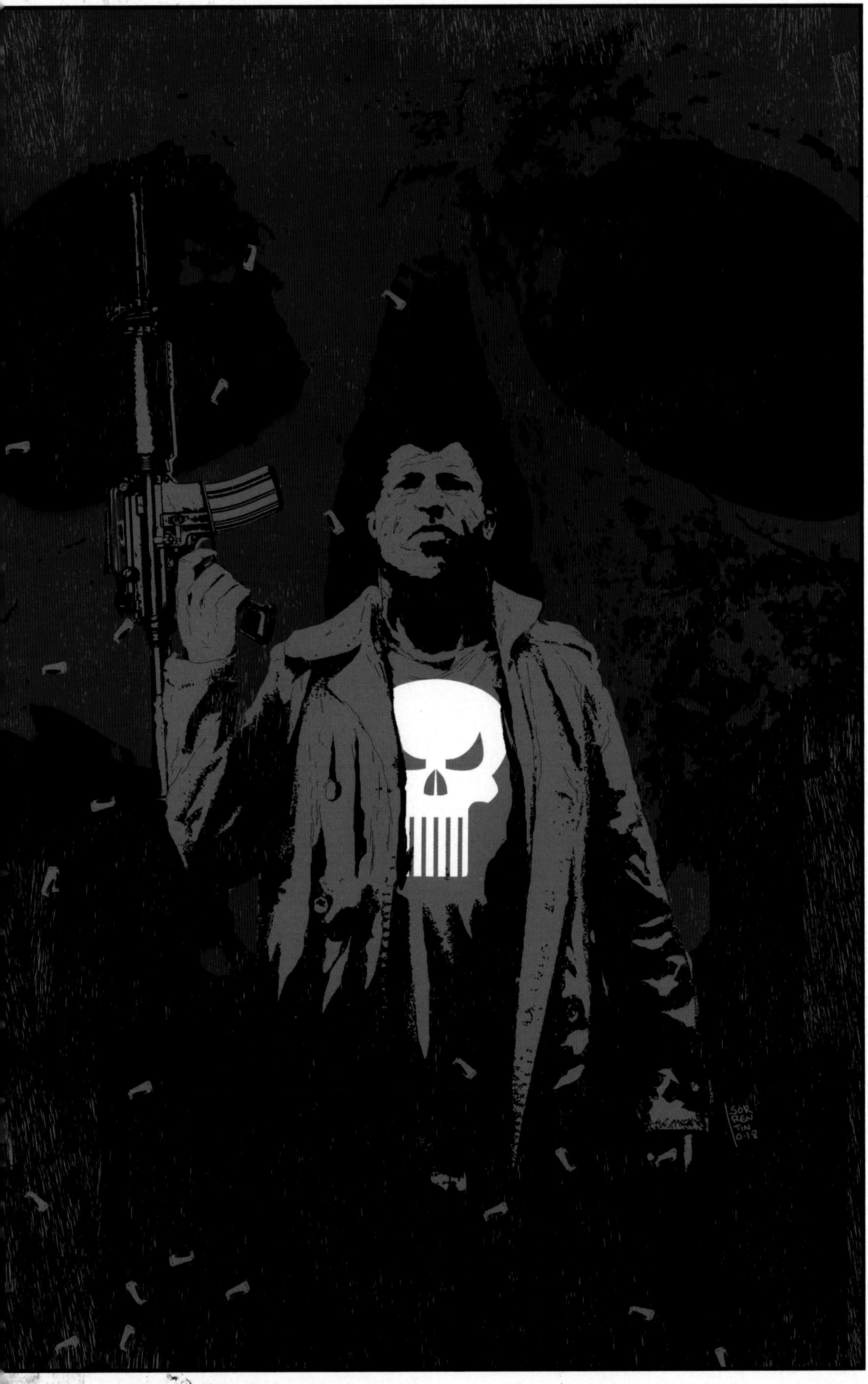
SOR
REN
TIN
O-18

#3 **VARIANT** BY ANDREA SORRENTINO

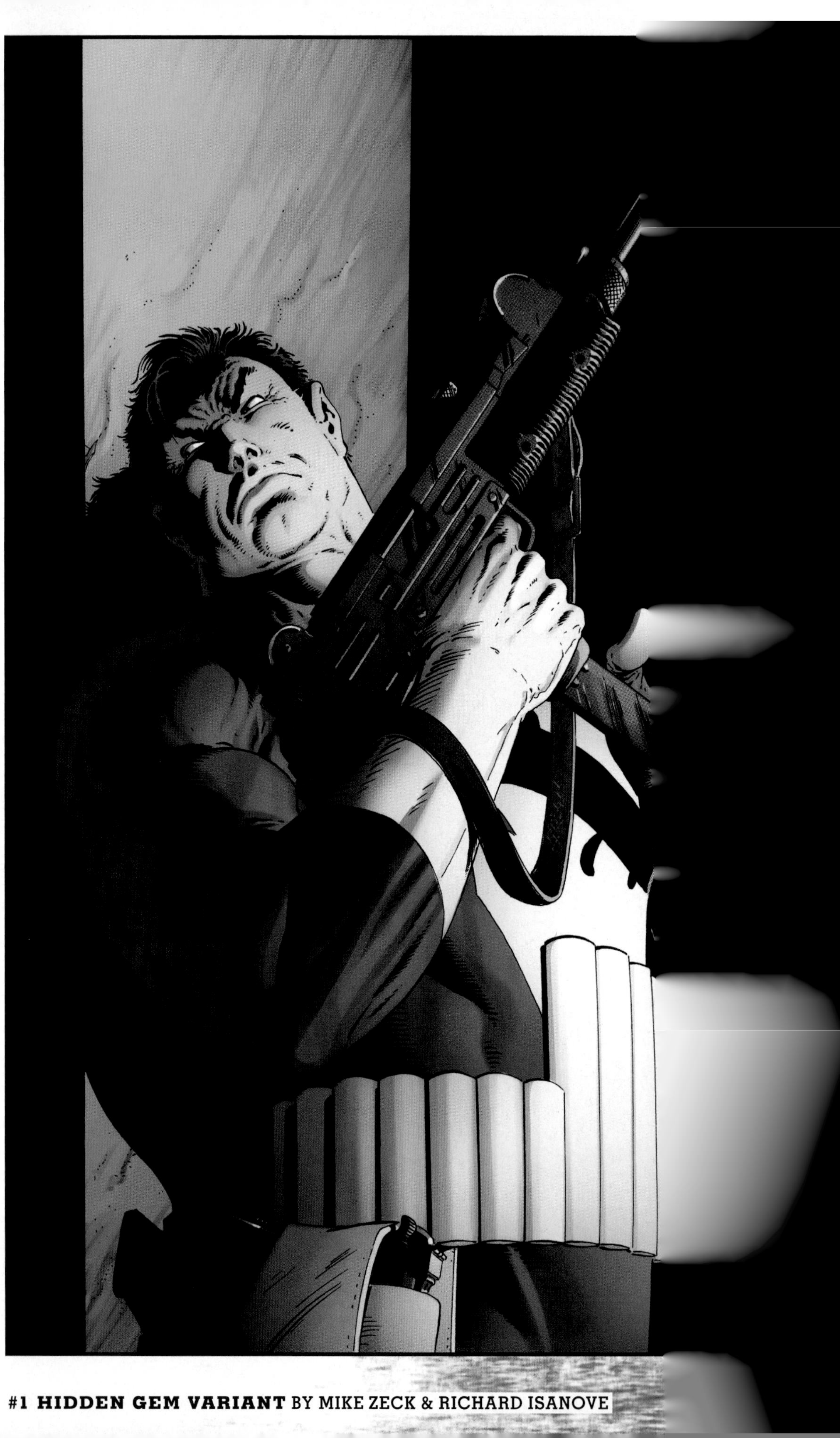

#1 HIDDEN GEM VARIANT BY MIKE ZECK & RICHARD ISANOVE

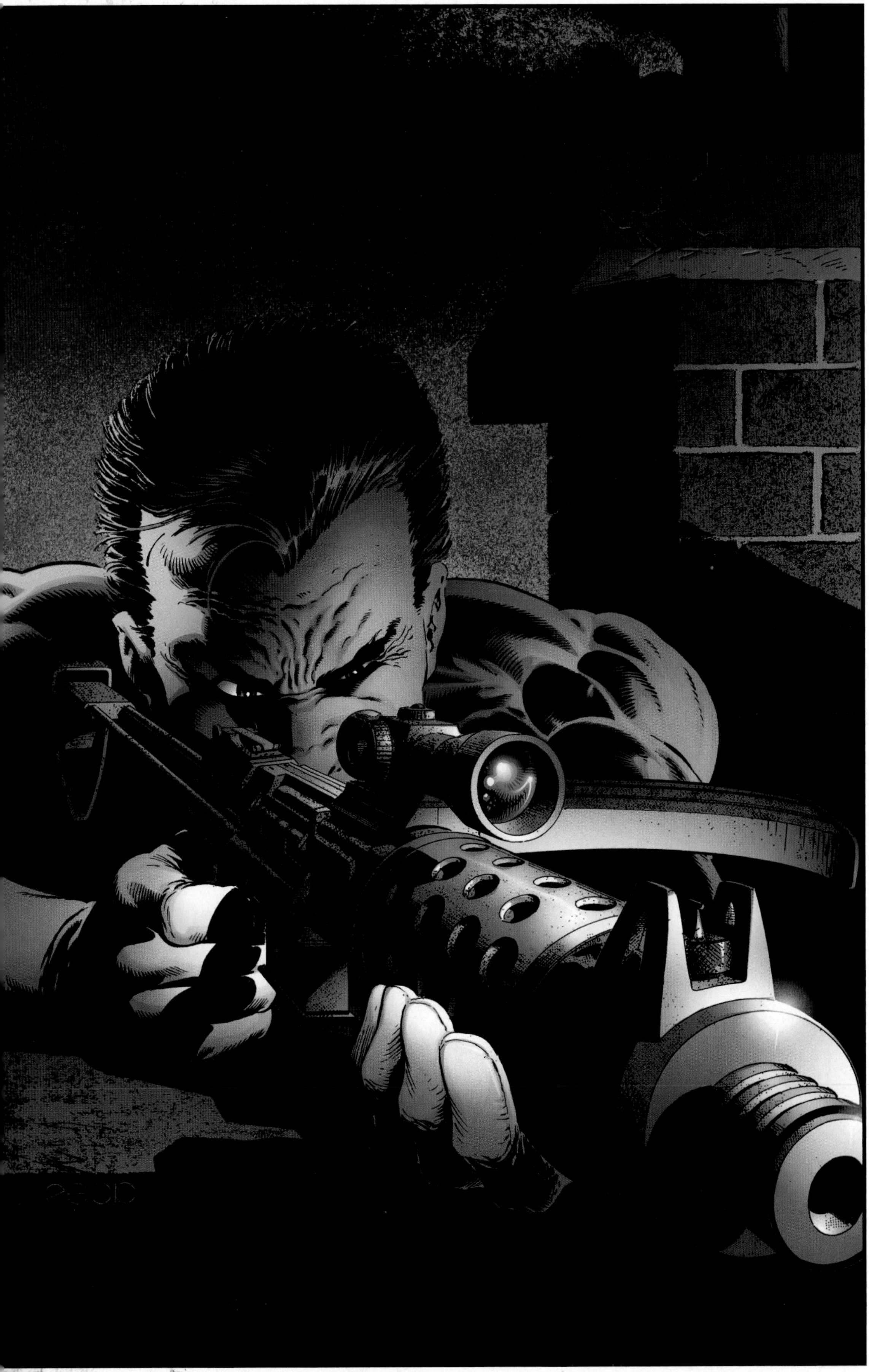

#2 HIDDEN GEM VARIANT BY MIKE ZECK & RICHARD ISANOVE

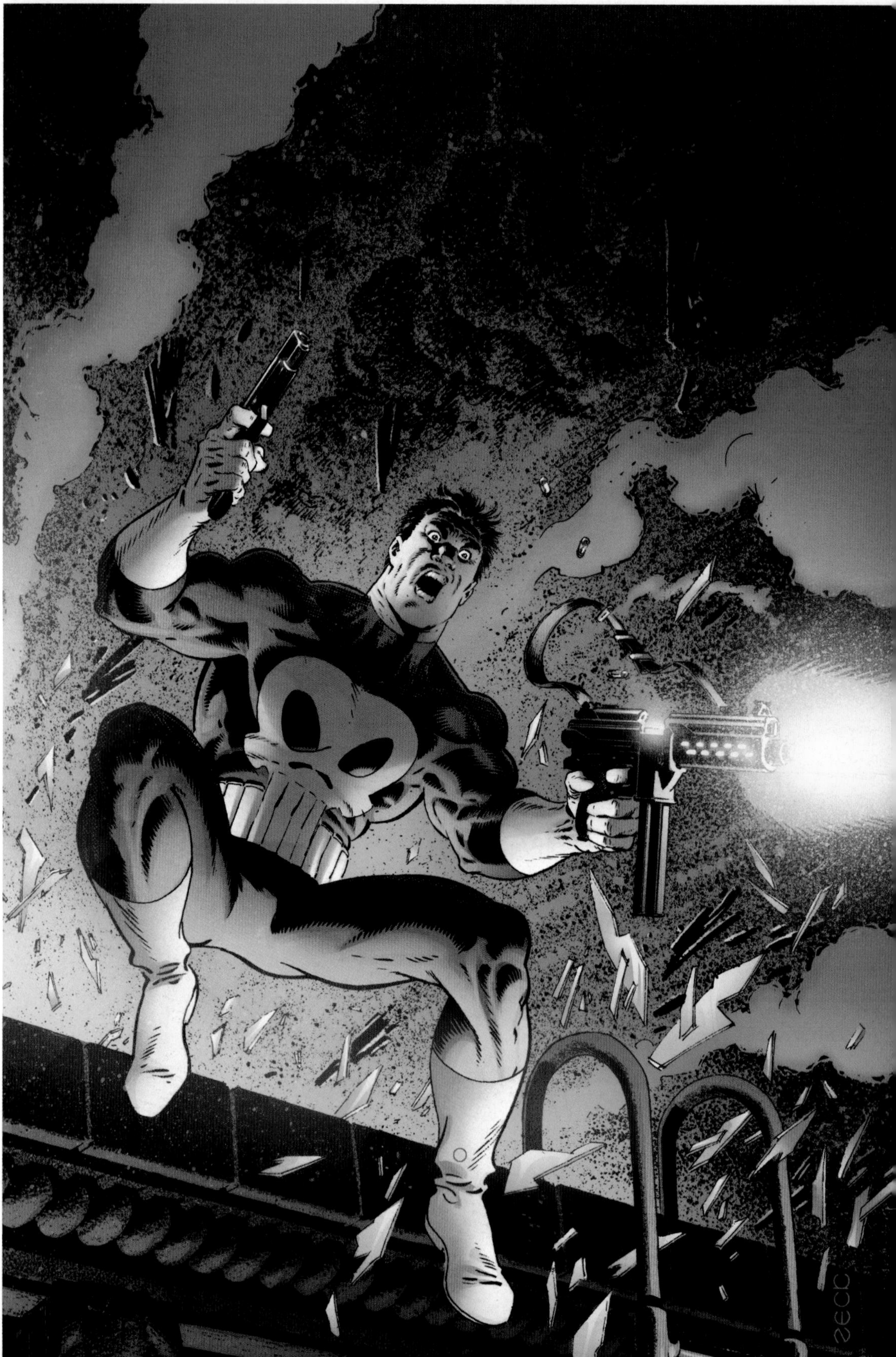

#3 HIDDEN GEM VARIANT BY MIKE ZECK & RICHARD ISANOVE

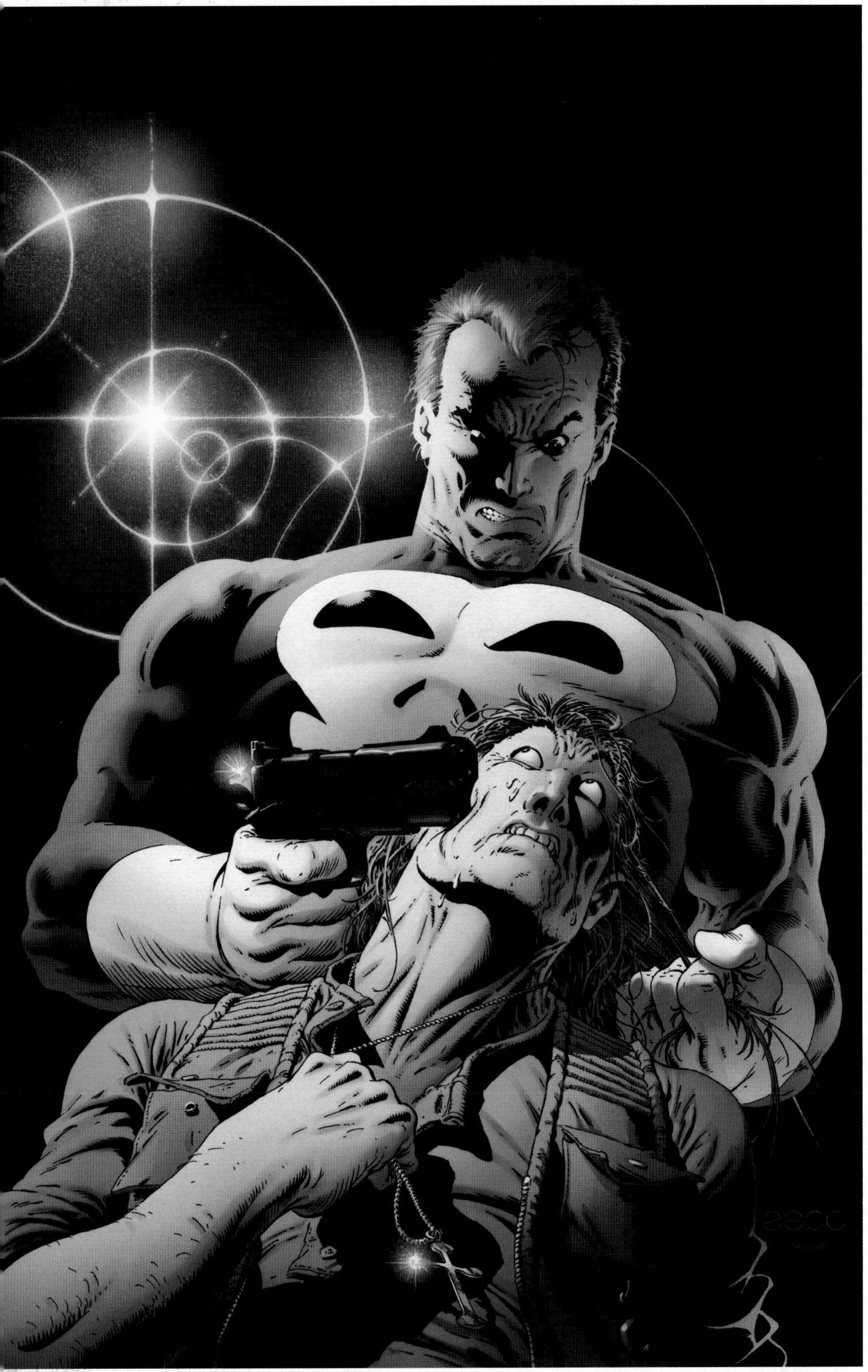

#4 HIDDEN GEM VARIANT BY MIKE ZECK & RICHARD ISANOVE

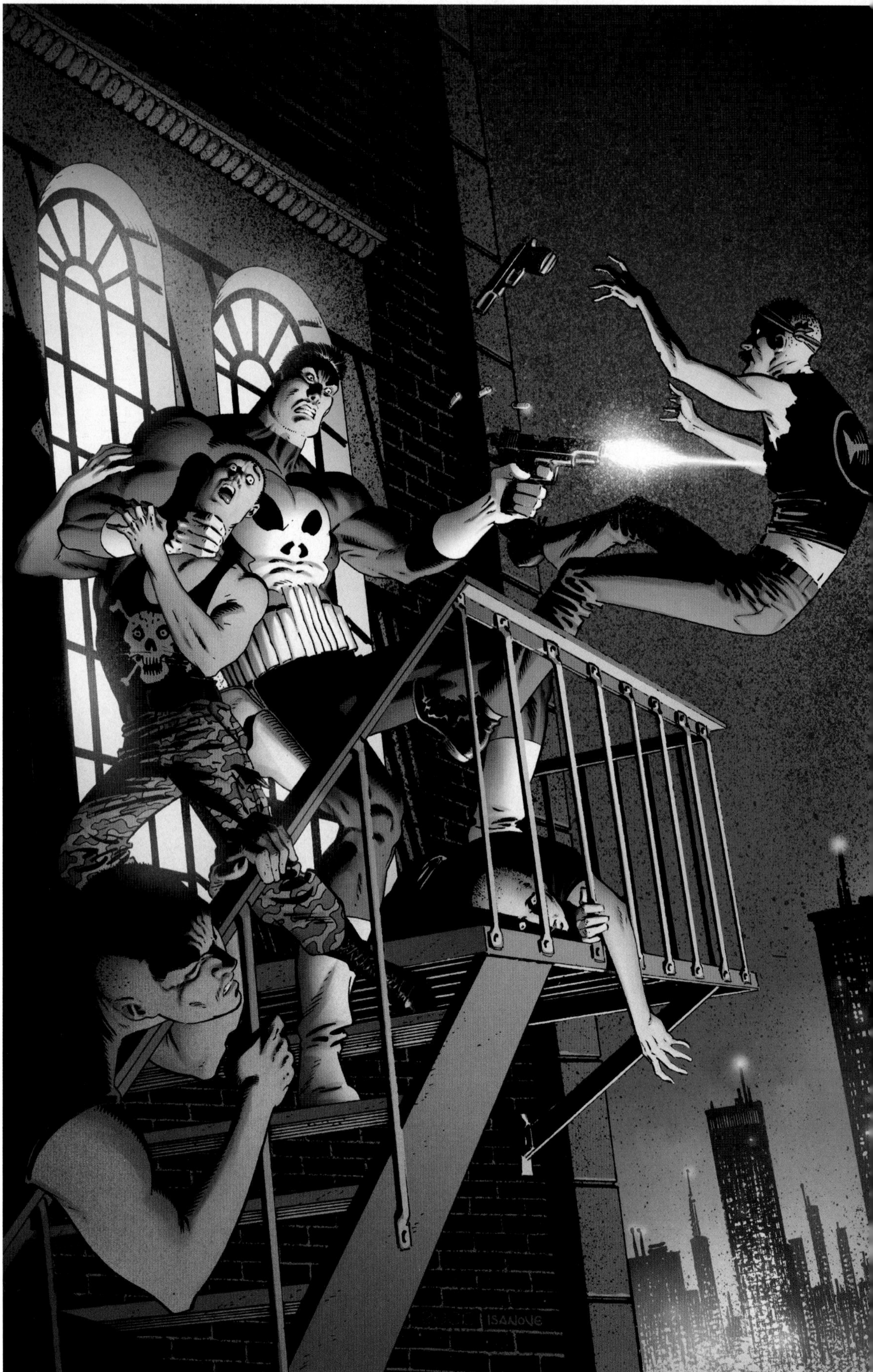
ISANOVE

#5 HIDDEN GEM VARIANT BY MIKE ZECK & RICHARD ISANOVE